R. Gupta's®

POPULAR MASTER GUIDE

IB-ACIO

Intelligence Bureau – Assistant Central Intelligence Officer

Grade-II/Executive

TIER-II (Descriptive Exam)

&

Interview

By
RPH Editorial Board

RAMESH PUBLISHING HOUSE, New Delhi

Published by
O.P. Gupta *for* Ramesh Publishing House

Admin. Office
12-H, New Daryaganj Road, Opp. Officers' Mess,
New Delhi-110002 ☎ 23261567, 23275224, 23275124

E-mail: info@rameshpublishinghouse.com
Website: www.rameshpublishinghouse.com

Showroom
● Balaji Market, Nai Sarak, Delhi-6 ☎ 23253720, 23282525
● 4457, Nai Sarak, Delhi-6, ☎ 23918938

Book Code: R-1918

ISBN: 978-93-86845-41-2

1st Edition: 1710

HSN Code: 49011010

Contents

$$\boxed{\textbf{S\small CHEME OF E\small XAMINATION}}$$

Tier/Mode of Examination	Description of Examination	Total Marks	Time (minutes)
Written Exam			
Tier-I	**Objective Type MCQs,** divided into 4 parts containing 25 questions of 1 marks each on: (a) General Awareness (b) Quantitative aptitude (c) Logical/analytical ability (d) English language.	100	60
Tier-II	**Descriptive Type:** (a) Essay on one of the given topics (30 marks), & (b) English comprehension & précis writing (20 marks).	50	60
Interview:	100 marks		

Note: (a) There will be negative marking of ¼ mark for each wrong answer in Tier-I.

(b) No marks would be awarded for an un-attempted question.

(c) **Only those candidates would be called for Tier-II exam who come up to a certain standard in Tier-I. For Tier-II examination, there will be a minimum cut off marks of 33%.**

(d) On the basis of their combined performance in Tier-I and Tier-II, the candidates would be short listed for the interview.

(e) Based on the combined performance in Tier-I, Tier-II and interview, the candidates would be short listed for final selection subject to successful completion of their Character and Antecedent verification followed by medical examination.

———————

Model Paper–1 (Solved)

IB-ACIO—Grade-II/Executive
Tier-II (Descriptive Exam)

1. **Write an essay in English language only on any one of the following topics in about 400 words:**

   (*a*) The Onus of Maintaining Healthy Relations with Nepal is on India

   (*b*) Farmers' Suicides in India : A Sign of Impending Disaster

   (*c*) India Needs to Redefine the Relations Between the Centre and the States

   (*d*) Is Development Possible at the Cost of Environment?

   (*e*) Revamping our Banking System is the Need of the Hour

   (*f*) Urbanisation of India is Nothing but Blind Westernisation

2. **Attempt a precis of the given passage in one-third of its length. Do not suggest a title. Write, as far as possible, in your own words.**

   There is no better illustration of human folly than the narrative of Sheikh Chilli. Who in India is not aware of the story of this incorrigible fool who chose to ignore the sane advice of a passer-by of not cutting the same branch on which he himself was sitting. Obviously fools fail to learn from others' experiences and pay a heavy ·price in the process. They have use neither for their own intelligence nor for that of others. They live in their own world, while apparently they may be in the middle of a group of people.

Fools by nature are enemies of thinking, both reflective and prospective. They never doubt their intelligence, are cocksure of their sense of judgement. They think they are benefactors of society and are anguished that the world fails to recognise their talent. All fools possess a degree of impatience in their desire to make the world realise their worth, wishing to improve its lot by setting a personal example before it. They are sure that the folks around them lack an innate sense of discretion and require to learn from them.

Fools have been immortalized by literature across the world. Like Sheikh Chilli's account in India, the legend of Don Quixote, the fictional Spanish knight, is equally famous in the West. He is known for thriving in a make-believe world where he is the lone saviour of humanity. The good thing is that these self-proclaimed samaritans often inhabit the world of imagination, limiting their capacity to cause damage to the real world and producing in the process hilarious effects through their irrationality. But there are instances when such fools have come to occupy the centre stage of history. Their actions then had disastrous effects on our welfare, as well as on our existence. We all know how people like Hitler brought the world to the brink of destruction through their disastrous leadership. The condition of the world continues to be precarious and its future insecure due to foolish scientists who have handed over the destructive secrets of nuclear power to vicious politicians.

1

There goes a saying that it is no use crying over spilt milk. Now what we need to become vigilant about is the danger posed by fools to our survival. Academic curricula across the world need to educate learners about the negative potential of fools to challenge the safety and security of planet earth.

(402 words)

3. **Read the following passage and answer the questions that follow:**

It is an obvious trait of black incomes that they cannot be declared to the fiscal authority for fear of large penalties. As under-declarations multiply, the tax base shrinks and price controls begin to blunt the edge of fiscal policy. One instrument of control gets into the way of the other and makes it ineffective. Tax evasion is large not necessarily because the rate of tax is high, as businessmen often proclaim, but because the income on which tax is to be paid, and the activity from which income is received, cannot be declared. It follows that even if taxes were halved, so long as the income is black, taxes will be evaded. However, to the extent taxation fails to catch undeclared incomes emanating from controls, it becomes a bad instrument for balancing aggregate demand and supply and for controlling inflation. In an enthusiastic attempt to make taxation do the balancing trick, tax rates on honest tax-payers become penal. This leads to a second round of tax evasion, this time because tax rates are intolerably high. More and more tax-payers at the margin avoid tax payment, become dishonest and in the course of time get used to dishonesty. While black money does so much damage to public policy, it also dries up the sources of real growth in the private sector of the economy. The capital market, the main vehicle of growth, consequently dries up, and capital formation both in the public and private sectors suffers a serious decline.

Questions:

(*i*) How is the circulation of black money detrimental for private entrepreneurs?

(*ii*) Why isn't reduction of taxes useful for sprucing up taxes?

(*iii*) How do honest tax-payers suffer on account of tax evaders?

(*iv*) How does black income impact a nation's economy?

(*v*) 'Large scale evasion of taxes takes place due to exorbitant taxes.' Argue for or against the statement on the basis of your reading of the passage.

ANSWERS

1. (*d*) **Is Development Possible at the Cost of Environment?**

India's growing population has been accompanied by massive urbanisation. Census of India estimates show that between 1991 and 2011 the urban population in the country increased from 26% to 31%. However, this rapid urbanisation has been accompanied by an alarming rate of environmental degradation and a growing scarcity of natural resources. Estimates from the WHO suggest that India has now replaced China as the country with the largest number of cities (13!) in the world's top 20 most polluted cities in terms of air quality. Delhi, incidentally, is the worst-ranked city.

Our rivers are just as polluted, with many stretches (particularly in and around the cities) becoming dry in lean season. The garbage in cities is growing by the day, with worrying increases being seen in plastic waste and e-waste; the scarcity of landfill sites poses another challenge.

Water scarcity is fast becoming urban India's major concern, with residents having to deal with depleting supplies due to falling groundwater levels, vanishing water bodies, severe pollution and urban floods. Further, a large number of people depend on the land, the forests and the water around them for their livelihood, but the population growth along with the increased urbanisation has led to deterioration of these resources and the environment, threatening their livelihoods.

In a democratic country such as India, public perception, opinion and response also hold a high value, especially for policy makers and politicians, leading to more informed decisions, improved design, effective policies and better acceptance and implementation of policies.

Further, the behaviours and actions of the residents play an important role in promoting sustainable standards of living. Lack of community input and involvement in environmental and resource policy development and management creates community indifference to environmental issues. We often find communities embracing the benefits of development and ignoring the negative impacts, at best seeing them as problems that the government needs to address.

The government, in turn, may have little knowledge of the priorities of the communities and the degree to which the public recognises environmental concerns to have direct implications on the quality of their lives. In fact, The Energy and Resources Institute (TERI) conducts an annual environmental survey in selected cities in India with an objective to assess people's perceptions, behaviour, awareness and opinions towards the environment and its related indicators such as air and water quality, waste and waste management, water pollution and conservation and contribute in a modest way to understanding the realities underlying what people feel about the environment.

Engaging communities and encouraging their participation in the policy-making process, having transparency in environmental management, ensuring strict compliance to environmental and forest clearance conditions and adopting market-based instruments can help us to do things differently to reinvent the development process. We need to internalise negative externality of pollution. People need to be more aware, to behave in a responsible manner and to participate in the reinvention process.

2. Precis

Fools never use their own minds and of others as well. They do not learn from others' experiences too and do the harm.

Fools naturally do not think in any way. They are always sure of their own insights. They think they are doing good to the society while the society doesn't oblige them. They are mostly impatient to display their worth and set their own examples before others.

Many fools like Sheikh Chilli and Don Quixote have also found place in the world of literature. Fortunately they remained in the imagination only and could not cause any damage to the world through their foolishness. But when such fools like Hitler appeared before the world, they almost destroyed it by their foolish ideology. Then there were some foolish scientists who made the world a dangerous place and threatened its very existence by disclosing the atom-bomb formula to wicked politicians.

Now, when the damage is done by them we need to be alert from its dangers. The people of the world need to be educated to learn to avoid the dangers to the saftey & security of the earth caused by foolish people.

3. (*i*) The circulation of black money is detrimental for private entrepreneurs as it is often difficult for them to declare the activity and the income received. This turns their activity illegal and income goes to black money which hampers their growth of business and white money.

(*ii*) Reduction in taxes isn't useful for sprucing up taxes as the whole income from an illegal source goes to black money irrespective of the rate of taxes.

(*iii*) Honest tax-payers suffer on account of tax evaders as the taxation authorities increase the tax rates to balance the revenue figures. Thus, honest tax payers have to pay more taxes.

(*iv*) Black incomes impact the nation's economy gravely. They damage the public welfare policies and dry up resources of real growth in the private sector. The capital market and growth of capital also suffers.

(*v*) **Argument for:**
Large scale evasion of taxes takes place due to exorbitant taxes as they encourage under-declarations at a large scale and cause the tax base to shrink.

Argument Against:
Large scale evasion of taxes doesn't take place due to exorbitants taxes but because of the illegality of the income and the business activity on which the tax should have been paid.

IB-ACIO—Grade-II/Executive
Tier-II (Descriptive Exam)

1. **Write an essay in English language only on any one of the following topics in about 400 words:**

   (*a*) Sardar Patel's Role in India's Freedom Movement and Afterwards

   (*b*) Financial Inclusion is a Must for Inclusive Growth

   (*c*) Role of Governor in Indian Polity

   (*d*) Disaster Management System in India

   (*e*) NET Neutrality is a Must for Digital India

   (*e*) Sino-Pak Alliance and India's Security

2. **Attempt a precis of the given passage in one-third of its length. Do not suggest a title. Write, as far as possible, in your own words.**

There is a fatal imbalance between what man is and what he wishes to be. This discord is responsible for our unrest. We talk like wise men but act like lunatics. We cannot prepare for war and at the same time for a world community. We are tormented by inner uneasiness and pangs of conscience. The warring sides of our nature require to be reconciled. If we are to defeat fratricidal tendencies in us, we must break our self-will, the pride of egoism which is widespread in all sides of our life. In man, there is always an urge to self-transcendence, but until it becomes absolute unselfishness, narrow loyalties and destructive rivalries will prevail. The unrest in the world is a reflection of our inner disharmony.

A people are saved not by their military leaders or industrial magnates, or by their priests and politicians, but by their saints of implacable integrity. Religion is the discipline by which we are helped to overcome the discord in our nature and integrate our personality. If we reflect on the history of religious development, we will be surprised at the amount of intellectual ingenuity, passion and zeal spent on the task of defining the Supreme to which silence or poetry would seem to be the most appropriate response. Self-righteousness breeds fanaticism. None but fools and fanatics are quite certain of their views of God. With crusaders there is no arguing.

Before God there is neither Greek nor barbarian, neither rich nor poor, neither master nor slave. They are all citizens of the one commonwealth, members of one family. A truly religious person cannot hold back but should lead. He cannot remain silent when he should speak up. He should not compromise when he should stand fast. Ethical values have relevance to social facts. We must face up to the ugly facts of sin, pride and greed. Human nature is essentially good and it is opposed to tyranny, injustice and authoritarianism. Religion appeals to the hearts of men to root out fear, guilt and faith in force.

The tradition of tolerance, not merely in a negative, but in a positive sense, that is an appreciation of other faiths, has been with us for centuries. Tolerance is not apathy, but is conviction without condescension. Aggressiveness is not an essential part of human nature. Combativeness can be replaced by meekness and gentleness. The Cross indicates that the love which suffers is more powerful than the force which inflicts suffering.   [413 words]

3. **Read the following passage and answer the questions that follow:**

The most prominent obstacle to cultural unity is the variety of languages. When told that there are fourteen regional languages and many more dialects belonging to four different linguistic families in India, foreigners are inclined to think that Indians are not one people but, like the inhabitants of Europe, a motley group of peoples with different cultures showing some common elements. There can be no doubt that on account of linguistic barriers, people from different parts of India generally meet as comparative strangers on all levels other than the religious one. Unless he happens to know English or Hindi, a man from the non-Hindi speaking regions finds it extremely difficult to make himself understood outside his own linguistic area. No doubt if he spends some time in a new place, he can pick up enough of the local language to get along but in spite of a common background of religious beliefs and thought in general, he cannot come in intimate contact with the people around him because there is no common medium for the exchange of deeper thoughts. So, until there is a link language and it is known throughout the country, an effective cultural unity is not possible.

But more variety of languages could not be a positive danger to the unity of India if it were not accompanied by linguistic communalism amounting in many cases to chauvinism. It is this poison in our social organism that makes the movement for linguistic states, which is perfectly justified on rational, historical and practical grounds, an object of great concern to all who have the good of the country at heart.

To avoid any misunderstanding we should make it clear what we understand by the term "linguistic communalism". The consciousness of a group of people speaking the same language that makes them form a distinct community is natural and legitimate. But if it is associated with the feeling that those sons of the country living in the same area or an adjacent area who speak a different language are outsiders in the worst sense of the term and should be treated as such, then it assumes the ugly shape of linguistic communalism which is harmful to national unity and is highly objectionable. Far more harmful and objectionable, however, is the tendency in a linguistic majority to withhold from the minority the safeguards guaranteed by the Constitution for preserving and promoting its language and culture, including the primary education of its children through the medium of the mother tongue, or to discriminate against individual members of the minority in state services and other matters. It is this chauvinism, unfortunately present in India, which has created a painful situation after the states were reorganised on a linguistic basis, the cultural and other rights of linguistic minorities in each state have been disregarded in many cases. So, when the question of redefining the boundaries of linguistic states comes up for consideration, one finds the worst tensions and conflicts in the border areas where each of two or more language groups agitates for the inclusion of the area of its domicile in the state where its own mother tongue would be the official language. If groups living in each border area could be assured that to whichever state the area went they would all receive equal treatment and their constitutional rights would be safeguarded, a major difficulty besetting the problem of linguistic states would be removed.

Questions:

(*i*) Why are the foreigners inclined to think that Indians are not 'one people'?

(*ii*) "So until there is a link language and it is known throughout the country, an effective cultural unity is not possible." Elucidate.

(*iii*) What according to the author is 'linguistic communalism'? When is it 'harmful to national unity'?

(*iv*) What happens when the question of 'redefining the boundaries of linguistic states' crops up for consideration?

(*v*) How could the major difficulty besetting 'the problem of linguistic states' be solved?

ANSWERS

1. (*e*) NET Neutrality is a Must for Digital India

Before shedding light on India's need to have NET Neutrality, it needs to be elucidated as to what it means in today's dream of making Digital India. Net neutrality means Internet that allows everyone to communicate freely. It means a service provider must allow access to all content and applications irrespective of the source and no websites or pages should be blocked, as long as they are not illegal.

Today, there is a race among the developing countries to become digital, and India among them should not lag behind as it is already treasured with IT professionals despite being constantly suffering from the scourge of brain-drain. Since, India is emerging as an enviable market with the attraction of small businesses as also of foreign investments, NET neutrality has become vitally important for small business owners, startups and entrepreneurs, who can simply launch their businesses online, advertise the products and sell them openly online. The giants like Google, Twitter and many others are born out of net neutrality.

With the augmentation of Internet penetration in India, the country is evolving into a breeding ground for startups and entrepreneurs but lack of net neutrality is a matter of grave concern for us in today's perspective. The Internet cannot function in absence of net neutrality

that means Internet Service Providers (ISP) will be able to charge companies like YouTube or Netflix as they consume more bandwidth, and ultimately the load of the extra sum will be burdened upon the consumers. In the same way, ISPs can then create slow and fast Internet lanes, meaning all websites cannot be accessed at the same speed and one can do so only by paying an additional sum.

Therefore, in the current scenario, if India wants to flourish in multiple domains, especially in education and commercial spheres as dreamed by its PM Narendra Modi to make it Digital India, it is quintessential that India has access to Net Neutrality, as it can be a leading factor behind realising the dream of making her Digital India.

2. Precis

The greed, ego, envy and selfishness of man have almost eaten into the virtue of altruism. If such vices continue, the unrest will continue to prevail. It is not physical force, but one's own conscience and God's fear in heart that can strengthen human integrity. Real crusade lies in eschewing the act of arguing for self-gains and going against fulfilling one's covetousness. Every human being is equal in God's eye. True adherence to religion lies in crusading against the evils in hearts and striving for virtues in life. Human nature stops man from wrongdoings and it is religion that teaches him to shun all the misanthropic acts. Aggressiveness is not an essence of human nature; it is tolerance that can create an ambience of integrity as the Cross indicates that love despite falling prey to the harshness of force, is ultimate winner.

(142 words)

3. (i) Foreigners are inclined to think that Indians are not one people. They think so because a variety of languages are spoken in India and thus, people from one state or area face difficulty in understanding the language of other states' people. Unless one happens to know English or Hindi, a person from the non-Hindi speaking regions finds it extremely difficult to make himself understood outside his own linguistic area. That is why the foreigners think that Indians are linguistically divided, thereby creating a linguistic barrier in becoming one people.

(ii) An effective cultural unity in India cannot be possible until a link language is used throughout the country. The major hindrance to cultural unity is the variety of languages spoken by the people of different states and areas. When told that there are fourteen regional languages and numerous dialects belonging to four different linguistic families in India, it is to be ensured that there is promoted a link language like English or Hindi so that people from linguistically different states or areas have no difficulty to understand and thus, a cultural affinity can be created and shared widely.

(iii) The consciousness of a group of people speaking the same language that makes them form a distinct community is natural and legitimate. But if it is associated with the feeling that those sons of the country living in the same area or an adjacent area who speak a different language are outsiders in the worst sense of the term and should be treated as such, then it assumes the ugly shape of linguistic communalism which is harmful to national unity and is highly objectionable.

(iv) When the question of redefining the boundaries of linguistic states comes up for consideration, one finds the worst tensions and conflicts in the border areas where each of two or more language groups agitates for the inclusion of the area of its domicile in the state where its own mother tongue would be the official language.

(v) If the groups living in each border area are assured of receiving equal treatment irrespective of the state or area they originally belong to, and their constitutional rights are safeguarded, a major difficulty besetting the problem of linguistic states would be removed.

IB-ACIO—Grade-II/Executive
Tier-II (Descriptive Exam)

1. **Write an essay in English language only on any one of the following topics in about 400 words:**

   (*a*) Nexus between Health Practitioners and Pharmaceutical Companies, a Concern

   (*b*) Inter-State Water Disputes in India

   (*c*) Role of Social Reformers in the Struggle for Freedom

   (*d*) Impact of Falling Value of Rupee on Indian Economy

   (*e*) China's Policy of Aggressive Dominance in South-East Asia

   (*f*) Effect of Media Publicity on Terrorism

2. **Attempt a precis of the given passage of 450 words, in one-third of its length. Suggest a suitable title. Write the precis, as far as possible, in your own words. State the number of words at the end of the answer.**

Indian literature has a long tradition and is a reflection of its culture through the ages. This fact is often overlooked, since literature in English is popular amongst the urban middle class. The British attempted to categorise the main regional languages. Despite the Orientalists' admiration of the Sanskrit tradition, the need to communicate with the locals or convert them to Christianity prompted the British to learn the local languages. As a result, a number of grammar books were written to understand these better. The nationalists also recognised the importance of regional languages. Members of the Congress party realised that if they only spoke in English, they were alienated from their own people, as it was considered to be synonymous with cultural domination.

In 1910, the Hindi Sahitya Sammelan (Conference on Hindi Literature) was held by the conservatives of the Independence movement. In 1916 the Benares Hindu University was founded with a similar ideological aim — to defend the great Hindu tradition. Gandhi, who endorsed it in the era between the two world wars, disassociated himself from it in the 1940s, and reproached the conservatives for promoting a very Sanskritised Hindi. He advocated a synthesis, Hindustani, which could be used by all the speakers of Urdu and Hindi. After Independence, the government supported Hindi, which eventually became the official language of the nation and the mass media promoted a very Sanskritised form. Later, the increasing power of the Hindu nationalists also encouraged the use of Hindi. Paradoxically, the English-speaking intelligentsia also encouraged it as they did not want the communalists to monopolise the cultural traditions of the country.

The growing domination of Hindi, which is evident due to a demographic balance of power, has however not eclipsed other regional literatures. In 1954, the Sahitya Academy was established by the government. It considers Indian literature as "a literature in several languages." Two of its fellows, U.R. Ananthamurthy and K. Satchidanandan, write in Dravidian languages — in fact, Ananthamurthy was awarded the Jnanpith Award in 1994 for his work in Kannada. If the Academy makes allowances for Hindi literature, notably by giving prizes, it supports all other regional literatures equally. It acknowledges more languages than the Constitution, including Maithili, Dogri, Rajasthani and English, and tries hard to support them by following an active publications policy. The States Reorganisation Act of 1956 rearranged the states according to a linguistic principle. This too helped foster regional literature as the state governments supported it. The Sahitya Academy seeks to focus on the common cultural traits that underlie literature written in Indian languages. The unity is associated with the structure of Indian society, its caste divisions, its religious communities and gender inequality. This social dimension of Indian literature is important.

(450 words)

3. **Read the following passage and answer the questions that follow:**

Ever since the dawn of civilisation, class inequality has existed. Among savage tribes at the present day, it takes very simple forms. There are chiefs, and the chiefs are able to have several wives. Savages, unlike civilised men, have found a way of making wives a source of wealth, so that the more wives a man has the wealthier he becomes. But this primitive form of social inequality soon gave way to others more complex. In the main, social inequality has been bound up with inheritance, and therefore, in all patriarchal societies, with descent in the male line. Originally, the greater wealth of certain persons was due to military prowess. The successful fighter acquired wealth, and transmitted it to his sons. Wealth acquired by the sword usually consisted of land, and to this day land-owning is the mark of the aristocrat, the aristocrat being in theory the descendant of some feudal baron, who acquired his lands by killing the previous occupant and holding his acquisition against all comers. This is considered the most honourable source of wealth. There are others slightly less honourable, exemplified by those who, while completely idle themselves, have acquired their wealth by inheritance from an industrious ancestor; and yet others, still less respectable, whose wealth is due to their own industry. In the modern world, the plutocrat who, though rich, still works, is gradually ousting the aristocrat, whose income was in theory derived solely from ownership of land and natural monopolies. There have been two main legal sources of property: one, the aristocratic source, namely, ownership of land; the other, the bourgeois source, namely, the right to the produce of one's own labour. The right to the produce of one's own labour has always existed only on paper, because things are made out of other things, and the man who supplies the raw material exacts a right to the finished product in return for wages, or, where slavery exists, in return for the bare necessaries of life. We have thus three orders of men — the land-owner, the capitalist, and the proletarian. The capitalist in origin is merely a man whose savings have enabled him to buy the raw materials and the tools required in manufacturing, and who has thereby acquired the right to the finished product in return for wages. The three categories of land-owner, capitalist, and proletarian are clear enough in theory; but in practice the distinctions are blurred. A land-owner may employ business methods in developing a seaside resort which happens to be upon his property. A capitalist whose money is derived from manufacture may invest the whole or part of his fortune in land, and take to living upon rent. A proletarian, in so far as he has money in the savings bank, or a house which he is buying on the instalment plan, becomes to that extent a capitalist or a land-owner as the case may be. The eminent barrister who charges a thousand guineas for a brief should, in strict economics, be classified as a proletarian. But he would be indignant if this were done, and has the mentality of a plutocrat.

Questions:

(*i*) How is social inequality bound with inheritance?

(*ii*) What is the irony in the most honourable source of wealth?

(*iii*) What are the two legal sources of property?

(*iv*) How does the writer distinguish the three orders of men?

(*v*) Who is a plutocrat?

ANSWERS

1. (*f*) Effect of Media Publicity on Terrorism

Recent history, specifically the past decade, has provided plenty of examples of the mutually beneficial relationship between terrorist organizations and the media. As some remarkable terrorist attacks in history indicate, whether it is in the United States (US), Europe, or the Middle East, it is by and large the case that the architects of terrorism exploit the media for the benefit of their operational efficiency, information gathering, recruitment, fund raising, and propaganda schemes.

In the words of Nacos, whether it is the relatively inconsequential arson by an amateurish environmental group or mass destruction by a network of terrorists, the perpetrators' media-related goals are the same: attention, recognition, and perhaps even a degree of respectability and legitimacy in their various publics. Media, in return, receives the attention of the public that is vital for its existence and benefits from record sales and huge audiences.

To put it briefly, just as terrorism has to be communicated to have effect, the media has to cover the incidents in such a way to benefit from the public's eagerness to obtain information about terrorist attacks.

Indeed, the goals of terrorists are not solely confined to winning the attention of the masses. In addition to that, through the media, they aim to publicize their political causes, inform both friends and foes about the motives for terrorist deeds, and explain their rationale for resorting to violence. They further aim to be treated like regular, accepted, legitimate world leaders, as the media gives them a similar status.

The above suggests that terrorists need the media to receive free publicity for their cause, transmit their messages, and garner support, recognition, and legitimacy. Given the emerging trends in the media and communications technology, it is likely that terrorists will employ more innovative tactics to achieve their goals.

The media plays a central role in the calculus of political violence and are put into positions where they can magnify or minimize these kinds of acts and their perpetrators, or, of course, they can provide coverage that avoids either one of those extremes.

Terrorism is a category of political violence, which is intended to influence foreign and domestic governments, as well as communities. Terrorism uses its immediate victims and material targets for semiotic and symbolic purposes. Attacks are designed to create an atmosphere of fear or a sense of threat. In the same vein, terrorism can also refer to politically motivated deeds perpetrated by groups or individuals for the sake of communicating messages to a larger audience. In any case, the terrorists' need for media publicity and media's need for a greater audience and profits form a symbiotic relationship between terrorism and the media.

This symbiosis is not inevitable. Implementing certain policies that are different than the previous failed policies can facilitate the breaking of that cycle by forcing at least one side of the equation — the media — to act in a more responsible, more conscious, and more cooperative manner. Only then starving the terrorists of the oxygen of publicity on which they depend can become possible and more robust steps can be taken to win the ideological and actual battle against terrorism.

2. **PRECIS**

Title: Social Aspect of Indian Literature

Literature of India is traditional and Indian culture is reflected through it well. Though English literature has been quite popular in urban India through the pre-independence times but to connect with the rest of India it is important to learn the local and regional languages and culture. Even the British tried this when there were here. After independence, though Hindi being the official language of the nation dominates yet not overshadows other regional literatures. The government also encourages other language literatures through Sahitya Akademi which apart from Hindi literature awards the literatures of other regional and local languages as well. Though the states of India were reorganized on linguistic basis yet the Sahitya Akademi focuses on common cultural traits that exists in the unity of Indian society despite diversities in castes, structure, religions and genders. This social aspect is the best part of the Indian literature which cuts across all social barriers and supports the literature of all languages.

(160 words)

3. (*i*) The greater wealth of certain persons was due to military prowess. The successful fighter acquired wealth, and transmitted to his sons. In this way, social inequality has been bound up with inheritance.

(*ii*) The most honourable source of wealth is considered the wealth acquired by the sword, which usually consisted of land. The irony is that their honourable possessions were acquired by killing the previous occupant and holding them against all comers.

(*iii*) The two main legal sources of property are — the aristocratic source or the ownership of land, and the bourgeois source or the right to produce of one's labour.

(*iv*) The writer distinguishes the three orders of man as — the landowner, the capitalist and the proletarian or the working class.

(*v*) A plutocrat is a person whose power derives from his wealth.

DESCRIPTIVE EXAM

Essay Writing

An essay is a written composition containing an expression of one's personal opinions or ideas on a subject. A good essay must hold its readers' attention from the beginning to the end. For this, it must possess certain qualities which make a piece of writing readable and enjoyable.

Every essay depends on two things: (a) its subject matter, and (b) its language.

To write an essay you require 'material'—clear ideas based on experience, reading and observation. These ideas have to be put into words and these words must convey what you wish to say. For this you should know the right words and the most appropriate way to put them together.

IMPORTANT TIPS

An essay is generally divided into three parts:

1. The Introduction. 2. The Body. 3. The Conclusion. And each of these requires careful attention.

(i) **The Introduction Paragraph:** It is the first paragraph of your essay. It introduces the main idea of your essay. A good opening paragraph captures the interest of your reader and tells why your topic is important. The introduction should be designed to attract the reader's attention and give the reader an idea of the essay's focus. Begin with an attention grabber.

(ii) **The Body or Supporting Paragraphs:** Supporting paragraphs make up the main body of your essay. They develop the main idea of your essay.

To form a perfect body of your essay, you should:

1. List the points that develop the main idea of your essay. 2. Place each supporting point in its own paragraph. 3. Develop each supporting point with facts, details and examples.

To connect your supporting paragraphs, you should use special transition words. Transition words link your paragraphs together and make your essay easier to read. Use them at the beginning and at the end of your paragraphs.

(iii) **The Conclusion or Summary Paragraph:** It comes at the end of your essay after you have finished developing your ideas. It summarises or restates the main idea of the essay. You want to leave the reader with a sense that your essay is complete. Restate the strongest points of your essay that support your main idea. Conclude your essay by restating the main idea in different words. Give your personal opinion or suggest a plan for action. Use a transitional phrase, which summarises a point in your essay instead.

In a short essay, you can deal with a very few points only. It is of no use to write down a lot of things that have nothing to do with the subject. Write down facts that will help you in your essay. Write down your own ideas. Find the main idea of your essay. Choose the most important point you are going to present. Organise your facts and ideas in a way that develops your main idea. Once you have chosen the most important point of your essay, you must find the best way to tell your reader about it. Develop each supporting paragraph and make sure to follow the correct paragraph format. Write simple sentences to express your meaning. Use simple words; be clear as well as brief. Focus on the main idea of your essay.

Check your essay for mistakes and correct them. Make sure that your handwriting is clear and legible. The examiner may not have enough time to take pains to try and read illegible words carefully. An illegible handwriting might only put off his interest in reading your essay even though it might be good.

An essay can be written just about anything, even a poem. Hence, it will be difficult to predict which essay you may be asked to write about in your exam. Here are a few selected essays for your study.

SELECTED ESSAYS

THE DOKALAM ISSUE

India and China have ended their military standoff by agreeing to speedy disengagement on the Dokalam plateau in Bhutan. This welcome development has come just days before Prime Minister Narendra Modi's scheduled visit to China for the BRICS summit (September 3-5, 2017) in Xiamen city. The separate announcements by India and China that the Dokalam military stand-off has ended are a welcome sign that diplomacy has prevailed over the harsh rhetoric of the past two months.

The essence of the deal—mutual disengagement and restoration of the situation before the Chinese construction of a road towards the Indian border and the deployment of Indian troops blocking that activity is close to what India wanted. China, which had demanded an unconditional Indian withdrawal from Dokalam, has had a greater difficulty in presenting the return to status quo as victory. But the Indian decision to announce the withdrawal first seems to have given sufficient political space for China to accept the outcome while affirming its sovereignty over a territory that is also claimed by Bhutan.

India has got China to suspend the construction of a road that New Delhi cited as a big security threat. China, in turn, got the Indian army to pull out its troops from Dokalam.

Dokalam is a narrow plateau lying in the tri-junction region of Bhutan, China and India. Dokalam is situated roughly 15 km southeast of the Nathu La pass that separates India and China. On the western edge of the Dokalam plateau is Doka La, which connects Sikkim with either Tibet (Chinese Government Claim) or linking Sikkim to Western Bhutan (Bhutanese and Indian claim).

On July 12, 2017 China signalled its intent to end the standoff between Indian and Chinese troops in the Dokalam area at an early date, if Indian forces withdraw to what it called the "Indian side of the boundary". The standoff had been continuing since first week of June 2017, adding tension to the Sino-Indian relations.

The standoff started in June 2017 when People's Liberation Army (PLA) of China started constructing a road towards Doka La. The Royal Bhutan Army tried to intervene but they were pushed back. Bhutan maintains no formal diplomatic ties with China and depends on military and diplomatic support from India. The Bhutanese Army thus approached the Indian troops for help. India has officially accepted that its troops blocked PLA road construction inside Dokalam as it would "represent a significant change of status quo with serious security implications for India."

Until 1959, China made no claims on Dokalam, asserting in one official communication that there were no discrepancies in its maps and those of

Bhutan at that time. But now, China cites the 1890 China-Britain treaty, which states that the border runs west from Doka-La along the ridgeline - that is, south of the Dokalam plateau. Bhutan disputes this, noting that the 1890 convention applies to the borders of India and China, not Bhutan and China. Bhutan knows it is taking a risk but it is counting on the fact that China would loath to be seen as a bully - and that India would stand by it militarily.

The Dokalam area is dangerously close to the narrow Siliguri Corridor (or the Chicken's Neck) that connects the northeastern states with the rest of India. Undisputed control over Dokalam will give China tactical and strategic advantage in the region. The corridor is extremely important for India because rail and road networks towards the North East run through it. This allows it to sustain the armed forces posted in the North East which will form an important piece of the puzzle should a conflict arise between India and China.

Proximity to the region through road near the Siliguri corridor gives China two-fold benefit - India's north-eastern troops fall in disarray and India gets another headache of maintaining order in the North East. Since 1998, China has been developing infrastructure in the region. Reports suggest that it has already built a crisscross of basic roads there. China now intends to build all-weather highway in the region to gain strategic advantage.

Beijing has been intensely distrustful of its two economically powerful neighbours - Japan across the sea and India across the mountains. Since it has surged way ahead of India in terms of economic development, China wants to zealously guard the advantage, pricking India from time to time to register its military superiority. India, however, is also a huge market for Chinese consumer goods. And that is an opportunity Beijing does not want to forgo. But India's growing economic and diplomatic clout ruffles China. India's unflinching opposition to China's grandiose One Belt One Road (OBOR) idea marks a setback for Beijing's strategic, economic and political pursuits. In Beijing's view, India is a critical 'swing State' that increasingly is moving to the U.S. camp, undercutting China's ambition to establish a Sino-centric Asia.

Both New Delhi and Beijing have respected the wishes of the Bhutanese government, which wanted an early end to the crisis before the bitter winter set in. Diplomats must now begin the heavy lifting required to repair the rupture in ties over the past few months which led to actions such as cancellation of the Nathu La route for Kailash-Mansarovar pilgrims and calls for boycott of Chinese products in India. India and China must revert to the spirit of the Border Defence Cooperation Agreement of 2013, which laid down specific guidelines on tackling future developments along the 3,488-km boundary the two countries share.

TRIPLE TALAQ IS UNCONSTITUTIONAL

On 22nd August, 2017 a five-judge bench of the Supreme Court in a split verdict ruled that the practice of instant triple talaq in the Muslim community is unconstitutional. The bench set aside the practice by a majority of 3 : 2.

Three judges of the bench said that triple talaq must be struck down as it goes against the Constitution and is unacceptable. They said that the Muslim Personal Law (Shariat) Application Act of 1937 recognised and enforced triple talaq, therefore, it should not be considered a personal law but a statutory law. Hence it comes under the ambit of Article 13(1) of the Constitution. Article 13 mandates that any law, framed before or after the Constitution, should not be violative of the fundamental rights. Triple Talaq is manifestly arbitrary and was violative of Article 14 (the Right to Equality) and did not enjoy the protection of Article 25(1) of the Constitution.

Two judges ruled that triple talaq enjoys the status of fundamental rights as it is a part of Muslim personal law. They were in favour of putting the practice aside for a period of six months allowing Parliament to legislate on it. They asked political parties to set aside their differences and introduce a new law on the practice, taking into account concerns of Muslim bodies and the Sharia law.

Article 25 of the Constitution guarantees religious freedom as Freedom of Practice and Propagation of Religion. Like all other Fundamental Rights, it is subject to restrictions and does not protect religious practices that can negatively affect the welfare of citizens. Hence, Article 25 is overridden by Article 14, which guarantees the Right to Equality as triple talaq denies a Muslim woman's equality before the law. Article 25 is also subject to Article 15 (1) which states that the State "shall not discriminate against any citizen on grounds only of religion, race, caste, sex…" Since triple talaq does not work in the favour of women, it violates Article 15 (1) of the Constitution. However, section 2 of the Muslim Personal Law (Shariat) Application Act of 1937 recognises triple talaq as a statutory right, bringing it under the ambit of Article 13 of the Constitution. Article 13 defines 'law' and says that all laws, framed before or after the Constitution, shall not be violative of the fundamental rights.

There are three forms of talaq (divorce) in Islam: Ahsan, Hasan and Talaq-e-Biddat (triple or instant talaq). Ahsan and Hasan are revocable but Biddat is irrevocable. Triple talaq is a practice mainly prevalent among India's Muslim community following the Hanafi Islamic school of law. Under the practice, a Muslim man can divorce his wife by simply uttering "talaq" three times but women cannot pronounce triple talaq and are required to move a court for getting divorce under the Sharia Act, 1937. Triple talaq divorce is banned by many Islamic countries, including Pakistan, Bangladesh and Indonesia.

The issue has been making news since a Muslim organisation, Bharatiya Muslim Mahila Andolan (BMMA), launched a campaign to ban triple talaq and "nikah halala" - a practice where divorced women have to undergo second marriage to retain the first marriage. In 2015, Sayara Bano, a resident of Uttarakhand, filed a petition in the Supreme Court seeking a ban on the practice after her husband ended 15-year marriage by sending a letter pronouncing the word talaq thrice. In 2015 only, the SC registered a suo motu public interest litigation (PIL) petition titled 'In Re: Muslim Women's Quest for Equality' to examine if arbitrary divorce, polygamy and nikah halala violate women's dignity.

In the Shah Bano Case (1985), the SC gave 62-year-old Shah Bano the right to alimony from her husband by invoking a provision in the Criminal Procedure Code, 1973, a legislation for compensation that is to be given by the husband as maintenance to his divorced wife. However, The Muslim Women (Protection of Rights on Divorce) Act, 1986 was passed was the then Central government which was seen as an attempt to dilute the effect of Shah Bano Case judgement. In 2001, Danial Latifi & Anr v. Union of India case, SC reiterated the validity of the Shah Bano case judgement upholding Muslim women's rights.

There is no doubt that triple talaq violates women's rights to equality and freedom, including freedom within the marriage, and should be invalidated by the Supreme Court. The larger question, however, is whether the court will stick to its old, narrow, colonial—influenced jurisprudence, and strike down triple talaq while nonetheless upholding a body of law that answers not the Constitution, but to dominant and powerful voices within separate communities; or will it, in 2017, change course, and hold that no body of law (or rather, no body of prescriptions that carries all the badges and incidents of law) can claim a higher source of authority than the Constitution of India?

RESERVATION POLICY IN INDIA

Two thousand years ago, the great philosopher Aristotle said, "injustice arises equally". This profound statement is what lies at the heart of equality—a fundamental human right. Every human simply by virtue of being a human being is entitled to equal treatment.

The most significant, pervasive and violent discrimination in our country is the centuries old caste system. It was abolished by the Constitution in 1952 and untouchability was declared a crime. There was a category of people called dalits outside this system who were discriminated and treated as untouchables. They were thus given reservation by the government.

Reservation in India is the process of setting aside a certain percentage of seats (vacancies) in government institutions for members of backward and under-represented communities (defined primarily by caste and tribe). It is a form of quota-based affirmative action. Scheduled Castes, Scheduled Tribes and other backward classes are the primary beneficiaries of the reservation policies under the Constitution with the objective of ensuring a 'level' playing field.

The Constitution of India states in Article 15(4) that, "All citizens shall have equal opportunities of receiving education. Nothing herein contained shall prevent the state from providing special facilities for educationally backward sections".

It also states that, "The State shall promote with special care the educational and economic interests of the weaker sections of society and shall protect them from 'social injustice' and all forms of exploitation". The Article further states that nothing in Article 15(4) will prevent the nation from helping SCs and STs for their betterment.

In 1982, the Constitution specified 15% and 7.5% of vacancies in public sector and government-aided educational institutes as a quota reserved for the SC and ST candidates respectively for a period of five years, after which it was to be reviewed. This period was routinely extended by the succeeding governments. The Supreme Court of India ruled that reservations cannot exceed 50% and put a cap on reservations.

However, there are State laws that exceed this 50% limit and these are under litigation in the Supreme Court. For example, caste based reservation stands at 69% and the same is applicable to about 87% of the population in the State of Tamil Nadu.

In 1990, then Prime Minister VP Singh announced that 27% of government positions would be set aside for OBCs in addition to the 22.5% already set aside for SCs and STs. This was followed according to the Mandal Commission which was established in India in 1978 by the Janata Party government under Prime Minister Morarji Desai with a mandate to "identify the socially or educationally backward".

Now, the question arises whether there is a need to review the reservation policy in India or should continue with the tradition? The basic idea of reservation was undoubtedly superb as it was in all good intent, meant to improve till now the status of those sections of the society which had hitherto been left uncared for. However, as we see it today, the policy of reservation has completely changed in the past few years. There has been unlimited extension of the policy for no one knows how long, it appears as though the policy has come to stay forever and its extension is also as though unlimited, with several more sections joining the band wagon of the classes under reservation.

If we look at the reservation policy in India, we are the only country in the world that provides affirmative action based on individual caste identities. It is a well established fact that reservations are tools of upliftment for those disadvantaged groups who have suffered years of discrimination and oppression at the hands of the higher castes.

We the people of India, believe in the concept of 'Vasudhaiva Kutumbakam' where we take each and every person on equal terms and also take the path of fraternity into its ambit. The reservation policy in India gave a change to the backward and downtrodden people to be on equal terms with the other classes of the society. It not only helped them in improving their lives and status in the society but also provided them with an opportunity to represent themselves in various aspects of the decision-making part of society, something which has denied to them for a long time.

Reservation has come up in educational institutions, in jobs, in state assemblies, in

Parliament and in every feasible sphere. It will be a wonder if this system is really going to help us to raise our standards in every sphere or will this become just a tool in the hands of a few, to forward their own interests, as has been upto this juncture. The reservation policy has taken only few families of weaker sections and not the masses, in general, in its purposed ambit. If we do not revise this preferential discrimination policy, we are going to see more division, more resentment and more violence. We need a policy which really helps people who are deprived of education and means of better life. Reserving certain percentage of seats in the higher education of institutions and jobs in the high ranks of the government is not going to help solve problems of 85% of total backward castes population.

The government need to review its reservation policy instead of extending its benefits to the other sections also who call themselves backwards. The criterion for reservation should be totally restructured as we need to set certain definitions straight all over again before we decide whom to give reservation or not to give it at all. If equality is the aim, reservation should be given to people with lower income group so that they feel at par with the rest of the society.

Economic background must be considered if reservations are actually to help deserving people. The current reservation policy and its persistence is likely to increase the caste gap which is most likely to solidify distinctions in the society producing unnecessary rancour. It should be kept in mind that lowering the standard of education for anyone is not the solution, it is important to raise the standards of facilities provided to people so that they become self-reliant and come out of the vicious circle of caste and quotas. Reservation should not be looked at as the only tool for empowering the marginalised backward communities of the society.

CYBER CRIME

The past two decades have witnessed an invasion by technology in almost all the spheres of human life. This has led to an increased dependency on technology. Thanks to information technology, the world is making paradigm shifts from the offline to the online domain. Everything from banking, stock exchange, healthcare, education can be controlled and monitored using technology. As there are two sides of a coin, the technology also has two sides to it *i.e.*, its pros and cons. One of the major cons of the technology is cyber crime.

Cyber crime is defined as a crime in which a computer is the object of the crimes such as, hacking, phishing, spamming or is used as a tool to commit an offense (child pornography, hate crimes). Cyber criminals may use computer technology to access personal information, business trade secrets or use the internet for malicious purposes such as online monitoring of another person's activities, unauthorised users who can access their personal and sensitive information.

A person who gains unatuthorised access to the system is known as a hacker. Theft involves the download of copyrighted material by violating the copyrights. In the case of electronic fund transfer crime, a person illegally gains access to another person's bank details and this may lead to financial losses. E-mail bombing involves sending a large number of mails over the network in order to crash the server. A very common cyber crime act is sending the virus as an attachment via mails. This virus can be used to extract the data from the system and jeopardise it in some cases.

National and international financial institutions, banks and security agencies fall victim to the cyber criminals. In many cases, they have to pay a lot of money to the criminals in order to prevent the misuse of their data. The social media is driving the world crazy. But, at the same time, it has become a breeding ground and platform for cyber crime. Thanks to the sharing culture of social media, people tend to share a lot over the social media platforms. This information is used by cyber criminals to extract personal and sensitive information of others which can be misused later on. The imposters create fake social media accounts and post misleading information about the concerned person. This commonly happens with public figures and is done with an intention to malign and harm the image of the person.

In this world dominated by technology, smartphones have become imperative. The smartphones have given way to mobile applications. A large number of private and public sector banks, e-commerce websites, railways and airlines have launched their mobile applications. The ease of operations of smartphone applications prompts the users to install and operate them. With millions of users, these applications are a lucrative source of data.

Many times, the users unknowingly grant certain permissions to the application, which allows it to access their personal information. This gives the application provider with personal information about the individual. So, the user need to be careful while installing mobile applications and be sure of the permissions granted to them.

India is taking giant strides towards digitalisation with initiatives such as 'Digital India'. This necessitates the people to learn to tackle with the different aspects of cyber crime. Although, people have become tech-savvy, their knowledge about cyber crime is limited. The cyber crime needs to be dealt at two levels—one will be at the individual level and the other will be at the service provider level.

People need to be very careful about their acquaintances and the degree to which they divulge their personal information on social media. It is best to stay away and not accept invites, as well as requests, from unknown people. One should avoid sharing sensitive information such as passwords with anyone. The passwords need to be strong enough so that the hacker cannot crack them. In order to increase the strength of the password, one can make use of alpha-numeric values and special symbols. In fact, one needs to make sure that there is never a common password for all accounts.

It is best to refrain from clicking on the pop-ups and unknown website links. One needs to make sure that all the transactions that are done online happen through a secured gateway. One must abstain from saving the bank account details on the websites. The mails which make claims about winning a prize money are malicious and must be ignored. A good quality anti-virus must be installed in the system. This anti-virus must be regularly updated.

E-mail service providers as well as many other online platforms have started multi-step verification process in order to secure the user's account. It is always better to spend some extra amount of time and go in for the verification in order to secure one's account. The service provider can encrypt the data in order to protect it. Encryption is a technique to convert plain text into cipher text. Cipher text is the coded text and it is only the recipient of the data who can decrypt it using a special private key. In this way, except for the recipient, nobody can access the information. A wall can be created between the users and possible intruders. This wall is known as the Firewall. The firewall allows the flow of information only to the computers which are registered and recognised by the host. Digital signatures can be used in case of banking and other such industries. These are created by cryptography and are safe to use.

The biggest concern with regards to cyber crime is that it gets tough to uncover the identity of the criminal. A skilled law enforcing agency is required to deal with this crime. The Information Technology Act, 2000 passed by Indian Government deals with the domain of cyber crime. But this act has certain loopholes that need to be plugged in order to strengthen the cyber security. Besides, it is important for the government to create awareness among the people about the exponentially rising cyber crime and ways to deal with it.

There will always be new and unexpected challenges to stay ahead of cyber criminals and cyber terrorists but we can win only through partnership and collaboration of both individuals and government. There is much we can do to ensure a safe, secure and trustworthy computing environment. It is crucial not only to our national sense of well-being, but also to our national security and economy.

CHILD LABOUR IN INDIA

Childhood is considered to be the golden period of one's life but this doesn't hold true for some children who struggle to make their both ends meet during their childhood years. At a tender age, which is supposed to be an age of playing and going to school, they are compelled to work in factories, industries, offices or as domestic helps. Child labour means employment of children in any kind of work that hampers their physical and mental development, deprives them of their basic educational and recreational requirements. It is a blot on our society and speaks volumes about the inability of our society to provide a congenial environment for the growth and development of the children.

Earlier, the children used to help their parents in agricultural practices such as sowing, harvesting, reaping and taking care of cattle etc. But industrialisation and urbanisation have in a way encouraged child labour. Children are employed in hazardous work such as bidi rolling, cracker industry, pencil, matchbox and bangle making industries etc. In the bidi industry, children are expected to perform all the chores of rolling, binding and closing the ends of bidis using their nimble fingers. The cracker industry poses threat to the lives of the children due to their direct exposure to the explosive material. The bangle and pencil making industries make the child susceptible to different respiratory problems and lung cancer, in the worst cases. Besides, children are employed as labourers in the garment, leather, jewellery and sericulture industry.

A number of other factors could be attributed to the rise of this menace. In the poor and lower strata families, children are considered to be an extra earning hand. These families have a conviction that every child is an earner so, more the number of children more the earning. The children are expected to shoulder their parents' responsibilities. Parental illiteracy is also one of the contributors to this problem. Education tends to take a backseat in the lives of these children. The uneducated parents consider education as an investment in comparison to the returns which they get in the form of earnings of their children. The child labourers are subjected to unhygienic conditions, late working hours and different atrocities which have a direct effect on their cognitive development. The young and immature minds of the children find it difficult to cope with such situations leading to different emotional and physical problems. Employers also prefer child labourers in comparison to the adults. This is because they can extract more work and still afford to pay the children lesser amount. Bonded child labour is one of the worst forms of child labour. In this, the children are made to work in order to pay off a loan or debt of the family.

It can be considered as a form of slavery where the children assist their parents as they inherit the debt from them. Bonded labourers are most commonly employed in the agriculture sector. Bonded labour has resulted into trafficking of the children from rural to urban areas in order to work as domestic helps or in small production houses.

The government has an important role to play in this fight against child labour. As poverty is one of the major cause of child labour in India, the government needs to assure that it provides basic amenities to all its citizens and there is an equal distribution of wealth. It needs to generate sufficient jobs to assure employability to the poor.

At the same time, NGOs can provide vocational training to people in order to get them good jobs. The government, in collaboration with NGOs, should reach out to the poor people to make them understand the importance of education. The parents as well as the children should be made aware of the government's initiative to provide free education to all the children between the age group of 6-14 years. The parents must be encouraged to send their children to schools instead of work places.

To prohibit the child labour in India Nobel Prize winner Kailash Satyarthi took an initiative. He is the founder of Bachpan Bachao Aandolan (BBA), and organisation dedicated towards the eradication of child labour and rehabilitation of the rescued former child workers. Educated citizens can contribute significantly in doing away with child labour. They can play an important role in spreading the word about the harmful effect of child labour on the oerall development of a child. Affluent and high income group families can pool in funds to support the education of poor children. In fact, the schools and colleges can come up with innovative teaching programmes for the poor children. The principle of 'Each one, teach one' can be followed. Children of the support staff (peons, clerks etc of schools and colleges) can be offered free education.

The Indian Government has enacted many laws to protect child rights, namely the Child and Adolescent Labour (Prohibition and Regulation) Act, 1986, the Factories Act, 1948, the Mines Act, 1952, the Bonded Labour System Abolition Act and the Juvenile Justice (Care and Protection of Children) Act, 2000. Most of these acts prohibit the employment of children below the age of 14 years in factories, hazardous occupations or in bondage. The Right of Children to Free and Compulsory Education Act, 2009 mandates free and compulsory education to all children between the age group of 6 to 14 years. Apart from this, it also reserves 25 per cent seats in every private school for Economically Weaker Sections (EWS) of the society.

The National Policy on Child Labour, 1987 looks into the rehabilitation of children working in hazardous occupations. The Article 39 of the Indian Constitution declares the duty of the state to provide the children the facilities to develop in a healthy and congenial environment and in conditions of freedom and dignity. In May 2015, the government approved a proposal allowing children below 14 years of age to work in family enterprises or entertainment industry with specific conditions.

But there should be a total ban on the employment of small children in any activity other than going to school and getting educated. The government needs to ensure that it has foolproof laws and they are properly executed as well as implemented. Strict measures need to be taken against those who encourage child labour in any form.

Children are the future of a country and it is the childhood which has a profound impact on the future of a child. So, it becomes the collective responsibility of the citizens, society and the government to provide them an environment which helps them to bring out the best of their capabilities, thus participate in the nation building process.

Children are the future citizens of a country. Childhood experiences and foundation will have a great impact on these children's overall development. A nation full of poverty ridden illiterate children cannot make progress. It should be the collective responsibility of the society and the government to provide children with a healthy and conducive environment which will help them to develop their innate capabilities and use their skills effectively.

The need of the hour is to expand the machinery for enforcing the various laws on child labour. If child labour is to be eradicated from India, the government and those responsible for the enforcement need to do their jobs sincerely. Success can be achieved only through social engineering on a major scale combined with broad based economic growth.

ONE BELT ONE ROAD (OBOR)

Chinese President Xi Jinping announced one of China's most ambitious foreign policy and economic initiatives at the end of 2013. He called for building of a Silk Road Economic Belt (SREB) and a 21st Century Maritime Silk Road, collectively referred to as One Belt One Road (OBOR). OBOR is arguably one of the largest development plans in modern history.

Originally this project was envisioned to increase Chinese trade as it needs more raw materials and markets now and also to develop its northeastern Xinjiang region but the most important reason was to grow in a world power.

However if we gain a deeper insight we notice that it is going to affect India as well. On one side we can debate upon that it would result into better integration with Central Asian countries but on the other side we notice that it will harm India in many ways.

Firstly the most important concern is the threat that comes from China-Pakistan Economic Corridor (CPEC), which is an integral part of SREB. Due to the fact that the CPEC project runs through Pakistan Occupied Kashmir (POK), it poses a serious fear that in the near future China may emerge as a direct party in Kashmir dispute and undermine India's strategic position. The China-Pakistan Economic Corridor's mandate includes the development of energy infrastructure, roads and railways. Its influence ends in Gwadar, which is fast becoming a de facto Chinese staging post in the Persian Gulf area. It will also allow transport energy sources like petroleum from Middle East Countries via Pakistan. China signed 51 MoU's with Pakistan worth $46 billion as an extension of China's Silk Road initiative. Regional transport, energy security and blue economy are the key reasons. Apart from serving as a commercial port, Gwadar is also deep enough to accommodate submarines and aircraft carriers. Thus it may be used as a military port by People Liberation Army Navy in future.

The development of more projects such as Gwadar could significantly trouble India's current dominance in its backyard—the Indian Ocean region. Also OBOR is a unilateral idea of China and there is a lack of transparency in its working. The process is not participatory and collaborative in nature.

Another harm is that China is developing ports in Bangladesh, Sri Lanka, and Pakistan under Maritime Silk Route (MSR) and trying to enlarge its influence using its economic might in the Bay of Bengal and the Arabian Sea. So MSR is nothing but an economic disguise to the "Strings of Pearls" Theory. The fact that China is investing a lot in India's neighbouring country and it can play its cards against India can also not-derelict, for example, China-Pakistan Economic Corridor gives de facto legitimization of Pakistan's rights in POK (Pakistan Occupied Kashmir) which is against India's interests.

As far as security issues are concerned, through OBOR, China is trying to counter the strategies of India in North East region and is promoting its greater presence in North East India, part of which China claims as its own territory.

Now if India joins OBOR it will give legitimacy to the alleged state-sponsored terrorism from Pakistan which can spread to the rest of J&K. Besides that the fact that the economies of China, India and Pakistan are not complementary and can actually spell doom for India's economy.

DEMONETISATION

In a historical move that will add record strength in the fight against corruption, black money, money laundering, terrorism and financing of terrorists as well as counterfeit notes, the Government of India had decided that the 500 and 1000 rupee notes would no longer be legal tender from midnight, 8 November, 2016. Prime Minister Narendra Modi made these important announcements during a televised address to the nation on the evening of 8 November 2016. He said that these decisions will fully protect the interests of honest and hard-working citizens of India and that those five hundred and one thousand rupee notes hoarded by anti-national and anti-social elements will become worthless pieces of paper.

Though the unprecedented financial measure may have come as a rude shock to many, Narendra Modi also gave enough opportunities and threw enough hints in this regard. However, he waited for the festival season of Dussehra and Diwali to get over. The first such initiative came when the Narendra Modi Government, in its very first Cabinet meeting, constituted a Supreme Court-monitored Special Investigation Team (SIT) on Black Money.

This was followed by the launch of the Pradhan Mantri Jan Dhan Yojana (PMJDY) on August 28,

2014. Prime Minister Narendra Modi took personal interest in the scheme. He made it a mission to ensure that the scheme was successful. The scheme would be of immense help in the present circumstances. Now, that old ₹ 500 and ₹ 1000 currency denomination notes have been banned, transactions from banks will acquire importance. Opening of accounts even in the remote areas will help the rural villagers. They will not feel the pinch of demonetisation of the currency notes.

Had the bank accounts not been opened, the people would have faced immense problems. But not now, at least for those who have bank accounts.

The government renegotiated the Double Tax Avoidance Agreement (DTAA) with Mauritius to impose Capital Gains Tax if such Capital Asset is situated in India. The Narendra Modi Government also negotiated an Automatic Information Exchange Agreement with Switzerland. Agreements are also being negotiated with other tax havens. From 2017, Organisation of Economic Cooperation and Development (OECD) countries have agreed to share information on foreign account holders with their home countries.

The scheme was launched to bring back black money stashed in foreign countries and tax havens. The scheme ended on 30 September, 2015. The Act also had various stringent provisions for penalty and prosecution of foreign black money holders unearthed during future investigation by the tax department.

The Income Declaration Scheme (IDS) which opened on June 1, 2016 gave a chance to black money holders to come clean by declaring the assets by September 30 and paying tax and penalty of 45 per cent on it. The Narendra Modi Government wanted to capture the entire parallel economy flowing in the system of ₹ 7 lakh crore in India. The government was upset with the output of IDS scheme. Though the Income Tax department had identified 90 lakh high value transactions without PAN, the final disclosure of black money was to the tune of ₹ 65,250 crore.

The Narendra Modi Government imposed a penalty of 20 per cent on all cash transactions exceeding ₹ 20,000 to purchase or sell a property (real estate). This was aimed at curbing the role of black money in real estate transactions. Another important step to check high value cash transactions and create an audit trail was to impose Tax Collection at Source at a nominal rate of 1 per cent on cash purchases exceeding ₹ 2 lakh.

The Parliament passed the Benami Transactions (Prohibition) Amendment Act, 2016 (BTP Amendment Act) in August. It came into force from November 1, 2016. The new law seeks to give more teeth to the authorities to curb benami transactions. The notification issued by the Income Tax department, stated that after coming into effect, the BTP Amendment Act, the existing Benami Transactions (Prohibition) Act, 1988, shall be renamed as Prohibition of Benami Property Transactions Act, 1988 (PBPT Act).

Narendra Modi is the second Indian Prime Minister to demonetise high-value rupee notes in independent India. But he will be the first to introduce the ₹ 2,000 and ₹ 200 notes. In 1978, the then Prime Minister Morarji Desai had banned all currency notes above ₹ 100. In both instances, it was the menace of black money that had compelled the government to scrap the existing high-value currency notes.

The Prime Minister has time and again said that the Government is committed to ensure that the menace of black money is overcome.

E-BANKING/INTERNET BANKING

Computers and internet have brought revolution in our lives in many ways. Our banks and banking system are also revolutionized by these. Now-a-days you may do all bank-related work without even entering the bank premises, sitting at home or in the office. You do not have to bother about the bank distance, timings, holidays, negligent staff and long queues. This type of banking is known as internet banking or electronic banking. Even to withdraw or deposit cash you do not have to visit your bank's branch. All you have to do is to visit the nearby ATM and use your ATM card to do this. Even if your branch is located in another city you can do all type of banking transactions sitting in a remote place or city. Thanks to e-banking!

Banks are trying to make your life easier. Not just bill payment, you can make investments, shop or buy tickets and plan a holiday, all at your fingertips.

Each bank has tie-ups with various utility companies, service providers and insurance companies across the country. You can facilitate payment of electricity and telephone bills, mobile phone, credit card and insurance premium bills.

All you need is a computer with a modem or other dial-up device like a mobile phone, a checking account with a bank that offers online service. Just press a few keys and it is done.

You can transfer any amount from one account to another of the same or any other bank. You can now open an FD online through funds transfer.

Now you no longer need to rush to the vendor to recharge your prepaid phone or DTH. Just top-up your prepaid mobile cards and DTH account by logging in to Internet banking.

Leading banks have tie ups with various shopping websites. With a range of all kind of products, you can shop online and the payment is also made conveniently through your account. You can also buy railway and air tickets through Internet banking.

Through Internet banking, you can check your transactions at any time of the day, and as many times as you need.

There are many advantages of online banking. It is convenient, it isn't bound by operational timings, there are no geographical barriers and the services can be availed free of cost or at a minimal cost.

Customers should never share personal information like PIN numbers, passwords etc. with anyone, including employees of the bank.

PLACE OF WOMEN IN SOCIETY

Today, we find women walking shoulder to shoulder in all fields of life. They are there in the fields of education, medicine, law, engineering, administration, management, etc. Now, we have women teachers, doctors, nurses, air-hostesses, engineers, architects, clerks, officers and even pilots and drivers.

However, all this seems to be on the surface. Women form about one half of the population. Have they got a quota of 50% in all walks of life? The answer is big NO. So, liberation and empowerment of women is still a dream. Only a small fraction of women belonging to higher sections of society have been able to reach the top. Most of them are still languishing behind in this male-dominated society. The condition for women is particularly miserable in poor families and rural areas.

Our constitution gives equal rights to women along with men. Girls are getting education equal to boys at least in the urban areas. Reservation for women has been made in the Panchayati Raj. But such reservation is still not there in the union and state legislatures. In the Parliament and state assemblies, there is a vast gap between the number of men and women legislators.

Still, great cruelties are being inflicted on women. Some of the most heinous crimes in society are taking place against women. Thus, we have female foeticide, bride-burning, dowry system, rapes, molestations, murders of women, eve-teasing, etc.

It is imperative that laws pertaining to women such as anti-dowry laws, sex-determination tests, etc. should be made more stringent and much severer punishments should be given to violaters. Women themselves should also assert at all levels.

Women should be treated equal to men. Girls and women should be given the same type of food, education, clothing, employment opportunities, health opportunities, etc. as boys and men. In other words, women should be empowered further and made self-dependent to give them real freedom and empowerment. Seats for them should be reserved in educational, medical and engineering colleges and particularly in legislatures. It is commendable that Women's Reservation Bill has at last been passed in the Rajya Sabha on 10th March 2010 which gives moral empowerment to women in politics.

PRICE RISE

India is a land of problems. One of the most serious problem is the problem of price rise. Whenever we go to market, we often find that the prices of all the essential articles have risen. Now, the situation has become more serious because of unprecedented rise in the prices of food items.

It is very difficult for a common man to make both ends meet. The income of the common people does not rise so much as the prices of goods. The salaried people and those who live on pensions are hit the most as they have only a fixed income. The condition of those who live on interest income is even worse as the interests have so many times been decreased during the last few years.

One great reason for the rise in prices is the rapid increase in population. Another reason is that most of the people are trying to raise their standards of living. Now people are giving more attention to food, clothing, health, housing, entertainment, education of children, etc. Many people have ACs, cars, desert coolers, geysers, mixers, refrigerators, television sets, telephones, etc. in their homes which previously they did not have. All this increases their expenditure and prices of goods.

Goods are not produced at the same rate as the population and demand rise. Many people waste money on luxuries and functions and marriages. The government does not care to control its expenditure. Taxation system is also defective in our country. Then, there are so many ministers and legislators and government employees who have to be paid from treasury. Not much money is left with the government for development purposes.

India has to import a lot of petroleum products and gas to meet her energy requirements. There is much wastage of petrol on running luxury cars. Black money and corruption also lead to price rise. Some traders hoard essential items and raise prices to earn more profits. Famines, floods and strikes also cause price rise.

To check prices, population should be controlled. Strikes should be avoided. Taxation system should be overhauled. Wastage should be avoided. Black money and corruption should be dealt with strictly. Unnecessary imports should be avoided, particularly the imports of luxury items. More attention should be given to exports. Production should be increased. More attention should be given to energy resources.

Much expenditure has to be done on defence. This cannot be helped. However, it should be avoided wherever the security of the country is not compromised. Good relations with neighbouring countries should be established to minimise expenditure on wars and encounters.

With the coming of the GST system of taxation, people hoped that the prices of goods would by and large go down to a considerable extent. But this has not happened. Let the government and people cooperate with each other to solve all problems, including the problem of price rise.

POPULATION EXPLOSION

The rapidly increasing population may be a matter which can cause scare in the minds of all thinking people. It is a kind of explosion no less horrible than the explosion of an atom bomb.

At the time India got Independence in 1947, she had the population of about 35 crore. Now, she is inhabited by more than 125 crore people. The world over population has greatly increased. It is around 700 crore mark at present. It also means that every 7th person in the world is an Indian. Population is increasing more rapidly in developing countries than in developed countries. It means industrialisation or development is an answer to the rising trend in population.

India is second only to China in the matter of population. But in India, population is increasing much more rapidly than in China. It is estimated by the demographers that within the next two decades India may overtake China in the matter of population and will become number one in the world.

There are several reasons for this rapid increase of population. One of the reasons is the improved healthcare facilities. These facilities have reduced the number of infant mortality and increased the life span. Another reason is illiteracy. Many people, mostly in slum and rural areas do not have much knowledge of means of family planning.

Still, another reason is poverty. Many poor people want more and more children to increase the earning capacity of their family as they put their children to some sort of work at a very early age. Child marriages and early marriages are other reasons.

It is very important that awareness should be brought about among the people to adopt the means of family planning especially, the traditional and religious-minded people of poor families should be brought around to adopt these methods.

FEMALE FOETICIDE

Of all the crimes and immoral acts, perhaps female foeticide is the most heinous. Female foeticide means killing the girl child in the womb. It is no different from killing a girl who is born, as a girl in the womb is as much a living being. She is only at a developing stage.

The main reason for female foeticide is that the girls are not a desirable child in our society. It is mainly because of our faulty social customs. A girl is considered a burden on the parents. It is because as per the common social practice in our country, the girl's parents have to give a very rich dowry on her marriage. In fact, they have to continue giving money and material to the girl's in-laws all her life. Therefore, if the problem of female foeticide is to be solved in right earnest, the problem of dowry system must also be solved on equal footing along with it.

Indians are fond of having a male child to continue the lineage. Those who have one or more girl children go in for female foeticide till they get a male child. In this respect, the use of ultrasonic machines has played a negative role. As a matter of fact, these machines are very useful for scanning purposes to determine the presence of any abnormality in the body. But they are being used unscrupulously for knowing the sex of the infant in the womb. No doubt, there is an Anti-prenatal sex determination law, but the unhealthy practice of knowing the sex of the unborn child is going on secretly. For this, the greedy practitioners charge a hefty amount which the parents of the unborn child gladly pay.

The sex ratio against girls has been declining during the last few decades. It is particularly the condition in some of the northern states, Punjab and Haryana in particular. The situation has become alarming after the arrival of ultrasound scanning machines.

If this trend continues, a stage may come when girls will be a rare breed. Already there are so many crimes against women in society such as rapes, murders, bride-burning, immoral trafficking, etc. We will certainly shudder to think of final stage and that is the world without women. If there are no women, there will be no mankind. So, if we do not take any drastic steps right from now, we may be heading towards a womanless world which means the end of mankind. Hence all the educationists, students, teachers, parents, government, NGO's and the media should strain every nerve to enlighten the people and put an end to this unhealthy practice positively.

RELIGION IS THE OPIUM OF THE MASSES

Religion is the most dominant social force in the society and is next only to technology and materialism. It is surprising to note that but we are bound to hit the next century within a year we have not been able to overcome the harmful effects of religion. The opium of religion is still intoxicating our people and we have received more harm than good due to its existence.

Take the modern urban man as an example. His contribution towards religious causes is very low. He devotes a small time period in temples, mosques or churches; his busy schedule does not allow him to get overindulgent in religious affairs. He is a machine which must churn out money and materialistic assets. Then, how could he possibly devote his entire time to religion? Strange it many seem but we must take note of the fact that ignorance of religion in the urban areas is harmful to the urban masses. The peace of mind and mental satisfaction are no longer the keywords in urban settings. The lust for money, power, cars, mobile phones and factories is increasing and this is giving more tantrums to the urban society. We therefore, feel that "fear of God" and a will to remain on the right path should be inculcated by religion in the urban areas. The "cog in the machine" concept has made the urban people devoid of religious feelings; even if they rely upon religion, it is only an escape for their sins or a platform for their politico-religious machinations.

Now let us have a look at the rural religious landscape. The rural masses are credulous and gullible. They are simple and do not have evil depths in their hearts. They take the statements at their face values and are sans all evil manipulations. So the religious leaders and the politicians use their innocence to their own advantage and exploit them to the core. The sixth anniversary of Babri Masjid demolition fell on December 6, 1998 and there were fears of reprisals from the Muslim militants and fundamentalists. The USA had warned her citizens residing in India that there could be bloodshed on December 6, 1998. The rural areas are the worst hit by the religious turmoils. The master manipulators, politicians, the resource rich people and antisocial elements exploit such tense situations to their advantage. It must be noted that in a total contrast to the urban scenario, the moral values are upheld properly in the rural areas. But still, the rural people are more conforming to religious practices than their urban counterparts. They need not cleanse themselves as they do not have wicked hearts. But they are forced to take a diabolical recourse to religion. What an irony!

This blood and gore would have to be stopped. India is a multi-cultural and multi-ethnic society. We are secular to the core. There are no communal differences or strikes in the rural areas. The political and religious groups create these differences for their vested interests. The ultimate losers are the villagers, the farmers, the rural industries and finally, the national economy. We have to put a check on the communal frenzy at all costs. Our record as a "diverse but united nation" must remain intact.

The communication revolution — through satellite television, Internet, cable TV networks and telephone networks — could deliver the message of communal harmony to the rural masses. Community workshops must be organised in sensitive pockets in order to preach non-violence and brotherhood among the masses. Cinema and theatre could play vital role in this context. If facts are put before the public in the right perspective, then the public would take the criminal elements to task. The police and judiciary should extend all cooperation and support in this regard.

It is very important to educate the masses so that they could distinguish between communalism and religion. An educated individual would have a conscience but an uneducated individual would only have a religion-based motivation for performing any task. Education would inculcate logic, rationale and communal brotherhood among the various communities. After all, we have been living together for the past 5,000 years. A few stray incidents cannot tear our national fabric. We are a strong and united national organism and time has made this glaring fact known to the world.

Religion should dominate our personal and spiritual lives. It should be separated from politics and economic problems. We have entered the new millennium. We have to shed most of the features of the past. Communal violence and hatred is one such evil, which must be done away within the national context. Already, this demon has consumed lakhs of people and property worth billions. Let this demon know that we all are united and would oppose all those forces, which tend to divide us. We shall emerge victorious in the long run as we are on the right path. Our sacrifices would not go in vain. We have already faced enough of communal violence.

SECULARISM

All the politicians in India commit themselves to national unity and security. They pledge their allegiance to a secular India. But all of them play the communal card to their advantage as communalism propagates their interests. They always try to rake up communal issues in some part of the country or another. This helps them in tarnishing the image of other political party and consolidating their own positions in the ensuing elections. If we listen to the gibe of any politician, we would never find him to be telling a lie. They seem to be so natural and patriotic that one may be forced to think that they could have done very well in theatre or cinema.

India is a secular State. The word 'secular' has been inserted in the Constitution (42nd Amendment) Act, 1976. Our secular character has been kept intact by our previous governments and should be kept so in future as well. Our record as a united nation (despite many cultural and religious diversities) is very enviable viz-a-viz our other Asian and African neighbours. How can India cease to exist as a secular entity while it is a glaring fact that our leaders and nation-builders emphasised upon this fact while starting our journey from the dawn of independence in 1947? We had some ideals to cherish, some dreams to realise and some moral values to adopt and nurture. Is our secularism so phoney that it could break under the stress of communal riots merely after 50 years of Independence? No! There is something wrong with our political, social and moral systems and during the task of nation building, we have not been able to take care of some

important aspects of our secularism and nationalism. Let us analyse some of the issues at stake :

We did not take adequate care of the interests of the minorities. We tried to reserve seats for SCs, STs and OBCs. We tried to give more privileges to all the tribal masses. But we did not understand that people were proud to be Muslims, Christians and Sikhs. They were in minority but they needed our affection and care. They did not ask for reservations as Muslims, Sikhs or Christians but they deserved our love and empathy.

The planners of our country did well to promote our country as a secular one. But they did not understand that a Hindu, a Muslim or a Christian lives according to his social beliefs, customs and religious rituals. Religion touches his life on a daily basis. We cannot ignore the fact that he needs religion on a day-to-day basis even if he breathes in a secular country. Our 'secular' character cannot overshadow the religious devotion of the masses. For example, a Muslim is an Indian but he is a Muslim as well. He has to attend the mosque for prayers five times a day. He has to fast during the *Ramzan* days and he would certainly celebrate Eid. Our Constitution guarantees the right to accept and follow any religion and the State does not interfere in this right of the individual.

Our leaders failed to understand that the right of all the minorities are equal to the rights of the majority. Therefore, if a citizen of India misuses religion and tries to disrupt the secular fabric of the nation (e.g., terrorism in Punjab), then the State must not tolerate such type of deviation on the part of that citizen and it can use long arm of the law to counter such moves. But if the poor citizen is leading a peaceful life and his religion does not hurt others, then the State does not have any right to impose any ritual, prayer, religious compulsion or tax upon him. For example, it is quite natural that the Hindu Code Bill is not applicable to Muslims as they are governed by Muslim Personal Law.

In this context, we can rightly conclude that the attacks on the minorities, their religious places or places of worship, the incidents of communal carnage and the illegal support of the ruling majority to the anti-social elements (for suppressing the minorities) are deplorable and would not suit the long term secular interests of our nation. We would live in better manner and would grow to new heights if we continue to retain our secular character on national and state levels. We respect and love all the faiths and need blessings of all the forms of Almighty in order to become a stronger and a more prosperous nation.

INTERNET : NEW CHALLENGES

In October 1990 Tim Barnes Lee produced the first ever Internet browser in European Particle Physics Laboratory (in the Swiss Alps). This software could scan every document, photo or video on the Net. This was a wonderful tool, which was named world wide web (www). Thus, the web became an instant hit because it was created by users. The web (www) democratised the Net. The age of Information, Communication and Entertainment (ICE) has made it indispensable and the human evils would make it lethal.

In the new era dominated by paperless offices, E-mail messages, E-cash transactions and virtual departmental stores, it would be cynical to imagine without the Internet. People would soon find their parents and siblings working through the Net from their own homes. The concepts of Small Office Home Office (SOHO) would be the most convenient derivative of Internet technologies in India. And why should we ignore the world? Nearly 30 per cent of business transactions in Europe and the USA are being carried out through this information superhighway. There are many more advantages of the Internet, which confirm the fact that it is a trusted friend of the surfer, businessman and the young mind of today. Let us outline them in a nutshell, as follows :

1. Information exchange is facilitate through the Net. Speeds vary from 56 KBPS to 1.2 GBPS. In the West, these speeds are higher. In India, if bandwidth is raised, then these speeds of data transfer will be mind boggling, thus leading us to a new era of high-speed information exchanges.

2. E-business has received boost in the West, though the progress of Net-related business activities is very slow. These trends would take a healthy course (in India) in the times to come.

3. Western nations depend upon the Internet, we would be forced to use it. So, we should adopt it quickly in our business operations, lest we should lose vital orders that can be won if we are Net-enabled.

4. There is no doubt about the efficiency of the Net as an entertainer. Children are amazed by the mind-boggling variety of games, software, entertaining programmes and what not? Adults and senior citizens also enjoy it (perhaps more than the idiot box). And housewives do not forget to switch on the computers of their husbands or children for getting information about the latest in women's world (whenever they find time).

5. Logistic costs would rise in the times to come. Further, busy people would not find time even to buy the bare necessities for themselves. The Net would help them (through WAP-enabled services) procure whatever they want (while they are on the move). Blue Tooth and DTH would also transform their business and social lives. Virtual departmental stores are already operational. People need not go to a grocery shop to purchase a cake of washing soap; they should use the mouse-click instead.

6. Internet would revolutionise the concepts of services. All the services would be available with the click of the mouse on it. Medical assistance, railway assistance and booking, road transportation, tourism services, booking for air cargo, booking for a theatre show, pest control services, etc., are only a few examples that would be (or, are being) provided through the Net.

In sum, we can state that the Net is a friend of mankind.

However, there are some critics of the Net who contend that its birth has created more chaos than harmony. Let us Consider their views as well, which are as follows :

1. The Net is a free platform; it has no legal or moral codes of conduct to govern it. Even if they exist, their coercive powers have not been established as yet. Cyber crime is the latest issue being studied by the police departments of the world. Police is "virtually patrolling" the Internet chat rooms for identifying those hackers, chat lovers and criminals who might be keen to foment trouble. Viruses such as **I Love You** have caused great harm to many a vital web site. E-cash can be stolen if the hacker gets an access to the passwords of E-cash accounts. And an intelligent hacker can siphon off billions of money from such accounts because he knows the Internet jargon fully well.

2. Interent pornography is another serious issue and worth giving a thought. Children are also being lured into this sleazy profession. This new and horrible development has forced the Net critics to come out openly against it. Moral assassination would eventually lead to societal decay, especially in the traditional societies like those of India.

3. Internet servers do break down sometimes. A server is not repaired or put in service so easily. This leads to wastage of time and loss of precious business deals. Further, when Net traffic increases (due to high numbers or E-mail transfers), important messages may not be transferred. This also leads to wastage of time and business opportunities.

4. Teenagers use the Net for satisfying their hitherto latent needs. The American Psychological Association has admitted that several youths have developed a disease due to too much surfing through the Net. It is called Internet Addiction Disorder (IAD) and the Association has added it in the list of mental disorders. Further, surfing through the websites for long hours exposes the human body to harmful radiations and weakens the eyesight too.

5. Internet connections are cheap and so are computers. At least, we can state this fact in the context of global markets. In India, prices will come down and many of us will use the Net more extensively. But this fall in prices will lead to our fading interest in physical sports and athletics. Our bodies will not remain agile and active. And a sound mind lives in a sound body. Thus, we might witness the creation of a society that is Net-addicted and physically weak. Our interest in sports will display a waning trend. Thus, we may become a physically weak or crippled species within 30 years from now.

6. Scientists have defined a new term, "the digital divide." Those, who use electronics gadgets, computers, the Net and associated avant-garde technologies, stand to gain. But many people of the world do not have access even to safe drinking water. How can they imagine that they will ever ride the Net wave? Thus, people on the "other end" of this digital divide must be made capable enough to afford these devices and technologies. If this were not done, the reprisal from the "have nots" would destroy both "haves" and "have nots."

Thus, if we go by the views of the critics, we will imagine the Net to be heartless navigator that churns out nothing but useless data, videos and money. It may be deemed by many of us as an octopus in our skies, ready to engulf the humanity through its all-pervasive websites, connections and lewd messages.

We can conclude that for some, the Net is a friend and for others, it is a foe. We must try to remove its limitations through global consensus. In India the Net is not generating much business but the harm caused to our young generation cannot be counted in numerical terms. India needs the Net but our strategy would have to be defined clearly so that this Net does not choke the lifetimes of our society and economy.

NATIONAL SECURITY— POINTS TO PONDER

India faces several military and non-military threats to its National Security. While there are military threats from its neighbours, Pakistan and China, it is mainly the threat from Islamic terrorism and ethnic insurgency which is ever growing due to external support.

Military Threats to National Security

These threats are largely from Pakistan and China. Threat from Pakistan is ever-existing, however from Chinese side, it is medium and long term. Not immediately. China is determined to see that the next Dalai Lama would be a man of its choice and that his selection would be under its supervision. This could lead to a ferment in Tibet after the exit of the present Dalai Lama, with a fall-out in the Tibetan Diaspora in India, West Europe and the US. This could once again hot up the Sino-Indian border. Till the Dalai Lama's succession issue is resolved, Beijing would prolong the border settlement talks in order to keep the border dispute alive for possible exploitation by it, if necessary.

Threat from Pakistan arises from its inferiority complex and from its paranoia and jealousy about India as well as its determination to frustrate India emerging as the paramount military and economic power of the region. Pakistani and Chinese objectives and intentions are similar, though each, while covertly co-operating with the other, would overtly follow its own modus operandi.

China, while openly advocating Indo-Pakistan detente, would continue to secretly arm Pakistan and add to its nuclear and missile capabilities in order to keep India confronted with the possibility of a two-front war.

Nuclear weapons have given us the deterrent capability vis-a-vis China and Pakistan, but, at the same time, have also added to our vulnerabilities. India has two other nuclear powers as across-the-land-border neighbours. To protect the civilian population against the dangers of a nuclear strike would be much more difficult for India than for any other nuclear power. No Government in India has paid attention to developing a dependable civil defence capability against nuclear weapons and nuclear accidents.

Non-military Threats

Religious, ethnic and ideological terrorism/ insurgency: Ideological terrorism manageable since it no longer has external sponsors after the collapse of communism in East Europe and after China stopped exporting its communist ideology.

Ethnic terrorism/insurgency has external sponsorship-not of States, but of non-Governmental organisations functioning under the cover of human rights, charitable and humanitarian organisations. Threats to national security from these organisations would continue in the short and medium term, but manageable.

Terrorism by some Sikhs effectively controlled, but not yet eliminated. Danger of revival would persist so long as Pakistan continues to give shelter to Sikh extremist leaders and to train and arm them.

Islamic terrorism: Its threat will continue and even increase due to external support from the State of Pakistan as well as from the Islamic funda-mentalist organisations of Pakistan, Afghanistan and Saudi Arabia. The old Communist international has been replaced by an Islamic International, consisting of various Islamic fundamentalist organisations with roots in Pakistan and Afghanistan. Their objective vis-a-vis India: To "liberate" the Muslims of not only Kashmir, but also the rest of India from "Hindu control". They talk of two more independent homelands for the Muslims of the sub-continent—one in North India and the other in the South.

There is an urgent need for a coherent policy to counter Pakistan's covert war. While the present Government talks of a proactive strategy, it doesn't seem to be clear in its mind about the components of this strategy. Amongst the components should be: a determination not to let Pakistan come out of its economic morass till it stops its covert war; a readiness to hurt the Pakistani State and society at a place of our choice in terrain favourable to us. In Kashmir, the terrain is not favourable to us except in the Jammu sector. To really hurt Pakistan, we have to direct our proactive strategy at its Punjab and Sindh, and particularly at Karachi. While India has a credible nuclear deterrent, it does not have a credible covert warfare deterrent, whereas Pakistan has developed its covert warfare capability over the years, with American assistance.

Pakistan-based Islamic fundamentalist organisations have been increasingly turning their attention to South India. After Tamil Nadu and Kerala, they are now focussing on Andhra Pradesh. Israeli counter-terrorism experts had been warning since 1992 of attempts to export Islamic jihadism to Tamil Nadu, but their warnings were not heeded. One understands that some Western counter-terrorism experts suspect that there has been a considerable flow of funds to the Al Ummah of Tamil Nadu and its Allied organisations in Kerala from Pakistan-based Islamic Jihadi groups, possibly through the Gulf and even Colombo.

There has never been a convincing analysis of why Pakistan's Inter-Services Intelligence (ISI) had been flirting with the LTTE, despite the latter's anti-Muslim activities in Sri Lanka's Eastern Province. One possibility, not yet proved, but suggested by foreign counter-terrorism experts in the past is that in return for the ISI's assistance, the LTTE, through its supporters in Tamil Nadu, had been training the cadres of the Al Ummah and other Jihadi organisations of South India and providing them with material assistance.

We need a separate strategy to deal with threats from the foreign-based Islamic Jihadi organisations. Such a strategy should tackle prevention of illegal migrations of Muslims from Bangladesh and Pakistan, identification and deportation of past illegal migrants, the flow of foreign funds for mosques and madrasas, the scrutiny of the credentials of foreign Muslim students who are admitted to educational institutions in India etc. In the past, even counter-terrorism experts of Islamic countries such as Algeria and Egypt had expressed surprise over the ease with which students blacklisted in their countries because of their association with extremist organisations managed to get admission to educational institutions in India without any background check.

Globalisation of the economy, of our telecommunication infrastructure through the Internet and of the printed and electronic media networks is adding to our economic strength as well as to our national security vulnerabilities. Surprisingly, in the formulation of policies relating to globalisation, national security implications have been given very little attention. Our analysts, who cite China as a model to be emulated, do not highlight the fact that China has clearly identified sensitive sectors with national security implications such as telecommunications, the Internet, defence industries, printed and electronic media etc and has been fiercely resisting Western pressure to open up these sectors to foreign participation. So has France been doing for many years. We seem to be opening up these sectors without any regard to its impact on our national security.

Mushrooming of NGOs and the unregulated flow of funds to them directly as well as through third world countries such as Nepal.

National Security Tools

Intelligence collection and analysis: Improving, but still weak with serious gaps in coverage and monitoring. Anticipation and prevention continues to be the weakest link in our national security management. While the strengthening of the intelligence collection capability of the central organisations such as the IB, the RAW and the various military intelligence directorates has been receiving attention, equal attention has not been paid to improving the intelligence collection capabilities of the States. The Centre has to play a more proactive role in this regard.

Assessment and follow-up action: Even the best of intelligence would be useless if it is not assessed promptly to identify looming threats and initiate follow-up action. This has not been given the attention it deserves. For this purpose, the National Security Council (NSC) needs a full-fledged Secretariat. In all countries with the NSC mechanism, the Secretariat is the nerve-centre and permanent watch-dog on all matters likely to affect national security. We still seem to have a miniscule Secretariat with no teeth.

Enforcement of physical and infrastructure security: Very weak as seen by the ease with which the Jihadi suicide squads have been penetrating high security areas in Kashmir and the Harkat-ul-Mujahideen terrorists had hijacked the Indian Airlines plane.

Crisis Management: It is again unsatisfactory. Past crisis management drills dealt only with conventional threats such as hijacking, hostage-taking, assassinations etc. We need separate drills supervised and co-ordinated by professional experts to deal with crises involving weapons of mass destruction (nuclear, chemical and biological) and weapons of mass disruption (hacking, injection of computer virus etc).

The Indian armed forces have to be leaner and meaner, backed by reserves and paramilitary units. Satellites should be launched to gain advance information on military and other threats and satellite imagery, missile prowess, and space-based laser platforms deployed to deter them. Longer term national security will depend on a holistic approach that integrates economic and security planning. For instance, with domestic oil and gas production falling below soaring demand, India has to ensure that the energy situation does not affect its future strategic decision-making.

ENVIRONMENTAL POLLUTION

Important elements constituting the earth are air, soil and water. These together comprise the environment. The earth has a cover of air around it which is called atmosphere. More than two-thirds of the area of the earth comprises oceans and seas which contain water.

All the elements together form climate. All the living beings can live only in a particular type of climate. We are living on the earth because a climate suitable for our living is available on this planet. Our earth took more than 400 crores of years to evolve the present climate.

It is quite clear that if the climate at present available on the earth is disturbed excessively, life on this planet may be in danger. Unfortunately, this is what man is doing at present. His actions are causing the depletion of ozone and oxygen and increasing the production of harmful gases such as carbon dioxide, carbon monoxide, sulphur dioxide, etc. These gases are produced by the smoke released by chimneys of factories, automobiles, burning of wood, etc. Such gases also cause greenhouse effect. They cause increase in temperature all over the earth. This undue increase in temperature is melting the snow on mountain-tops. This can lead to increase in the volume of water in oceans. The result of this can be the merger of many islands and coastal areas in many countries under the water.

Man is at present cutting down forests recklessly. Forests cause rain and maintain a balance of oxygen in the atmosphere.

The excessive use of pesticides and insecticides and the use of spurious fertilizers is polluting the soil. The water channels are being polluted due to the toxic matter released by factories. Non-disposal or improper disposal of medical and domestic waste is also polluting the soil and water.

Another kind of pollution is the noise pollution. We have so much noise in cities and towns. We hear sounds of factory hooters and generators, noises made by hawkers and customers in markets and loudspeakers used at religious places and functions of all types, including religions and political functions and social gatherings such as marriages, etc. Loud noises have an adverse effect on human nerves and they affect the brain and the hearing system of the body.

If man wants to continue living on this planet, he will have to mend his ways. Otherwise, there is no certainty that mankind will live for more than a century on it.

DRUG-ADDICTION

When the Hippies came to India, they brought not only strange dresses but also drugs. It is common knowledge that the young people are greatly influenced by anything strange and new.

At present, our country is under the grip of drug-addiction. Most of the drug-addicts live in cities. They include both boys and girls. University, college and school hostels are particularly full of drug-addicts.

Drug-addiction is, however, not restricted to urban areas only. Even in the rural areas there are so many drug-addicts. There are not only men but also women in large numbers who take drugs. This vice has invaded all sections of society. Many rickshaw-pullers, factory workers, government employees and even businessmen can be seen who are given to the habit of drug-taking.

Most often it so happens that a person takes a drug just for the thrill of it. Then he takes it the second or third time to repeat the experience. When he takes it a number of times, he forms the habit. Then a time comes when he wants to get rid of it. But he cannot do so because he feels restlessness if he does not take the drug.

Most of the young people start this habit in the company of their friends in hostels. One reason for this wide-spread practice is that drugs are easily available everywhere. There are so many peddlers who sell drugs. Drugs are of many kinds such as heroin, smack, LSD, opium, ganja, charas, etc. All drugs are habit-forming.

A drug-addict gets his health spoiled. He also wastes his precious money on drugs. Some of these drugs such as heroin are very costly. But those who are addicted to drugs cannot get rid of them easily. If they do not have money to purchase a drug, they steal money from home or from wherever they can.

They can even commit some more serious crime to get money for drugs.

Drug-taking makes a person lazy. It can cause even death. Young people should be taught in schools and colleges to avoid this bad habit. If a youth falls a prey to this habit, he should be taken to the drug-deaddiction centre as early as possible. Strict action should be taken against drug-peddlers, chemists, and others who sell drugs.

One reason for this menace is that the young people feel frustrated. They find the education system worthless. They do not get proper love from parents. They are unemployed and have no hope of getting a job. The parents, teachers, NGO's, social workers, government agencies and media should join hands to save the youth of our country from this menace.

MNC'S : SAVIOURS OR SABOTEURS

Multinational Corporations (MNCs) are those private companies that work in more than one country. They produce or provide goods or services of highest quality and according to the latest global norms. They also employ the best human resource in a country and thus build brand images that are unique, stable and, above all, saleable.

In India, MNCs had arrived in the mid-sixties of the last century. Colgate, Palmolive and Coca-Cola were the most trusted names of those times. The sixties also saw the presence of the drug giants. Glaxo, Nicolas and other drug majors gradually made deep forays into the Indian markets as the population demanded more medicines. But our economy remained a mixed one and our governments always looked at the MNCs with suspicion. During those times, the concept of MNCs was not born. The Japanese had just started their marathon run in the field of consumer electronics. They were disliked by most of the Indian consumers because of nil credibility.

However, Indians could not give full support to Coca-Cola due to political reasons. The company was sent packing during the seventies; those were the times when relations between India and the USA were at their lowest ebb. Glaxo, Biological Evans, Smith Kline & French and Pfizer were other drug majors, which firmly established themselves in India during the mid-seventies. And, then came the Japanese—highly efficient, cheap, determined and techno-savvy. They introduced products of the silicon age, which we fondly know as semiconductor revolution. Radio, television, wireless, electronics, telex systems, etc., were in vogue. Music got a new meaning when the Japanese majors like Sony, Matsushita and Sharp introduced hi-fidelity stereo system. The revolution had begun!

During the dying years of the seventies, the stage was set in India. During the last years of eighties, this stage was re-set by Integrated Circuits, CNC machines, drugs for fighting heart attacks and the like. So, the Indians had to rely on MNCs, which had become synonymous with technology, comfortable products and cheap rates. Most of MNCs entered India during the late eighties or early nineties. The government favoured their entry because of its changed (and liberal) policies related to economic reforms. Several MNCs established their offices and factories in urban centres of India. Some even went to villages and signed deals in collaboration (partnership) with the Indian firms. Sales soared and FMCGs became the hot goodies on the television shows and in advertisements. Cable TV networks, satellite connections and Internet connections did the rest of the job. Western culture brought the concept of consumerism or "fast eaters". Naturally, a nation that had a population of above one billion had to be given these new products, services and gizmos. And MNCs filled the void that was left by local manufacturers. It is surprising to note that not a single firm has been able to compete with Colgate Palmolive in the toothpaste market; it is the undisputed leader in this segment even today, despite the fact that there are nearly one dozen competitors.

This credibility did not seek in the minds of the Indian consumer in a day. It took several years and billions of dollars to make these products and services instant success. And there were fiascos too. The cases of Enron and Cogentrix are the two glaring examples, which bluntly tell us that we may not have any collaboration in the power generation sector. Although, Enron has displayed several flaws (like high price of power kwh at Dabhol Power Corporation), yet we cannot deny the fact that we also made a mess of the issue and moved in an unplanned fashion.

The free market economy of India has made the task of MNCs quite easier. Many readers may contend that we are not "completely free", if they keep scandals, scams, corruption and the PSUs in their view. But this ultimate change is inevitable. If ours is not a fully free economy today, it shall be one after fifty years. The MNCs realise this fact and so they have started establishing themselves in India—physically and psychologically. Several MNCs align their advertisements with local festivals, religions, beliefs and political sentiments. They have become a part of our culture quietly and in a stealthy manner. Thus, saviours may be deemed saboteurs by many a political outfit. We agree that the opponents of these global economic giants are not totally wrong. They are saviours on many fronts— medicines, heavy engineering, information technologies, medical diagnostic equipment, aircraft, chemicals, rubber products and electronic gadgets. New technologies and devices have put Indians on the path of ultimate progress. No wonder, we may become a developed nation soon due to inflow of capital, technologies, consultancy and manpower into this land. Thus, MNCs have contributed a lot to our economy and will do so in the future too.

MNCs are also being allowed to enter those sections which were hitherto deemed the exclusive areas reserved for the Indian firm. Ironically, we must state that the MNCs would do much better in those areas, thus putting out our own coin under shade. Banking, insurance, car production and telecommunication services are some of the areas in which they would outperform Indian firms. Thus, Indian firms would either be required to meet the challenge or fade into oblivion.

Finally, every MNC comes to India to earn money. In a free market system, any amount of money can be transferred by an MNC to its parent country. This would lead to drain on our precious foreign exchange reserves. We cannot check the flight of this capital. Had our own enterprises been efficient, productive and innovative, we would not have threats of this kind. It is a pity that we import shirts, jeans and electronics gadgets, whereas we can manufacture them at much cheaper rates in India. Our quality control norms are poor and so, customers get swayed by the quality of products and services of MNCs. Our own firms (like Tata, Reliance and HCL) are multinationals. So, we can easily emulate them.

We can conclude by stating that we need MNCs as we are a part of the global treading culture. We must allow them to operate in those high-technology areas in which, we lack the expertise. We should also import technologies through them but we should manufacture products (or services) in India. MNCs should not be viewed as saboteurs. But they must not be allowed to control the destiny of our nation.

CONSUMERS' RIGHTS

It has been rightly said that today, we are living in a consumer age. Never before in man's social life, have supermarkets and business centres been so dominant with their consumer food items and durables. Some 'malls' or markets of Western countries have arrived in multi-storeyed buildings of our cities. You get everything from pins to paste, household appliances to machine parts under one roof. There could be a whole floor dedicated to different types of perfumes, books and music systems.

While the manufacturers cater to every palate and taste, the consumer finds himself inundated with so much products that his powers of discrimination are challenged. It is obvious that many manufacturers take consumers for a ride. By advertising aggressively through media such as TV, the manufacturers almost hypnotize consumers into buying their brands. The goods are presented in such an artistic style as to suggest everything a consumer wants to make his life worthwhile — economy, grace, elegance and luxury. Life seems to be miserable for a housewife unless she buys "ultra-whiteners" for her husband's clothes. For the working woman or man, fast food has arrived as a boon. "Two minute noodles" is a blessing when the mother is exhausted and all the children demand food! There lies the trap. The consumer does not take the trouble to ascertain various facts about the food he or she buys.

A consumer has the following rights: *(a)* right to choose; *(b)* right to accept or reject the offer; *(c)* right to complain in an appropriate court of law for settlement of a dispute; *(d)* right to get information about the product / service; and *(e)* right to get good quality products.

Consumer awareness cells of the government have laid down guidelines to save the innocent and unwary consumer as follows:

1. Always ask for a bill for goods, which you have bought. This should mention properly the date, the name of the product and the price paid. You can use this bill to report a case of food-poisoning or of overcharging which you could discover later.

2. Look at the expiry date of a product marked on the tin or on the packet. Do not buy anything — drugs, foods, etc. — for which, the expiry date is almost near the date of your purchase.

3. You must ask for the guarantee card for the consumer durables you buy. You can claim for damage or can ask for a replacement later if need be.

4. Note the ingredients of a food item. Do they suit your health? In Western countries, it is mandatory to mention salt, sugar and fat contents on the label. Are the artificial colours used in the food item permitted? Quite often, artificial colours cause vomiting and stomach upsets. Certain types of ghee and some vegetable oils contain high contents of fats and salts which could harm heart patients.

Consumer courts are most active in the Indian subcontinent today, thanks to the efforts of the State and NGOs. Today, our consumers can go to a consumer court to seek compensation for financial losses incurred by them, if any particular product or service (purchased or availed by them) ever led to such losses.

In the West, not only is there very strict quality check on manufactured items but, also the compensation for damage could be exorbitant. A mother of a child, who eats a chewing gum which chokes the child, can sue the gum manufacturing company and can claim heavy compensation. We are lenient in India about such incidents. If we discover a spurious item or a food that was stale, we consume it as we are short on time or we grumble a little and forget. This has encouraged unscrupulous manufacturers and sellers to work in collusion and dupe the buyers. Consumer Cells remind you to bring every such case to their notice. Even collective protests by housewives or consumers can prevent such types of crimes.

Consumer courts have been set up in almost all the towns to redress such grievances. Usually, they have senior or retired judges and listen to pros and cons of each case and penalize the guilty manufacturer. Cases at those courts are decided summarily within a one or two years period. Constituted both at the state and district levels, these fora have statutory powers and legal status.

The agencies of the government like the Departments of Health, Food Agriculture, Social Welfare, etc., support consumers and protect their interests indirectly. These agencies have comparative rates of products advertized regularly in the newspapers. Consumers can read them, compare them and decide the product quality, price and the place of purchase. The print media include newspapers, magazines, handbills, pamphlets, etc., Radio and TV have a special role to play in educating the illiterate masses. These awareness cells also build awareness about foods by pointing out age-old misconceptions about fast foods and dieting. Thus, costly foods are not necessarily the most nutritious ones. The humble sprouted gram and the soyabean are far more nutritious than costly almonds and fruits. Seasonal fruits, which are usually cheap, are the best to eat. Mother's milk is the best for the baby and it does not spoil mother's health but improves it if she suckles her baby quite often. Certain food items like betelnut and other mouth fresheners are carcinogenic. Some soft drinks are habit-forming. All these facts help to make the consumer aware about the products that flood the markets and are advertised by multinationals and Indian corporate houses.

The Prevention of Food Adulteration Act (1954) makes the usage of harmful additives and preservatives a legal offence. Such additives cause chemical reactions in the foodstuffs. The cumulative effect of small doses of these additives may lead to serious debilitating diseases. There is no restriction on traditional preservatives like salt, sugar or spices but there is a restriction on the usage of sulphur dioxide which makes food toxic and may lead to vitamin deficiency. Sulphur dioxide is also the leading cause of rising number of cases of asthma. Too much of nitrites in food find their way into the bloodstream, which may prove to be fatal. Anti-oxidants like Butylated Hydroxy Toluene (BHT) in ghee and butter are banned in many countries as they lead to asthma or dermatitis. However, they are allowed in India. Such types of adulteration have serious implications for the masses on the health front. Artificial sweeteners like saccharine have lethal effects on the digestive system and cause several abnormalities. So, care has to be taken while buying processed foods. Consumer rights must be exercised in case of TVs, food items, clothes, toys, petroleum products and medicines as these products affect our lives everyday.

PATRIOTISM / NATIONALISM AND NATIONAL INTEGRATION

Some people believe that the concept of nationalism is new to India. They are of the opinion that this concept came in India with the British and the western education.

This, however, is a fallacy. Even in ancient times, people had the concept of India as one country. Their thinking might not have been entirely based on political reality. But the concept of India being one country even politically was not totally absent. Chandragupta Maurya, for instance, under the able guidance of Chanakya, wanted to establish his rule all over India. His capital was Patliputra which is modern Patna in Bihar. Chandragupta marched all over from Patliputra to north India to defeat Alexander's general Seleukas who had attacked India. After him, Ashoka's kingdom covered almost the whole of India and even a part of Afghanistan. Even earlier, India was called "Aryavrat" or "Bharat" which meant the whole of India.

Later, in the middle ages, Adi Shankaracharya established his ashrams in four corners of India. It is clear that people in general had the concept of India as being one country. They travelled to places of pilgrimages which were spread in different parts of the country. It must, however, be admitted that the concept of a nation state as at present was perhaps not there then among the Indians.

In earlier times, the common people pursued their occupation in their villages where most of them lived and they were not much concerned with the kinds of kings and governments ruling at the centre.

India was a vast country inhabited by people of different religions, castes, communities and races, all speaking different languages, wearing different dresses and having different food habits. So, separatist tendencies in people's minds could also not be ruled out. Such tendencies were responsible for the enslavement of the Indian people when one ruler did not help the other ruler who was attacked by some foreign invader. This was mostly witnessed in the middle ages. This enabled even the British rulers to play policy of "divide and rule."

With the emergence of the Indian National Congress towards the close of the 19th century, the love for freedom for the whole country was awakened among the Indian people and it became stronger and stronger as the Independence movement gained momentum. India was fortunate in having selfless, patriotic leaders like Mahatma Gandhi, Bal Gangadhar Tilak, Lala Lajpat Rai, Jawaharlal Nehru, Subhash Chandra Bose and others.

After attainment of Independence, India chose democracy to be the form of government. In this respect too, India has been fortunate for the reason of having such leaders as Jawaharlal Nehru, Lal Bahadur Shastri, Sardar Patel and others.

Later, though fortunately, the democratic set-up in the country has been allowed to continue, the nefarious designs of later narrow-minded leaders slowly landed the country where national integration could be endangered. They encouraged regionalism, linguism, casteism, nepotism and other parochial institutions. The result was a demand from different regions for autonomy, if not secession. Such voices were heard in Kashmir, Punjab, Tamil Nadu, eastern states, etc. By stages new states such as Himachal Pradesh, Haryana, Uttarakhand, Jharkhand, etc. came into being. Again, fortunately, for the Indian people, there has been no secession from the Indian union.

Constitutionally, no state can secede from the union. But what is more important is that the people should have emotional integration. They should consider the nation above any social, religious, communal or racial considerations. There should be a national cohesion among the people. For this, the newspapers, TV, radio and other means of media should play a positive role. Parents, teachers, social workers, students and leaders of all parties should join hands to achieve the end of national integration.

It should be understood clearly that we live if India lives. Who lives if India doesn't? So, national integration is the need of the hour. Let's meet the challenge bravely and unitedly whatever hard work we might have to do.

BITCOIN

Bitcoin is a peer-to-peer payment system and digital currency introduced as open source software in 2009. It is a cryptocurrency, so-called because it uses cryptography to control the creation and transfer of money.

Bitcoins are created by a process called mining, in which computer network participants, *i.e.* users who provide their computing power, verify and record payments into a public ledger in exchange for transaction fees and newly minted bitcoins. Users send and receive bitcoins using wallet software on a personal computer, mobile device, or a web application. Bitcoins can be obtained by mining or in exchange for products, services, or other currencies.

Bitcoin has been a subject of scrutiny amid concerns that it can be used for illegal activities. In October 2013 the U.S. FBI shut down the Silk Road online black market and seized 144,000 bitcoins worth US$28.5 million at the time. The U.S. is considered Bitcoin-friendly compared to other governments, however. In China new rules restrict bitcoin exchange for local currency. The European Banking Authority has warned that Bitcoin lacks consumer protections. Bitcoins can be stolen and chargebacks are impossible.

Commercial use of Bitcoin, illicit or otherwise, is currently small compared to its use by speculators, which has fueled price volatility. Bitcoin as a form of payment for products and services has seen growth, however, and merchants have an incentive to accept the currency because transaction fees are lower than the 2-3% typically imposed by credit card processors.

Buying and Selling Bitcoins

Bitcoin can be bought and sold for many different currencies from individuals and from companies. The fastest way to obtain bitcoins is to purchase them in person or at a Bitcoin ATM for cash. Participants in online exchanges offer bitcoin buy and sell bids. Companies buy or sell bitcoin in bulk on exchanges and offer their customers the option via ATM to buy or sell bitcoin at market price. Bitcoin ATMs allow bitcoins to be purchased for cash, and some also allow cash withdrawals from Bitcoin wallets stored on smartphones. Using an online exchange to obtain bitcoins entails some risk, since according to one study 45% of exchanges have failed and taken client bitcoins with them.

Since bitcoin transactions are irreversible, sellers of bitcoins must take extra measures to ensure they have received traditional funds from the buyer.

History

Bitcoin was first mentioned in a 2008 paper published under the name Satoshi Nakamoto. In early 2009, the first open source client (or wallet software), called Bitcoin-Qt, was released and the first bitcoins were issued. In 2009, a feature in the Bitcoin-Qt software was exploited and large numbers of bitcoins were created. This was due, in large part, because Bitcoin-Qt was the only software that facilitated bitcoin transactions and mining. This feature was later removed because specialized mining software turned out to be more efficient. Since then, the bitcoin open-source software has been maintained and enhanced by a group of core developers and other contributors.

By May 2011, interest in Bitcoin was growing as were concerns. The price of bitcoins has fluctuated wildly since its inception, going through various cycles of appreciation and depreciation, which have been referred to by some as bubbles and busts. In 2011, the value of one bitcoin rapidly rose from about US$0.30 to US$32 before returning to US$2. In the latter half of 2012 and during the 2012-2013 Cypriot Financial Crisis, the bitcoin price began to rise, reaching a peak of US$266 on April 10, 2013, before crashing to around US$50.

Alternative to National Currencies

Bitcoin detractors and supporters have suggested that Bitcoin is gaining popularity in countries with problem-plagued national currencies because it can be used to circumvent inflation, capital controls, and international sanctions. For example, bitcoins are used by some Argentinians as an alternative to the official currency, stymied by inflation and strict capital controls. In addition, some Iranians use bitcoins to evade currency sanctions. A link between higher Bitcoin usage in Spain and the 2012-2013

Cypriot financial crisis has been suggested. Mistrust in traditional financial institutions and central banks fostered by the financial crisis of 2007-08 has probably helped to bolster Bitcoin popularity.

World has more Bitcoins than Currencies

The world now has a larger number of virtual currencies than a total 180 recognised currencies in different parts of the globe, notwithstanding issues like bankruptcies and growing regulatory unease about bitcoin and its other digital peers. Within an ear shot of the 200-member mark, a total of 193 virtual currencies are currently being traded across the internet, although none of them carry an official stamp from the government or banking regulator from any of the countries. While bitcoin and other such currencies began coming into existence about four years ago, a frenzied proliferation in last two months has more than doubled their count. Apart from bitcoins, ripple, litecoin, auroracoin, peercoin and dogcoin have seen steady pickup in volume as well market value. The latest additions include tea-coin, aliencoin, magic internet money and heisenberg.

Speculation and Bubbles

Bitcoins are traded by speculators who want to profit on short to medium term price changes. A separate organization offers futures contracts against multiple currencies allowing speculators to short bitcoin. The European Banking Authority warned in December 2013, that the risks of engaging in speculation go beyond a potential loss of bitcoin value. Unable to find any intrinsic value, former Federal Reserve Chairman Alan Greenspan has called it a speculative bubble as has economist John Quiggin.

As an Investment

Bitcoin is a new and interesting electronic currency, the value of which is not backed by any single government or organization. Like other currencies, it is worth something partly because people are willing to trade it for goods and services. Its exchange rate fluctuates continuously, and sometimes wildly. It lacks wide acceptance and is vulnerable to manipulation by parties with modest funding. Security incidents such as website and account compromise may trigger major sell-offs. Other fluctuations can build into positive feedback loops and cause much larger exchange rate fluctuations. Anyone who puts money into Bitcoin should understand the risk they are taking and consider it a high-risk currency. Later, as Bitcoin becomes better known and more widely accepted, it may stabilize, but for the time being it is unpredictable. Any investment in Bitcoin should be done carefully and with a clear plan to manage the risk.

EXAMINATIONS : RIGHT OR WRONG

Life is all along an examination and all of us have to face one or the other tough task daily, wherever and in whatever position we may be.

Most of the students are virtually in a state of depression near the examinations, though strictly in medical terms, this state may not be technically admitted to be such a state. But, we can say with jubilation "The examination blues!" And jubilation not at the poor fellows who suffer these blues but at the finding out of a term even like Galileo who exclaimed, "Eureka! Eureka! Eureka!" on a new astronomical discovery.

We learn from the counsellors about the students' common complaints like lack of appetite, insomnia, fear of failure, fear of being rebuked by parents, fear of loss of status among the student community in particular and society in general, etc. Sometimes, even suicidal tendencies are noticed by these counsellors. In certain cases, students who have shown remarkable performance in the previous classes are afraid that they may not be able to repeat the performance and be taken to task by their parents. In certain cities, helplines are available round the clock. Even the CBSE has been running such helplines for students.

Some of such helplines for students in blues, to make some queries to get rid of them, are Disha,

Snehi, Sarthak, CBSE, etc. It deserves to be noted that not always calls are made by the students themselves, sometimes, even parents make a fervent call about their ward and at times even express their anger over the phone at the defective examination system, which reduces the students to robots and automatons, snatching all the emotions, charm and joy from their life.

Since many of us will be inclined to say that after a lot of experimentation in several ways, the net decision for the present seems to be that examinations in one form or the other are unavoidable. They may be called a necessary evil. In whatever form they may be, they are, after all examinations and there is hardly a student who does not shudder at the sheer mention of the word "Examination."

A great bane of the modern examination system is that we have too many examinations. Even to get admission in the nursery or pre-nursery class, the child has to take a test. Not only the child but also its parents have to appear for an interview. Then throughout the career of the poor child, there are tests and examinations galore such as daily, weekly, monthly, bimonthly, semester-related, annual, etc.

If a student has to seek admission in any other institution for any reason, he has to take a test. Even after getting a certificate, diploma or degree, one has to appear in a test, examination and/or interview or viva voce, group discussion and what not in order to join a vocational, technical or professional course or a job.

We have a pertinent saying: "Excess of everything is bad." This should and does equally apply to the examinations. The examinations always keep the students on tenterhooks. They are often a worried lot. It is hard to find a ray of cheerfulness on the faces of most of the students. Then in this world of hard competition and pressing demands on the students from their parents and teachers, many students fall a prey to such unethical practices as copying. Gone are the days when students like Gandhiji refused to copy the spelling of a word from another student's exercise book even when he was urged by his teacher to do so. Now, not only the students themselves but also many times even their parents and well-wishers try to exhort the student to indulge in the unhealthy practice of copying.

Another great menace, perhaps the greatest of all other menaces, is the menace of leakage of papers of various examinations. There have been reports about the leakage of PMT papers right from the beginning. Similarly, leakage of papers of many other examinations has sporadically taken place in the past. During the recent few years, however, the leakage of papers pertaining to various examinations has taken the shape of an epidemic.

The leakage of All India Pre-Medical Test (AIPMT) was detected in Delhi. It is a different matter that two students were arrested. And, now we hear a well-organised racket has been caught in Chandigarh engaged in facilitating copying in post-graduate medical course admissions tests through high-tech devices such as bluetooth and pen-scanners. They are even said to have placed dummy candidates for this job.

Such a state of affairs can make the students lethargic. They can seriously and sincerely think that if they can get through an examination just by buying a question paper a few hours or a day before the examination, why should they lick the books the whole year? What they now actually need is a few lakhs of rupees for which their parents may be willing even more. Let the nation, society and the world go to hell! So this is what the present examination system makes them and from what. How raw they were and how crude, rude and rough now they are!

Let some methods be devised to uplift the moral standard of not only the students but also the parents, teachers, government functionaries and all others concerned.

India's education and examination systems are now being lauded all over the world for being of quite high quality, though we still find several deficiencies in them. A positive factor in this context is the will for constant rethinking and making changes where necessary. An example can be given in the matter of rethinking about the examinations pertaining to Class X. One of the proposals mooted mainly by the CBSE was concerning making class X examinations optional. The boards, however, did not find favour with this proposal. Instead, the council, allowing flexibility to students, agreed to implement the grading system and also made a case for including internal assessment in schools. It allowed students. The new idea emerged is that the annual examinations should be spread over a couple of months so that a student can take a few papers in one month and the rest in the subsequent months, instead of appearing in the examinations in one go. However, it was agreed that the results should be declared in one go. It was believed that the system would prevent the students from neglecting their school education.

UNITY IS STRENGTH

The advantages of unity have always been manifested themselves on the social, personal and national scales. The family, the society and the country survive only due to the coherence of their components. Unity is a very beneficial and exhilirating spirit of every phenomenon. A united society or a nation would be able to face any challenge or crisis. Let us analyse.

Now-a-days, the concept of nuclear family is catching up very fast. The joint family system is breaking up simply due to the fact that the young boys and girls move towards urban areas in order to earn and to achieve professional satisfaction. The unity of the joint family is sacrificed in terms of prosperity, protection from the world, aid during disease and other disasters. But the nuclear families do not have any such type of security. Hence, they suffer on account of lack of security from the joint family system. An individual cannot fight a war. But some individuals can fight a war together and in all probability, they would be able to win all the wars.

Another example could be given from the Indian history. We lost our crucial wars due to the cracks within our social, religious and political organisations. We have many traitors to curse; Mir Jaffer, Jai Chand, Jai Gopal, Najeebullah etc. are only a few names to mention. The traitors went to the groups of the powerful marauders and let the Indian natives suffer the worst ever defeats. For example, had Jai Chand not invited Muhammed Ghauri from Afghanistan, Prithvi Raj Chauhan would certainly have expanded his empire in the Northern and the Western parts of the country. He could have stopped the onslaught of foreign mercenaries and marauders with the senews of steel. But Jai Chand fought a savage battle with him through Muhammad Ghauri and the righteous king had to give up his life and kingdom in his last war. Our history is full of many such shameful examples.

Let us now turn to the modern times. India has fought five wars so far — in 1948, 1962, 1965, 1971 and in 1999. In all these wars, our brave soldiers, our courageous paramilitary forces, our committed civilians and above all, love for the motherland helped us fight the enemy forces bravely. We lost the 1962 war but we were united as a nation. We won the 1971 and 1999 war due to the courage and united efforts to win over the enemy forces. We were united and would always be united in our endeavour for peace, prosperity and global welfare. Our unity is our strength.

Similar examples of strength in unity could be quoted in the fields of business, warfare, sciences, engineering, sociology, environmental regulations, struggle for Indian independence, the two world wars etc. Human history is full of those stories which proved beyond doubt that when men of courage joined hands for a pious objective, they achieved their coveted aims with flying colours. The ecstacy of success was due to the commitment either to the group norms or to national ideals.

We are now convinced that unity is strength. Then why do we not implement the spirit of unity in our lives? The reason is simple. We are now more materialistic and individualistic than ever before. The lust for money forces us to think in individual terms. The individualistic culture has been developed in the urban areas of India due to Western influences. For example, many people in the West do not marry. They live as couples and leave the partners when they get 'bored' with each other. Similar culture is dominating the urban life in India. Rural areas would also be affected sooner or later. Hence, the individuals fight for money, jobs, family values, prestige, fortune or fame. They do not get any financial, moral or political support from their friends, relatives or parents. Hence, they loose most of the battles in their lives.

We must not ape the West. We must remain united as a family, as a society and as a nation. It is in our best interests to remain united as a nation as the nation would lead us to political, social, economic and moral salvation. Our society believes in unity in diversity. That is why, this multi-lingual, multi-racial and multi-cultural nation has survived for 5,000 years. This resilience itself proves that unity is strength.

ELEPHANT VS. DRAGON : WHO WILL SURGE AHEAD?

In the race between Asia's two major developing nations, China's dragon is, by most indicators, beating India's elephant, hands down. Its gross domestic product (GDP) is growing at a rate almost double that of India's, and the aisles of Wal-Mart are cluttered with products made in China. But the United States and the rest of the world had better keep an eye on the elephant and resist temptation to declare the dragon the victor quite yet, says a Harvard Business School (HBS) professor.

However, it is remembered that while China has successfully leveraged its governmental structure to attract the foreign companies fueling its manufacturing boom, India's indigenous entrepreneurship is thriving in a way that cannot be ignored. Despite - or perhaps because of - the fact that its government lacks the economic savvy of China's, India has bred homegrown entrepreneurial ventures that are thriving. So-called "knowledge" industries like software, pharmaceuticals and biotechnology, advertising, and even the film industry are giving India an edge over its neighbour.

A Brief Comparison

India is far ahead of China. For bringing home the point, measures like the Forbes magazine list of medium-sized fast-growing companies, which boasts far more Indian than Chinese companies, and international banks' ratings of many Indian firms as far better managed than other Asian companies, including several better-known firms from Japan and Korea can be easily cited. China, on many dimensions, is just the exact opposite of India. While authoritarian China has aggressively courted foreign investment, democratic India is "allergic" to it. Here you have two large, populous, ancient civilizations that formed modern nation states in geographically proximate locations at roughly the same time, yet have chosen radically different development paths, and have no interconnection with each other whatsoever. Their historic hostility has accentuated the independence of their development paths. There isn't even a direct flight between China and India.

The economic differences arise partly out of the different governmental structures in the two countries. In China, where there is little distinction between the bureaucracy and the government, rising through the ranks of the party has been based, since 1978, on how much one contributes to the local GDP. You have an incentive to promote not just local enterprise but any enterprise. So you open your arms and lay out the red carpet for foreign multinationals. India, on the other hand, is the home of "rampant bureaucratic incompetence." There, bureaucrats' incentives are unrelated to economic outcomes. "You have to work to attract investments, so why bother?"

Yet while China's government provides incentives to the state-supported commerce that has fed its economic success, indigenous enterprise has flourished in India as the government has turned its back. Increasingly, these enterprises are gaining ground in the international economy as in the case of Indian software giants Infosys and Wipro, the pharmaceutical company Ranbaxy, the bio-technology firm Biocon, and the manufacturing firm

Moser Baer. These companies have thrived despite the failure of the government to provide appropriate infrastructure. They're compensating for the failure of the government. ... And the nice thing that's happening in India is the government is finally letting them do it. The government is recognizing the limits of its competence, which is actually an extraordinary thing.

Whether India overtakes China or not, frankly, it's immaterial. Much more important is the fact that the United States and the rest of the world learn from China, India, and other developing nations like Brazil or Russia. There's a lot of competition that's going to come out of left field. An Indian entrepreneur, for example, has launched a business growing and shipping high-end produce to Europe. "You could feed a large part of Europe from India," . That means that if you're a Florida grower exporting to Europe, you might want to rethink your business model.

Using markedly different strategies and policy reforms, China and India have sustained high growth rates over a number of years. This has had and will continue to have profound effects on their social, economic, cultural and political structures. The rapid growth in China and India has brought about tremendous opportunities and challenges for other countries as well.

Why India Will March Ahead

The question of whether the dragon or the elephant would dominate the global market is a question that raises passionate debates between millions of Chinese and Indians, all filled with pride over their nation's own ascendancy. Since it is impossible to make a judgment call based on every factor, conclusion can be based on two current indicators which will be the key hallmarks of a potential economic superpower – a strong knowledge based industry, and the existence of a highly entrepreneurial high tech environment. On these two counts, India score higher than China.

India is more likely to take over the role of America as the leading player in the knowledge economy. The current edge obviously goes to India,

where marquee names have sprung up over the last few years. Tata Consultancy, Infosys, iflex Solutions, Ranbaxy have become powerhouses in their own fields. Besides having stellar homegrown IT enterprises, the solid infrastructure and a huge base of college graduates in the key cities have allowed it to become the first choice for IT outsourcing.

China, on the other hand, lacks the same kind of luster in its IT sector. This problem goes deep. The lack of IP protection and massive piracy has served as a lesson to a whole generation of Chinese that producing software is pointless. After all, if goods can be pirated, and patents bypassed, where is the incentive for Chinese entrepreneurs to innovate and produce software and drugs of their own? Also, as shown by a recent MGI research, China produces massive number of IT graduates, but a large number of them are technicians, as opposed to highly skilled engineers able to take up managerial and senior engineering roles. With competition for these capable graduates becoming fierce, the labor shortage might become a real issue impeding growth of the IT sector.

Changes in mindset around IP protection, as well as huge investments in education to meet the higher end needs of industry are needed to ignite the knowledge industry in China. One thing China has going for it though, is its strong manufacturing base, which would generate internal demand for advanced technology to help in automation and supply chain management. With its better reputation for IP, and established base of IT companies and colleges, India is definitely looking to be the next key knowledge based economy.

MERCY KILLING

Mercy Killing or Euthanasia refers to the practice of ending a life in a manner which relieves pain and suffering. It is a deliberate intervention undertaken with the express intention of ending a life, to relieve intractable suffering.

Euthanasia may be classified according to whether a person gives informed consent into three types: voluntary, non-voluntary and involuntary.

There is a debate within the medical and bioethics literature about whether or not the non-voluntary (and by extension, involuntary) killing of patients can be regarded as euthanasia, irrespective of intent or the patient's circumstances. According to few experts, consent on the part of the patient is not considered necessary. However, others see consent as essential. Medicalized killing of a person without the person's consent, whether non-voluntary (where the person is unable to give consent) or involuntary (against the person's will) is not euthanasia: it is murder. Hence, euthanasia can be voluntary only.

Euthanasia conducted with the consent of the patient is termed voluntary euthanasia. Euthanasia conducted where the consent of the patient is unavailable is termed non-voluntary euthanasia. Examples include child euthanasia, which is illegal worldwide but decriminalised under certain specific circumstances in the Netherlands under the Groningen Protocol. Euthanasia conducted against the will of the patient is termed involuntary euthanasia.

In a country like ours, the religious aspects also have to be considered before taking such decisions. The Bible says, "Thou shalt not kill" And even Islam does not allow anyone to take away life. Is our society mature enough to understand the implications of this? We have cases, where doctors are often beaten up if the patient was not treated properly, what would happen to a doctor if he merely suggested euthanasia to the relatives? Will the relatives be able to understand the suffering of the patient?

Life is a gift, and even a life of pain is a life at least. Some people feel we don't choose when to be born and we should not be given the right to choose when to die. On the contrary, others feel that a life of pain is not a life but an imposition and we should be at least allowed to end it in a dignified peaceful manner. Euthanasia could be legalized, but the laws would have to be very stringent. Every case will have to be carefully monitored taking into consideration the point of views of the patient, the relatives and the doctors. But whether Indian society is mature enough to face this, is yet to be seen, after all it's a matter of life and death.

PAGE THREE SYNDROME

Some readers might argue that page three syndrome is not a syndrome but an honour bestowed on the celebrity due to his or her special abilities. But this explanation of Page Three Syndrome is not correct. In fact, we have added the word 'Syndrome' to the phrase "Page Three" here. It is a disease, not a thrill. It is a bane for society, not virtue.

A Page Three personality is one that appears in the photographs and news coverage on the third page of a popular newspaper that is normally reserved to cover the celebrities. Hence, a Page Three person should be the happiest one on the earth, given that he is being photographed, interviewed and pampered. In reality, he is being used as an object to show-case the anomalities of modern society that are presented under the veneer of show-biz. Women are shown half-naked whereas men are shown drinking and dancing. The Page Three persons of today are projected as connoisseurs or artists but most of them crave publicity. Nowadays, publicity can be done only at a price and these people pay a heavy price to get themselves exposed by the media.

A movie made on Page Three personalities brought out the wickedness of the system that Page Three columns of print media perpetuate. A newspaper needs advertisements to chug along. These advertisements are clubbed with raunchy news and indecent comments about people. Readers read these comments and news. Then, they read advertisements on other pages of the newspapers and buy the products and/or services advertised therein. Hence, Page Three columns are the gateways for earning more advertising revenues. The newspaper's circulation increases; so do its advertising schemes. Poor celebrities become scapegoats in this process.

Exposure to the media to an extent is welcome. But when limits are crossed, the Page Three news becomes a mockery. The celebrity thinks that he or she would get more exposure and later, more contracts because he or she is being exposed. This hypothesis is not entirely wrong. But the dignity of the celebrity is at stake. Not many celebrities of the contemporary times would understand this fact.

Page Three features are a part of the endorsingly media too. TV programmes expose TV stars, cinema stars, political leaders, thinkers, writers and social workers in a dramatic manner. These programmes are almost always coupled with advertisements. People watch such programmes and gather the information about various products and services that are advertised in such programmes. Later, they buy these products and services. Hence, Page Three personalities of the audio-visual media are also being used to add fuel to the fire.

In order to became a Page Three personality, a female model can go to any limit. The casting couch syndrome of the cinematic world is equally alive in this arena as well. Male models, actors and individuals are also prepared to lose their dignity to get media mileage. This decay in character can be ascribed to the rising aspirations of people. Everyone wants to earn the maximum amount of money, enjoy luxuries of life and get the status of a star. Page Three columns of newspapers and raunchy programmes on TV help people satisfy their unfulfilled desires. Hence, there is no dearth of people trying to get exposed in any part of the world. India has only recently boarded the Page Three bandwagon. Moral values take a beating. Liquor and drugs flow freely during the parties. Further, dance programmes continue beyond the early morning hours.

The media paparazzi cover these happenings and feed lascivious content to the masses. The system of a free market-based society earns its fortunes and fame only through these mechanisms.

This trend has just started in India. Hence, bringing it to a halt is nothing but wishful thinking. What we suggest is that our valued readers should concentrate on their career-building exercises and not on such activities as would make them repent later. There is no short-cut to success. There is no alternative to hard work. There is only one virtue—character. If it is lost once, it cannot be retrieved. Concentrate on your goals, plan to achieve them and slog to achieve them through the right methods..

DRINKING HABITS AMONG YOUTHS

The three "Ws"—"wealth, wine and women" have always been considered the root cause of human fall, for centuries for excess of any of these things leads to physical or psychological or moral decline. Adam was thrown out of Paradise falling prey to Eve's temptations. Wealth brings even ordinary humans on cloud nine and his imaginations get free flight as it revolutionizes human physical entity and the suppressed desires and wishes to throw away the barriers of social, ethical and moral hurdles.

Drinking means alcoholic liquids which, in excess may cause sensuary imbalance among the people. Any drink apart from water which has alcohol as the leading ingredient may derail the mental thinking power which ultimately results in physical aberration like wine, whiskey and scotch.

India has a long association with drink as 'Madira' had been widely prevalent during ancient times. However wine as a regular drink has been widely prevalent in western societies for in European countries weather plays an important role. In metros bigger percentage are addicted to drinks where parties and celebrations would be unthinkable if alcohol is not properly served. Hence, the habit grows more out of fashion and etiquette than the physical requirements, and once it becomes a habit a lot of money is wasted in drinking.

Young men are more tempted to social trends and if professionals with tons of official pressure take refuge under the spell of a glass of scotch or whisky, the broad impact is perceptible. As metropolis are coming up with more and more bars, casinos and pubs where wealth, women and wine associate in an orgy of merry making the social barriers becomes a non-entity. Not only drinking becomes a personal habit but it is a human right as well. The government also supports drinking by lifting restrictions on alcoholic consumption in recent years as more and more 'wine shops' or 'beer shops' are being opened on the highway. Prices are slashed whereby long queues in front of these shops are constant scences coupled with unprecedented sales. For the aged and creative human, drink can be supportive, but to youths it infects more harm than benefits. Formative years are full of passion and sentiments and alcohol acts as fuel to the fire. If the habits get generated in unemployed youth, it takes the form of addiction and will always result in alarming consequences for if taken to soothe the restlessness born out of failure in love or examinations, it can lead to disastrous ends. A strong urge of drink and no money in the pocket will certainly lead the restless youth to follow the illegal path and anti-social norms. Wine is the mother of all crimes and wealth is the benevolent father of wine who exhausts itself out in order to please his daughter and women is the beloved of wine.

Youths must shun this habit as it not only hampers the studies and professional career but it also takes its toll on the physical, psychological and moral body. Hence, over-socialisation, partying and celebrations should be curtailed as peer pressure compel an individual to swim in alcohol irrespective of his/her health. But yes, at the same time there is no harm in enjoying on odd drink amid in moderate quantity when one feels like. Only it must not be made a regular habiit.

INDIAN SOCIETY NEEDS REFORMS

India is proud to be cradle of the oldest civilisation in the world. It has many firsts to its credit: the Vedas were written here; the Puranas were compiled here; the epics were written in this land. India indeed, had a glorious past. Its social cutsoms, moral values and knowledge levels were respected around the world and India was regarded as the moral and spiritual leader of the mankind during ancient and medieval period.

The concept of joint family system was promoted by Hindu sages. Strict marriage rituals, commitment to the ideals of the family, pride in one's work and profession, love for the nation, commitment towards one super-soul and finally, the willingness to acquire more knowledge about this universe were some of the positive aspects of our ancient culture. During those times, people never locked their homes as there were no thieves. There were only scholars, agricultural workers, courtiers, Kshatriyas and landlords. The country was divided into several kingdoms. The cultural influences and social beliefs were the same throughout India.

But this golden era came to an end. Huns, Pathans, Afghans, Dutch, British and French invaded India and looted her wealth for over 1,000 years. They also brought new cultural beliefs, procedures and a commitment towards materialism. Therefore, the synergistic effect of this combination (of Indian culture with the invading cultures) led to the development of a new Indian society. New religions, social ideologies and political concepts changed our national and social fabrics. Today, we are essentially a Vedic-Western cultural nation and no longer Indians in the strict sense of the word. There were influences of Islam, Christianity and Hinduism on our society and these have led to the creation of a new religious canvass across the nation; the Indian Muslim, the Indian Hindu and the Indian Christian—are the three vital components of this new religious hue.

Indian society needs a serious scrutiny. The chief limitation of modern Indian society is that it has been trying to retain those obsolete values with us which are beneficial only for a smaller section of the society and are not wiling to eliminate the evils of the society as they are still serving the base objectives. The examples of Sati, dowry, early childhood marriage etc could be cited in this regard.

Further, Indian people are aping the West in a shameless manner but have never accepted the norms of the West in terms of efficiency, productivity and hard work in social and business lives. In sum, this generation is more comfortable with the club culture, satellite TV and pornography but would not like to work for sixteen hours a day, as is being or done in the West. Why should India adopt these double standards?

The next vital issue is that of social awareness. Our illiteracy levels are very high. An illiterate mother cannot offer future to her children. The vicious cycle of poverty continues to engulf the rural masses as education has not been able to reach out to the mass levels.

The resistance to change is another vital area in Indian context. Indian mind wants to adopt new technologies and modern social beliefs at a very slow pace but are more than willing to get a cable TV connection so that we could entertain ourselves through indecent entertainment software. Indians do not want to adopt new computer software techniques, production methodologies and living styles as we not want to get out of our Indian shell. But we are always trying to get imported whiskies, electronic gadgets and items of luxury, which would not improve our psyche. This leads to reduction in actual production, efficiency and satisfaction at the economic, societal and industrial levels. We must remember that the society, the industry and the nation are living organisms and each one of these supports the existence and growth of one another.

Therefore, the following social reforms should be adopted:

- The evil practices of dowry, Sati and female foeticide must be stopped. They must be strictly punishable by law and the culprits must not be allowed to escape the law. The laws are there but their implementation is slow.
- The government must spend more funds on female education and education of female adults in the rural areas.
- Woman is the essential building block of our society. Therefore, she should be allowed to take decision-making positions in local Panchayats, PSUs, state governments and the Parliament. There should be reservation of seats for women in the Lok Sabha and state assemblies to the tune of 33 per cent.
- Middle class families have always guided Indian society for a change. So, these families must form clubs, social service organisations and NGOs for bringing for-reaching changes in Indian society. The lower-middle income groups are struggling for survival. The rich groups have no time for development. And the neo-rich are busy making more money. The responsibility squarely lies on the middle income society, which has acquired moderate levels of prosperity and also, has the thinking ability for solving the complex social issues.
- Social reforms could be accomplished only through strict laws, a powerful judiciary and timely disposition of the pending cases in the courts. The process of delivering justice to the masses is very slow. This is an important area, which deserves attention in the context of delivering social justice to the downtrodden.
- We are of the view that the reservations in educational institutions and the PSUs should be done on the basis of economic necessity of the candidates. Reservations based on castes must be cone away with.

Even in the new millennium Indian society is not ready to accept the challenges of this era. Nonetheless social reforms would help us in economic growth and overall national progress. The responsibility of these reforms is of the masses; we have to change our psyche in order to become a modern society. The State, the judiciary and the institutions would also have to play key roles in this herculean task. This process would be painfully slow and agonising.

JUDICIAL ACTIVISM IN INDIA

Judicial activism has introduced a new dimension regarding judiciary's involvement in public administration. Judicial activism was made possible in India, thanks to PIL (Public Interest Litigation).

After the Constitution (Twenty fifth Amendment) Act, 1971, by which primacy was accorded to a limited extent to the Directive Principles vis-a-vis the Fundamental Rights making the former enforceable rights, the expectations of the public soared high and the demands on the courts to improve the administration by giving appropriate directions for ensuring compliance with statutory and constitutional prescriptions have increased.

The judicial power under our Constitution is vested in the Supreme Court and the High Courts which are empowered to exercise the power of judicial review both in regard to legislative and executive actions. Judges cannot shirk their responsibilities as adjudicators of legal and constitutional matters.

A common criticism we hear about judicial activism is that in the name of interpreting the provisions of the Constitution and legislative enactments, the judiciary often rewrites them undermining the authority of the legislature and the executive by encroaching upon the spheres reserved for them.

Judicial creativity even when it takes the form of judicial activism should not result in rewriting of the Constitution or any legislative enactments. In the name of doing justice and taking shelter under institutional self-righteousness, the judiciary cannot act in a manner disturbing the delicate balance between the three wings of the State.

Judicial activist fervour should not flood the fields constitutionally earmarked for the legislature and the executive. That would spell disaster. Governmental machinery cannot be run by judges. Any populist views aired by judges would undermine their authority and disturb the institutional balance.

Judicial activism characterised by moderation and self-restraint is bound to restore the faith of the people in the efficacy of the democratic institutions which alone, in turn, will activate the executive and the legislature to function effectively under the vigilant eye of the judiciary as ordained by the Constitution.

CORRUPTION IS AN ACCEPTED NORM

The standard definition of corruption is — the use of public office for private gain. Its roots and seductions lie much deeper in the quality of human relationships that characterize a society.

Corruption and Indian society are inter-woven closely. Each and every office whether it comes under Central or State administration is no exception. Corruption is simply a consequence of the fact that the state has wide discretionary powers.

The motivations that produce and sustain corruption are of course complex. Avarice and ambition doubtless play an important part.

The experience of both state and society in India is profoundly alienating in more ways than one can list and many forms of corruption stem directly from this experience. Indian society is profoundly inegalitarian. Vast disparities of income and power exist almost everywhere, but the depth, to which in India inequality has subjected individuals to a million humiliations, small and large, is almost unprecedented.

Generally, all this corruption goes on under a cloak, although one can almost see it happening before one's eyes, Bureaucracy is also moulded and influenced to take decisions favourable to vested interest due to corruption. In case of large contracts rules are relaxed and then negotiated without transparency. Not a new phenomenon in India or in many other countries.

If the senior bureaucrat or officer disassociates himself/herself from wrong decisions and does so on the files, wrongdoing or corruption would diminish greatly.

But India is considered especially as a case of its own *i.e.* it is only when the higher bureaucracy or officer becomes compliant and suitably "cooks the case", then corrupt practice could occur. But any one with even a mild conscience will hesitate to do so.

It has been rightly pointed that in a society in which honesty and patriotism are laughed at and poked fun of; corruption is going to be all pervading because there is no moral barrier to it at any level. And also an honest officer is always looked down upon as incapable person who is not suiting to the present environment.

CRIME AGAINST WOMEN

Since time immemorial women have been the worst victims of male-dominated world whether it is war or riot or general law and order disturbance or robbery or domestic clashes, the fair sex has to bear the brunt of barbarism. Human history is full of atrocities committed on women in the form of forced abduction and marriage as in medieval period, as revenge killing and rapes in Bosnia, or as war prize in countless conflicts worldwide. "War" said Virginia Woolf, "is not women's history".

Women bear a disproportionate burden of the consequences of war from beginning to end. First, women are not involved in the decisions that lead to war, not engaged in the appropriation of funds that make weapons and war possible, but they are tortured, kidnapped and raped as revenge tactic. Women as victims of war and women's role in peace building has been an important topic of discussion in several forums, most notably the United Nations.

Women have been labelled as 'sub-ordinates', 'homely', 'weak', and 'trouble-inviting' and in India as well in other nations they have been granted low status in society, being considered as a commodity, and birth of a girl child is still lamented.

Crime against women (CAW) traditionally includes rape, kidnapping and abduction, dowry death, torture, molestation, sexual harassment, importation of girls, cases under the Immoral Traffic (Prevention) Act, Sati Prevention Act, Dowry Prohibition Act, Indecent Representation of Women (Prevention) Act. Crime against women is usually classified as marital and sexual crime. However, one that victimises women is robbery and dacoity. Women are prime targets of robbery because of the jewellery they keep at home.

Like most offences, CAW is steadily on the rise in India. Of the total crimes reported in the country, 7% constitute CAW.

Women comprise some 80 per cent of internally displaced persons and refugees when there is a war. Women as well as little girls are also victims of rape, domestic violence, sexual exploitation, trafficking, sexual humiliation and mutilation. However, their voice is seldom heard when "the important men" talk peace and war.

Women and girls are vulnerable both in times of peace and war, due to profound gender inequalities that still characterize societies. Reversing this situation requires political will and determination to fulfil all commitments concerning the protection and promotion of the women's rights.

Delhi Police has advertised 'Dos and Don'ts for Women' in leading newspapers and opened 'women helpline' with every DTC bus bearing the telephone numbers for immediate contact. Not only this, women can take the shelter of various NGOs working for this purpose like the Navjyoti Centre. This is a healthy trend as far as women safety is concerned.

RIGHT TO EDUCATION

The April, 1st 2010, was marked in history as India joined groups of few countries in the world, with a significant law, making education a fundamental right of every child coming into force.

The Right to Education bill was passed by the Parliament on 4th August, 2009. Six years after an amendment was made in the Indian Constitution, the Union Cabinet cleared the Right to education bill, which promises free and compulsory education to every child.

The Government of India by Constitutional (86th Amendment) Act, 2002 had added a new Article 21A, which provides that the state shall provide free and compulsory education to all children of the age 6 to 14 years as the state may by law determine. And further strengthened this

Article 21A by adding clause (K) to Article 51-A which provides—"who is a parent or guardian to provide opportunities for education to his child or ward between the age 6 and 14 years." On the basis of constitutional mandate provided in Article 41, 45, 46, 21A and various judgements of Supreme Court, the Government of India has taken several steps to eradicate illiteracy, improve the quality of education and make children back to school who left the school for one or the other reasons. The government schools shall provide free education to all the children and the schools will be managed by school management committees. Private schools shall admit at least 25% of the children in their school without any fee. The National commission for elementary education shall be constituted to monitor all aspects of elementary education including quality.

Soon after gaining independence in 1947, making education available to all had become a priority of the government. As discrimination on the basis of caste and gender has been a major impediment in the healthy development of the Indian society they have been made unlawful by the Indian Constitution.

While the right to education, is a fundamental right now, the government have yet to acknowledge its proper implementation. The National Commission for Protection of Child Rights (NCPCR) has been designated as the agency to monitor provisions of the Right to Free and Compulsory Education (RTE) Act. To ensure that the RTE Act is implemented successfully in letter and spirit, the NCPCR has taken the initiatives to build a consensus among institutions, government departments, civil society and other state holders. It had instituted an expert committee comprising officials from various government departments, persons of eminence and experience in field of education, to focus on roadmap for proper implementation of RTE.

This is a fact that mere laws and bills will solve the problem of education. Everyone has to understand their own social responsibility, that every child gets access to education.

The government of India has been working tremendously on the education system over the past few decades. Even with such laudable efforts, drop outs from school is in continuation. It has also been noted that they do not acquire the basic of literacy and numeracy as the additional knowledge and skills necessary for their all-round development as specified under RTE.

The RTE act provides a right platform to reach the unreached, with specific provisions for disadvantaged groups, such as child labourers, migrant children, children with special needs, or those who have a disadvantage owing to social, cultural, economical, geographical, linguistic, gender or other such factor.

But for the complete pursual of the act is dependent on so many factors. The success of any educational endeavour is based on the ability and motivation of teachers. Parents, guardians, families and communities have a large role to play to ensure child-friendly education for each and every one of the estimated 190 million girls and boys in India who should be in elementary school today.

With RTE, India can emerge as a global leader in achieving the millennium development goal of ensuring that all children complete their primary schooling by 2015. Though a challenge, but with the resources and political support, it is not an impossible task. The world is waiting for India to have rightful leadership role in education on the global stage. RTE will help in propelling this great nation to reach great heights of prosperity and productivity, when every Indian child, girl or a boy, will be touched by the light of education.

WHISTLE BLOWING : A BOLD CONCEPT

Whistle blowing is an act of providing secret information on an illicit or illegal transaction or corrupt practices in an office. This is a very old practice and came to limelight when False Claim Act-1863 enacted—a watchdog law to restrict illegal practices in USA. There were widespread abuses in

Government contracts during Civil War in which higher officials were exposed of malpractices. Since then American history has been full of whistle blowing that helped expose companies especially, Pharmaceutical industries involved in illegal practices. In 1987, 33 whistle blowing cases were filed which rose to 320 in 2002. However, the most popular was the Big Tobacco Scandal. Jeffrey Weigand—a famous whistle blower gained wide publicity for his role in exposing the Big Tobacco Scandal wherein the company had been involved in mixing carcinogenic ingredients in the cigarettes, a poisonous element.

A whistle blower is a person in a government office or in an institution who spies on the unofficial or illegal or corrupt practices and deals with the officials and then report the matter to the authority for action. In some cases, a whistle blower helps to expose the corrupt or to catch them red-handed. The practice is very healthy to keep the corrupt officials in check. But at the same time, known whistle-blower faces risk or danger to his life. To help whistle-blowers, US government enacted whistle-blower Protection Act-1989 furthering the provisions of erstwhile False Claim Act 1863. The reports of whistle-blower being intimidated came as a shock to the world. However, the trend continues in spite of risk involved in it. To provide new impetus to the whistle-blowing, 'Time' magazine in 2002 selected three whistle-blowers as 'Time's People of the Year Award 2002'. They were—Cynthia Cooper of World Com, Sharon Watkins of Enron and Colleen Ronley of FBI. These three whistle blowers were given the front page coverage.

India is perhaps the best playground for whistle-blowing as corruption has made inroads in every department, office, institution and establishment. Laws are many, departments are also enough and officials are in abundance to check corrupt practices, yet due to lack of evidence against the wrong-doers they are let off. And because not all officials in any department are corrupt, those who are fair must venture out to expose the wrong-doers or illegal transactions. This will be a great service to the nation.

Indian political history is full of scams and scandals whereby hundreds of thousands of crores have been siphoned off yet on the level of prosecution hardly any one is executed as trails linger too long. So, one process of checking corruption is to generate an environment of unknown fear that some one is watching or a pair of hidden eyes are keeping surveillance. Bringing the culprits to book is a legal process but holding back the wrong doers before he does anything corrupt is a moral trend. This can not only create a wave of fear among officials but would help increase the efficiency level as well.

Our country does not lack the daring souls who could go out to expose the unofficial deals and illegal transactions, even if there are big fishes in the pond. The government agencies give reward to such people who help nab the culprits. This trend needs to be followed at war footing if India has to survive the onslaught of corruption. In US the reward is very handsome, and at one occasion a whopping sum of $100 million is paid to a whistle blower or they can get a share of 15-30% stake in company's profit. What is needed in India is Whistle-blower Act that can help whistle-blower morally, legally and financially. This would certainly provide legal basis for exposing the corrupt colleagues who are sucking the life-blood of the nation. A cash reward would generate general awareness and would encourage the honest professionals or citizens to go all out in exposing the system, the deals and those who are involved in such murky affairs.

Remember, speeches, discussions and research papers won't help root out the corruption but the beginning from the fellow honest employees will do the trick. As Lanka was won over with the help of a genuine fellow in the court of the Ravana leading to the end of unjust rule and the ruler, same can be accomplished in today's environment if masses come out and recognize their moral duty of reporting the corrupt or illegal practice/persons.

STUDENTS & POLITICS

Our nation is growing democracy with complete political independence and are likely to attain economic independence by the year 2050 AD. Indian students are allowed to form students unions. As they are the future managers of the nation (and they have to steer our nation towards political, socio-economic and industrial prosperity, they must know the art and science of governance of this nation. This necessitates the growth of student unions in colleges and universities as the real training of a student starts from the educational institute itself.

The political parties support (or create) one student union and try to influence the students. Political machinations take evil turns and manifest themselves in the forms of phoney elections, arson, violence on campuses and even murders. Therefore, valuable property worth millions is destroyed; state transport buses or local buses are the worst hit due to rampage and violence of students. All types of guns and other arsenal are freely available in a free market economy. Therefore, in order to rule the college or university campus, the power of the gun is used quite often. Political parties initiate wicked election campaigns and cook their own recipes for ensuring their presence in the educational institute. The ordinary student suffers on account of loss of freedom and disruption in academic sessions. A few hooligans rule the roost and the majority of students remains neglected.

Academic schedules, sports and the intellectual development of the students suffer. The useful time of the young students is wasted in political campaigns, strikes and protests. The student suffers, his or her family suffers and the nation suffers in the long run. Politics on campus may have benefited a few but most of the students remain untouched by and large. What is the use of politics on campus if it cannot affect the lives of atleast 80 per cent of students?

Politics and educational institutes must be separate. This would eliminate wastage of time and precious human resources and public property. The idea of involvement of those students in politics who are really keen to take up politics as a career in their later lives will be a welcome trend. They could form organisations, clubs and unions in order to hone their political skills. But why bother the ordinary student whose parents await the completion of his or her graduation so that he or she could become a wage earner for the family? Political parties must keep their hands off the educational institutes. They develop students as their pawns and exploit them to achieve their bare political ends. The State must pass strict legislations (at the centre and state levels) to this effect. The temples of learning should never be allowed to operate as hotbeds of politics. The nation has already suffered on account of marriage of politics with hooliganism and our youth have paid heavy price due to this unholy alliance.

The youth of today would not study on account of a strike call issued by their unions. But they would not miss the nearest fast food joint either (as strikes and bandhs bring holidays with them). These double standards would have to be shunned. We would suggest that instead of participating in campus politics, our students should take up part-time jobs so that they could become financially independent and earn enough money for meeting their educational expenses. This would help their parents in meeting other financial obligations and the students would also be pleased to earn. Part-time assignments could include jobs in factories, computer operations, home coaching etc. Constructive and result oriented activities like painting, multimedia, fashion technology and Internet operations would also develop their vocational skills. Moreover, they would be able to get better jobs when they pass out from their institutes. Strikes, bandhs and petty student politics would not be able to develop their faculties, which could enable them to be independent after the completion of their academic tenures.

The political affiliations of students should be allowed only for those students who are studying political science or who are keen to accept politics as a career. Our college and university campuses should be able to grow sans political affiliations. The State would have to take far-reaching decisions for ensuring their apolitical operations.

CRIMINALISATION OF POLITICS

When we say criminalisation of politics, we mean to say that the political system has been eroded of the good political people or people with selfish gains have entered the political arena. These days people with criminal background find it easy to become members of Parliament or legislative assembly. This gives rise to a kind of situation where there are great deal of erosion of values, dearth of security of life, lack of transparency and accountability, rampant corruption etc.

Today in order to win an election a candidate requires only manpower, muscle power and money power. People with these three cannot think of losing an election—though a person with good leadership qualities and devotion to service to society may lose his security money. Bad practice seems to have driven out clean traditions of political behaviour. The voters, political parties and the law and order machinery are all equally responsible for the criminalisation of politics. These days political parties look for people with criminal background who will be having muscle power and who can extract money from general public to meet up their election expenses and win the election by hook or by crook. People within a party must have the courage to speak against and turn out such candidates from the elections.

Masses in India are not educated enough and can be easily influenced by money or muscle power. Middle class is either manipulative or apathetic to the whole electoral process, which provides scope for criminal elements in politics.

Under the current law, only people who have been convicted atleast twice can be debarred from becoming candidates. This leaves the field open for chargesheeted criminals. Does it not seem that the political parties themselves are not interested in changing the system? In certain constituencies it has been observed that people vote for a particular candidate not in support of his agenda or his previous work done but because of the dire consequences that they may have to face after elections. The failure of the state machinery in ensuring free and fair elections is apparent here. Political parties continue to seek support of the criminals for electoral malpractices like booth capturing and rigging.

Today the biggest problem in our country is the weak law enforcement and the Indian Penal Code. People take law for granted. Even on commiting a serious crime like murder, the criminal may escape punishment in lack of ample evidence or may get the benefit of doubt due to lackness of an investigating officer. These situations make the criminals more bold and they get encouraged.

In the interest of practical and immediate solution, it is easy to state that one must depend on the power of force and coercion to put an end to criminalisation of politics rather than vague notions of morality.

Assuming that the election process is sufficiently corruption free, voters only have themselves to blame if they elect a criminal. A voter's friends and family may vote for that party but it is upto the individual voter to reject that candidate if he or she suspects that the candidate may be corrupt. Highly educated and capable people generally do not opt politics as a career, they will rather prefer business or some other job or may even go abroad for further studies or job opportunities. It requires courage and bravery to contest an election. More the educated and capable people leave politics as career, more the criminals will enter into it. Violence and criminalisation can be effectively tackled by inspiring leadership. Political parties must break ties with armed gangs and shun violence in political activities. Election Commission should act to prevent convicted criminals from entering politics. Every citizen who fails to take part in the process of discouraging criminalisation of politics even in any small way should be held responsible for the degeneration of politics to such an extent that it is today dominated by convicts and historysheeters.

SEEING CHALLENGES AS OPPORTUNITIES

From time to time, each of us will find ourselves in a rut of boredom and disinterest. We seem to lose our zest for life and feel tired, irritable and unmotivated. We want to hide under the covers rather than face the day. Perhaps you're feeling overwhelmed by work, or sad about the pain and suffering in the world, or just bored with the routine of your daily life. You are not alone. We all go through periods like this at some point. The good news is that we can do something about it. Following are laid some tips to help break out of the rut and feel excited about life again.

Prolonged stress can wear us down and zap any enthusiasm we once had. Before doing anything else, take a few minutes to breathe and just be easy. Empty your mind of all stress and worry. This takes practice, but don't give up! As thoughts come into your mind, gently push them back out and continue to keep your mind empty and calm. Take slow, deep breaths and let all of your muscles relax. Sit quietly and recharge your batteries. Try to do this daily, or even twice daily (morning and night). We need quiet time as much as we need anything else in life. Give yourself the gift of inner peace.

Read something motivational, inspirational or uplifting. Look at some beautiful nature photos, or read something humorous. Consciously move your thoughts to a more positive place. Focusing on nothing but work and our daily tasks in life can leave us feeling pretty uninspired. It's easy to turn it around if we want to. We just have to seek out things that will lift our spirits and our moods. Make it a point to laugh, be happy, joyful and lighthearted each day. Don't wait for inspiration to come knocking on your door, go out and find it, or create it. Conjure up some funny or touching memories. Write them in a journal so you can go back and read them when you're feeling down.

Think about the things you have planned for the day, and rekindle the enthusiasm you once felt for them. When we first begin a new project, or start a new job, we are excited about the possibilities and eager to get moving! Over time, we can lose that enthusiasm for a variety of reasons. Travel back in time for a moment, and think about what got you so excited at the beginning. What made your heart beat a little faster? Recapture that feeling and hang onto it! Even if your tasks aren't anything to be really excited about, at least think of some positive benefits to doing them. For example, list the ways they will benefit your children, your spouse, yourself, your job or your home. Identify the payoff, and focus on that. Even mundane tasks have some benefits. Sometimes it's just a matter of switching our mindset to see the positive side.

Sometimes the hardest part is actually getting started. A project seems so monstrous that we cringe at the thought of all that time and energy we'll have to expend. Instead of overwhelming yourself, start small. Set a timer for 15 minutes and just start working on it. Allow yourself to stop after 15 minutes if you really want to. But most often, once we actually start working on something, we won't want to stop. Don't focus on the big picture, look at the smaller details and take them on one at a time. Any large task seems manageable once we break it down into smaller steps.

Sometimes our feelings of fatigue are caused by physical deficiencies, not mental. Be sure you are getting enough rest, eating food that nourishes your body, drinking enough water, getting enough exercise, etc. Especially when we're very busy, we tend to grab the quickest, easiest meals, which aren't always the best choice for our bodies. Eating a lot of highly processed foods and sugar is like putting watered-down gasoline into our cars. In order for our cars to run smoothly, we need to maintain them properly, and so it is with our bodies also. Remember, the body is the vehicle for the mind and soul!

Finally, remember to reward yourself from time to time, and be gentle with yourself! There will always be things that "need" to be done. But some of us take on way more than we can handle, and our lives turn into a pit of drudgery because of it. Try to eliminate the things that truly don't bring you joy, or at least minimize the time you spend on them. Do what you can, and let the rest go. Or ask for help. Don't feel you have to do everything yourself.

Remember that motivation, just like happiness, is something we choose. We may need to give ourselves a little push at the beginning, but once we get into the right mindset, it's simple to stay there if we choose to. Now I hope you must be ready to take on the challenges as your opportunities.

Seeing Challenges as Opportunities

Are you a person who loves challenges, or hates them? I must admit I've spent most of my life as a person who hates them. I always thought of challenges as frustrating, maddening obstacles keeping me from where I want to be. I even used to take them personally, feeling like the universe must hate me and like to see me struggle.

As I grow older and (hopefully) wiser - I find my competitive nature rising up to meet these challenges, and I'm learning to see them differently. Most of us know that great rewards require great sacrifice and effort. You know the old saying that nothing worthwhile comes easy? In a sense that's true. If everything we wanted was handed to us, we probably wouldn't have a lot of appreciation for it. On the other hand, when we work hard for something and then see it manifest before our eyes, we get such a powerful sense of pride and accomplishment. We can point to it and say, "I did that. It was tough, but I did it anyway."

Challenges are truly opportunities. Opportunities to grow and learn, to strengthen ourselves, to test ourselves and our faith. They reveal how badly we want to create the dreams in our hearts, and how hard we're willing to work for them. This is such a blessing. It may not seem that way at first, but with a tiny shift in attitude, we can see that we have been handed an incredible opportunity.

The next time life hands you a challenge, stop and consider for a moment what it means. Is the universe saying "no", or "I want you to try harder?" Don't look at challenges as an end, look at them as a door leading to your heart's desires. That door might be locked, but you have the key. Maybe you forgot where you put the key, or you forgot that you even had it to begin with. It might take some effort and patience to find it again - or you might even have to create a new one, but believe that you will, even if you're not sure how yet.

I'm learning that it's not important to have all the answers right now. When challenges rise up before us, we may not know how to get around them, or through them. It might seem hopeless at first. Challenges can seem so overwhelming when we don't have a solution. However, life itself is very much like this too. Sometimes life is akin to bumping around in a dark room, trying to find the light switch. It is possible to get through the room without finding the light switch immediately, we just need to step slowly and carefully. Moment to moment, we find our way.

Rather than giving up when obstacles appear in your path, look at them as welcome challenges. The biggest challenge is choosing your own attitude. Will you get flustered and angry, or will you get excited and determined? Will you lay down and cry, or will you roll up your sleeves and get to work? Some of us take on a victim mentality when obstacles arise, and I can see why this happens. It does feel like the universe is picking on us, doesn't it? I think we've all been there!

Why not change your mindset and think of obstacles as a personal challenge? Rather than feeling like the universe is picking on you, challenge yourself to figure out a solution. Say to yourself, "Okay, such and such has happened, now what am I going to do about it"? Put your problem-solving skills to work. Once we begin to change our attitude about obstacles and challenges, they can actually become fun. Our competitive human nature rises up and gets ready to win, no matter what. We develop a steely determination to not be beaten.

In fact, I like to pretend there is a great critic in the sky who laughs mockingly at me and says, "You can't do that." I simply grin wickedly, roll up my sleeves and say, "Watch me!"

CHANGING FACE OF TERRORISM

Terrorism means an activity that involves a violent act or an act dangerous to human life, property or infrastructure. It appears to be intended to influence the policy of a government by intimidation and to affect the conduct of a government by mass destruction, assassination, kidnapping or hostage-taking.

Terrorism came into existence during the French revolution when the then king unleashed a reign of terror on his opponents and the revolutionary organisations. Our freedom fighters adopted the same measures against the British. During the struggle for independence in India, the militant groups and organisations cropped up to take up the struggle in aggressive and retaliatory methods. They used to get involved in bombing, killing and ambushing the ruling class. However, in free India, militancy started during 1960s when naxalite movement was initiated by Charu Majumdar. Though a number of countries have been affected by terrorism since a long time but after the attack on the "Twin Towers" in USA (9/11 (2001) attack), and Paris attack on 19 November, 2015 terrorism came to limelight in the entire world. Almost all countries are now very much bothered with this problem. Terrorist groups like the Al-Qaeda or Hizbul etc. are very much advanced in their methods of operations. They have gone much ahead of the phase of the guerilla wars. They use suicide bombers, highly advanced artillery, they have very unique methods of communication amongst themselves using coded languages which are not very easy to decode. The attack in Mumbai on Nov. 26, 2008 was a massive attack that the commercial capital has suffered in last 16 years. Likewise, in Delhi the public places were the main target. Indians can never forget the devastating bomb blast in Sarojini Nagar market in New Delhi. Yet it seems the people of Mumbai and Delhi have got used to militant attacks and hence once again they get on with their daily lives the very next day without any fear of attacks.

The alleged plot to blow up planes from the United Kingdom mid-flight involved the detonation of explosive devices smuggled in hand luggage on to as many as 10 aircrafts. One theory is that the attack may have involved liquid explosive being carried to a plane in either drink bottles or cans. An overpressure of just 10 per cent would wreck the aircraft and possibly kill the people in it.

India became a signatory to the International Convention for the Suppression of Acts of Nuclear Terrorism at the United Nations headquarters in New York on July 24, 2006. The Convention was adopted by the UN General Assembly on April 13, 2005. As per the Convention, states are required to make punishable as serious offences under their domestic law, terrorists acts involving the use of nuclear materials. The Convention enjoys upon the signatory states to cooperate in prevention, investigation and prosecution of these offences through the sharing of critical information regarding disruptive activities, extradition and mutual legal assistance.

Carnage in the name of religion will remain a threat as long as terrorists have access to the infrastructure needed to assemble large scale operations. If follows that security services should look not so much at the intention of individuals to execute violent acts as at the capabilities available to them. The terrorist threat is alive and kicking even with greatly increased security levels across the globe.

SOLAR ENERGY : A SOLUTION FOR THE ENERGY CRISIS

The meaning of the word 'energy' is "capacity to do work". Hence, energy is the force that does work, or it is a driving force. We walk because we have energy. Motor cars, railway trains and aircraft are also driven by energy. All the big machines also operate because of energy. There was a time when man used to do all the tasks with the help of his own energy *i.e.*, his physical power. Slowly, he started utilising the animal power. Then, he started serving his purposes by extracting energy from the natural sources. The era of today belongs to machines and factories. In order to operate them, man has devised many a technique to get energy. Today in every field of the world and especially, in every segment of business, energy is being utilised in many ways. The basis of the total progress and pace of this world is energy. Energy is the life of agriculture, industry, transport and communications. These would come to a halt in the absence of energy. That is why, energy is deemed the decisive basic element of a civilisation and its growth. Today, the more the amounts of energy consumed in a country, the more developed and progressive it is considered to be.

There are many known sourcs of energy in the modern age and efforts are being made to find new energy sources. The conventional sources of energy are wood, coal, oil (petroleum and products thereof), gas and water. Among its new sources, nuclear energy is included. In the latest and non-conventional sources of energy, solar energy, wind energy, hydel energy, tidal energy, etc., can be named. Keeping the growing population of the world, fast growth of economic and industrial development and need for increasing the transport and communication modes in view, the energy crisis has become quite serious.

In such a situation, the attention of people is being diverted towards such alternative sources of energy as should be cheap, harmless, universally available and usable time and again. Those sources, whose deposits do not decay, solar energy is deemed the most important alternative. There are three advantages in the context of solar energy: (a) Solar energy is comparatively cheaper for cooking, street lighting, heating water, producing electricity and carrying out such activities as are beneficial to the masses; (b) the source of solar energy is the Sun and supply of sunlight would not come to an end; and (c) while getting energy from this source, there would neither be generation of pollution nor there would be a harm inflicted on the environment. In the context of possibilities of using solar energy, scientists are very much optimistic. A survey has revealed that the solar radiations falling on the earth are equivalent to 170 crore kilowatts of energy. It means that the sunlight of eight days is equivalent to the capacity of all the available energy sources, which would provide energy to the world for one year. The scientists involved in the research of solar energy have opined that if solar energy is properly developed, then it can meet nearly 80 per cent of energy requirements of the world for the next 50 years. In America, Britain, Japan and Australia, rapid research efforts are being made in the fields of solar energy research.

There are great possibilities of use of solar energy in India. From the viewpoint of (exposure to) solar radiations, India occupies the second spot in the world; the first spot is occupied by the Sahara desert. In India, solar energy equivalent to 5.6 kilowatts is incident everday over a flat surface area of one square kilometer. After the world oil crisis of 1973, more attention has been given to solar energy research in India. Scientists are of the view that solar energy is the most appropriate and cheap energy source for India. Some experimental solar equipment have been installed in many states of India and with the help of these, energy is being supplied (for domestic use) within a radial distance of 1-5 kilometers from these devices.

There is another facet of adopting new and old energy sources. There is a need for the technology and requisite equipment to get energy from any source. When a country decides a source as a basis and develops equipment and infrastructure related to them, then she has to spend a lot of money. For example, superthermal power stations have been constructed in India by investing large capital in them; such stations generate electricity by using coal. When the coal reserves would be depleted, or if we adopt solar energy, then these power generation stations, built with investments of crores of rupees, would be made redundant. Hence, every country should see to it, she should opt for new energy sources keeping her needs, the quantities of sources available in the country, expenses to be incurred to exploit them, their long term availability, pollution and ecology in full view. By doing so, there would be no need to effect changes in the techniques and equipment being used to exploit them.

The energy crisis is confronting all the nations of the world. For some nations, it is a current problem

47

whereas in some others, it could arrive in the next 25-50 years. Hence, its solution largely depends upon the development of solar energy.

PROTECTION OF HUMAN RIGHTS

Man is a social animal. He needs some rights to lead a respectable life in the society. The rights enjoyed (and used) by man are called human rights. By the term human rights, we mean (in the general sense) that man, irrespective of his gender, class or caste, belonging to any nation, state or region, following any religion, sect or community, rich or poor, must get the right for growth, protection life with dignity at the time of his birth. In almost all the nations of the world, there are provisions for granting Fundamental Rights to their citizens without disciminations. In Indian Constitution, there is a provision to grant Fundamental Rights to the Indian nationals. In fact, our Constitution has been created on the tenets of equality of Justice (social, economic and political), respect and equality of opportunities. In our Constitution, the spirit of democracy has been kept in view and under the provisions of Fundamental Rights and Directive Principles of State Policy, equality and freedom have been guaranteed for all the Indians.

The limitation of our Judicial system is that a lot of time has to be invested by the victim to extract justice from the judiciary. Keeping this fact in view, in 1993, the Human Rights Protection Act was passed in order to settle disputes related to human rights violation. According to this Act, there is a provision for the establishement of Human Rights Commission, State Human Rights Commissions and District Human Rights Commissions. In 1993, the Human Rights Commission was established in our country. Human Rights Commissions are being established in various states too.

The Human Rights Commissions take judiciary actions with respect to the complaints related to human rights violations. Efforts, are made to punish those who violate human rights, according to the provisions laid for the purpose. Several State Human Rights Commissions have been established. In Uttar Pradesh, a number of Special Courts are hearing cases related to human rights violations. The state of Uttar Pradesh leads in the cases of human rights violations.

Normally, under the gamut of human rights violation, detention of an accused in Judicial custody for a long duration, tortures by the police, exploitation of women, atrocities inflicted upon people by the security forces, exploitation and torture of *Dalits*, mass murders etc. are included. A few years ago, the number of such cases was low, but nowadays, spiralling growth trends have been witnessed in the number of such cases.

Although several incidents related to human rights violation in the entire nation, yet only a few of them are registered. In modern times, due to rise in literacy levels and mass awareness levels, increasing numbers of such complaints are being registered. In this context, due to efforts of literate and elite people, various political parties, women's organisations, self-help groups, enlightened people, and media not only an awareness has been developed among people, but also Human Rights Violation Commission/State Human Rights Commissions are informed about such violations and they are requested to intervene in these cases and bring justice to the needy victims.

Although the number of cases of human rights violations seems to rise due to these efforts, yet it is a valid conclusion that offenders of human rights are becoming more fearful of these Commissions. It is hoped that if these awareness trends continue at this pace, then the number of cases of such human rights violations shall certainly come down.

THE BLACK SHADOW OF BLACK MONEY

Money earned through illegal means or by way of covert activities is called Black Money. This money remains deposited with people. As it is earned through corrupt methods and income tax is not paid on it, it is very important to hide it. In the public jargon, it is also called "dirty money". The chief sources of black money are thefts and misappropriations in income tax, excise duty, property tax, wealth tax and customs duty. Money earned through smuggling is also deemed black money. Money earned through the activities of black-marketing also falls under this category. Funds received through the acts of bribery are also a part of black money. On the basis of these sources, one can easily conclude who are the people who could be having black money. In the category of such people come industrialists, owners of factories, traders, shopkeepers (both wholesalers and retailers), owners of buildings, landlords, individuals engaged in businesses of imports and exports, politicians and government officials on high posts. But this list is not exhaustive; many more names can be added to it.

Today, the activity of collecting and hoarding black money is flowering at a very fast pace. According to the broad estimates of the National Institute of Public Finance and Policy, people in India have black money deposits of ₹ 37,000 crore with them. Remember that this amount can be larger than this figure too, it is based on an estimate because those who have black money do not give their accounts to anyone. The International Monetary Fund (IMF) has also estimated the amount of black money of many nations. It has been stated in its estimate that the amount of black money is 50 per cent of her Gross Domestic Product (GDP). According to the estimate of IMF, the amount of black money in India ranges from ₹ 80,000 crore to ₹ 90,000 crore.

Why is the business of black money growing by leaps and bounds in our country? Some genuine reasons in this context are as follows: (1) Lust for money, (2) Too much of materialism, (3) Weak laws, (4) Complex procedures to earn money with honesty (5) Awareness of the fact that money can buy everything and all types of good or bad deeds can be get done by any person through its use.

The fact that this has become an uncurable disease is not a hyperbole. However, some suggestions can be given to check the spread and effect of black money: (1) The government should control its expenses and these should be monitored, (2) High-deficit budgets should not be made, (3) Expenses being incurred on the government projects should be strictly monitored, (4) In the government administration, the self-discretionary rights of senior officials in industrial licensing department, income tax department, company law department or any other department should be either made defunct or minimised. Bias, corruption and black money are created because of the perpetuation of these very rights. (5) The taxation system should be pragmatic; the rates should not be very high because if they are moderate, people would not resort to acts of tax evasion. (6) The departments which collect taxes should be efficient and honest. (7) There should be a provision for harsh punishment for the acts of tax-evasion. (8) In the Institutions like state legislatures, government departments, financial institutions, judiciary, etc., the work should be of high quality. All their tasks should be done at the right time and the administrative machinery should be transparent (which means that actions and data should not be kept secret).

If this is done, then the possibilities of corrupt practices and biased behaviours would be lessened. We can expect that the production of black money would be at least reduced due to the aforesaid remedies.

THE PANAMA PAPERS LEAK

The International Consortium of Investigative Journalists on April 3, 2016, reported a gigantic leak of offshore financial records exposing a world wide network of crime and corruption. The papers were initially released to German newspaper Süddeutsche Zeitung, which then partnered with the International Consortium of Investigative Journalists. For more than a year, 300 journalists reviewed approximately 2.6 terabytes of data before releasing their findings, now called the Panama Papers.

Mossack Fonseca, is a little-known but powerful law firm based in Panama that has been exposed to be one of the world's top creators of shell companies, corporate structures that can be used to hide ownership of assets in cities such as Zurich, London, Virgin Islands and Hong Kong. It has founded, sold, and managed thousands of such offshore companies. It administers these offshore firms for a yearly fee.

The firm is based in Panama but runs worldwide operation. Its website boasts of a global network with 600 people working in 42 countries. It has franchises across the world, where new customers are signed in. It operates in tax havens including Switzerland, Cyprus and the British Virgin Islands, and in the British crown dependencies Guernsey, Jersey and the Isle of Man. The Panama Papers include approximately 11.5 million documents - more than the combined total of the Wikileaks Cablegate, Offshore Leaks, Lux Leaks, and Swiss Leaks. The data primarily comprises e-mails, pdf files, photo files, data from Mossack Fonseca and covers a period spanning from the 1970s to the spring of 2016.

The confidential documents have revealed how the rich and powerful use tax havens to hide their wealth. The documents show how a global industry of law firms and big banks help the rich exploit secretive offshore tax regimes and offer financial secrecy to politicians, fraudsters and drug traffickers as well as billionaires, celebrities and sports stars by offering them a place to park their money.

The papers have exposed how black money flows through the global financial system, breeding crime and stripping national treasuries of tax revenues.

The millions of documents have exposed heads of state, criminals and celebrities who have used secret hideaways in tax havens. These include criminals and members of various mafia groups, Ponzi schemers, drug kingpins, tax evaders and at least one sex offender.

The files have revealed the offshore holdings of several politicians and public officials from around the world. Twelve national leaders are among 143 politicians who have been using these tax havens.

World leaders, their families and close associates from around the world known to have been using offshore tax havens. The data include the prime minister of Iceland, the president of Ukraine, and the king of Saudi Arabia, the children of the president of Azerbaijan and the prime minister of Pakistan. A $2bn offshore trail led to Russian President Vladimir Putin.

The leak also provides details of the hidden financial dealings of 128 more politicians and public officials around the world. The law firm's leaked internal files contain information on 214,488 offshore entities connected to people in more than 200 countries. They also include at least 33 people and companies blacklisted by the U.S. government.

The files include a convicted money-launderer, 29 billionaires featured in Forbes Magazine's list of the world's 500 richest people and movie star Jackie Chan, who has at least six companies managed through the law firm.

The records also show best soccer player Lionel Messi and his father were owners of a shell Panama company: Mega Star Enterprises Inc.

The list also contains 500 people from India which has raised serious debate about the issues related to money laundring.

Having an offshore company isn't illegal. For some international business transactions, it is a logical choice. Under national laws and international agreements, firms like Mossack Fonseca that create companies and bank accounts are supposed to be on the lookout for clients who may be involved in money laundering, tax evasion or other wrongdoing. They are required to pay special attention to 'politically exposed persons' or PEP, government officials or their family members or associates for any political corruption.

However, the documents show that banks, law firms and other offshore players in these holdings have turned a blind eye to such people and in fact, indulged in a lot of irregularities and illegalities, and gone the extra mile to keep their clients dubious finances secret.

Banks, including giants like UBS and HSBC have created thousands of companies which exist on paper only for clients.

The leak has created an upheaval globally and continues to do so. Governments have pledged to unearth the truth on the people named in the leaks and investigate other leads.

As names began to be exposed, it has caused a barrage of denials of any wrong doing. Mossack Fonseca said it has operated beyond reproach for 40 years and never been accused or charged with criminal wrong-doing. It refused to divulge any information about its clients as it was obliged to keep their secrets, it said.

Most leading figures and financial institutions also responded to the leak with denials of any wrongdoing as prosecutors and regulators began a review of the information leaked.

The impact of the leaked documents began to snowball and one by one heads began to roll. The first causality was Iceland's prime minister, Sigmundur Davio Gunnlaugsson, who stepped aside since the revelations were made public. The next was Spain's acting industry minister. British Prime Minister David Cameron, was implicated and had to pay taxes for the first time. Pakistan's Prime Minister Nawaz Sharief also has to resign after a court disqualified him on this account.

Mossack Fonseca had been largely operating in the shadows. But, now the law firm is under growing scrutiny in Germany and Brazil. Employees of the firm were among those arrested by Brazilian police under Operation Carwash. The leaks also sparked off tax haven debates and measures to counter large scale tax evasions.

Recently, European finance ministers announced a tax information exchange initiative at the World Bank-IMF Springs meeting in Washington and also urged G20 leaders to participate in the initiative.

To prevent such practices India along with G20 have come along to sign an initiative known as Base erosion and profit sharing. This will make the sharing of information's regarding taxes and black money more easy and dynamic. India is effectively taking steps to implement this initiative which makes the process of stashing unaccounted money dificult.

The release of Panama paper is slated to create huge uproar in civil society and in parliament of many countries. Government of India has already ordered enquiry against this backdrop. However the need of the hour is to expedite such cases of money laundering through establishing of special courts and punishing the offenders so that it create an effective deterrence to repeat/commit such crimes.

WHY INDIA DESERVES A PERMANENT SEAT AT UN SECURITY COUNCIL?

Ever since taking over the leadership of the world's largest democracy, Indian Prime Minister Narendra Modi has doggedly concentrated on giving a new shape to India's foreign policy. Modi's global aspirations and desire for international recognition became known the moment he extended a formal invite to the leaders of neighbouring South Asian countries to attend his swearing-in ceremony at Raisina Hills in 2014.

Modi has repeatedly struck one masterstroke after another during the course of his foreign trips. Be it addressing a public meeting of NRIs inside jam packed stadiums in USA and Australia or articulating the nation's external policy at the United Nations or National Assemblies of Nepal and Bangladesh, Modi has made the world take notice of his eloquence and oratorical skills. He has been exceedingly sharp in visiting places which were mostly off the radar of Indian diplomats be it the state of Mongolia which is strategically sandwiched between Russia and China or the energy rich nations of Central Asia i.e. Turkmenistan, Tajikistan, Kazakhstan, Kyrgyzstan and Uzbekistan.

Prime minister's foreign visits have been high on symbolism and soft power. He has been quick to sight old ties by invoking the teachings of Buddhism and Islam. He hasn't missed out on an opportunity to visit a temple or gurdwara and successfully steered the holding of the first ever International Yoga Day. Predictably, foreign policy is one area where Modi has tasted relatively more success as compared to domestic issues. The hateful rhetoric of the Hindu right concerning love jihad, ghar wapsi and forced sterilization definitely embarrassed the ruling establishment headed by

Modi and the impasse in Parliament on the issue of Lalitgate has sent the much awaited reforms in cold storage. Amid all this gloom, Modi can stare at the horizon of foreign policy and give himself a pat on the back.

But Modi will have to do a lot more if he wishes to establish India's position as a country wielding global clout. The simplest way of achieving that objective would be by attaining a permanent seat in the United Nations Security Council (UNSC) which Nehru allegedly turned down in the 1950s. India has served seven terms as a non-permanent member of UNSC and has echoed the need for expansion and reform in the Security Council. A permanent seat in UNSC would elevate India to the status of USA, UK, France, China and Russia in the diplomatic sphere and warrant India a critical say in all global matters.

Interestingly, India is not the only country in the world eyeing a spot in UNSC. Other competing nations include the likes of Japan, Germany and Brazil. The very notion of a reform or expansion in UNSC leads to the rise of a few fundamental questions: How many countries will join the existing brigade of P-5? What will be the basis of inclusion of more countries in UNSC? Will it be economic status, regional parity or human development? If another Asian country is to be included in UNSC then will it be Japan or India?

India commands three distinct characteristics which make its case for a permanent seat compelling. Currently having a population of 1.28 billion, India will become the most populous country in the world by 2022. Such a large portion of the planet's population cannot be altogether ignored or kept at a distance from the decision making table of UNSC which brings with itself the "veto" power. Secondly, India happens to be the second fastest growing economy in the world making it an ideal destination for foreign investment and future growth. Thirdly, India is ruled by a democratic, secular government which has never been upstaged by an army coup and can be labelled as a "responsible" nuclear power.

India's last stint as a non permanent member of UNSC in 2011-12 was supported by regional rivals Pakistan and China but Pakistan might turn out to be a big thorn in India's way if a global consensus is reached in proving India with permanent membership. Pakistan is bound to raise the issue of regional imbalance if India is in a position to acquire permanent membership and draw the world's attention towards the persisting Indo-Pak conflict regarding Kashmir.

Despite prospects of a bright economic future, India has reasons to fear competing powers Japan, Germany and Brazil. India's GDP (nominal) makes it the ninth biggest economic power in the world. At present, Japan, Germany and Brazil's economic size is bigger than that of India with Japan being the third largest in the world and second largest in Asia after China, Germany being the largest in Europe and fourth globally, while Brazil commanding pole position in South America and seventh globally.

As far as per capita income is concerned, India is nowhere on the list. As per International Monetary fund (2014), India ranks 125 globally with a per capita income of mere $5,855. Japan, Germany and Brazil rank much higher at 18, 28 and 74, respectively. Human Development Index Report (2014) of United Nations Development Program (UNDP) ranks India 114 in the category of "medium human development." Japan and Germany are countries with "very high human development" ranking 6 and 17, respectively whereas Brazil ranks 51 and is christened as a country with "high human development."

Simplistic breakdown of facts and figures certainly lowers India's prospects of a permanent seat when compared with its rivals. But India has a silver lining when it comes to its track record in terms of its contribution to UN Peacekeeping forces which have played a pivotal role in combating violence and maintaining peace. India is the fourth largest contributor to UN Peacekeeping behind Bangladesh, Ethiopia and Pakistan. Though India has a large physical presence in UN Peacekeeping, it finances a minuscule 0.13 per cent of UN peacekeeping operations. The P-5 has lesser boots on the ground but rules the roost when it comes to financing peacekeeping operations with USA pitching in with over 28 per cent financial contribution. Japan comes in second with 10.83 per cent followed by other permanent members.

It is a complex situation. India is growing economically but lags behind when it comes to per capita indicators. Owing to its military strength, it is contributing in huge numbers to peacekeeping but cannot match up to the financing levels of P-5 or Japan in relation to peacekeeping operations. The story is a paradox. But the most important element of the story is yet to be spoken about i.e. P-5. A reform in UN Security Council would necessitate the need for an amendment in the UN Charter which is possible only when a resolution is adopted by two-third member nations in the UN General Assembly. It has to be further ratified by the constitutional process of two-third member nations including P-5.

Will the P-5 agree to share their power and authority with other nations? White House Press Secretary Josh Earnest is on record stating "President (Obama) would support the inclusion of India in that process (reform of UNSC)" but cables leaked by Wikileaks quoted Former US Secretary of State Hillary Rodham Clinton ridiculing countries like India as "self appointed front-runners" for a permanent membership of UNSC. The two statements, one on-record and the other off-record, hint at the underlying duplicity of USA. If the "Great Indian Dream" of attaining permanent membership has to be accomplished then India will surely have to cultivate a global consensus which will include the P-5. The penultimate question is: Can Modi pull off a Himalayan miracle?

CAN RELIGION AND POLITICS CO-EXIST?

On the outer margins of the debate over the place of religion in politics, there are two extreme positions, each fuelling the fundamentalism of the other. Now, religions do not advocate suicide bombing, though there is no doubt that many abuses are carried out in the name of religion. And religions do not need to be theocratic: They can easily co-exist with secular forms of government without attracting divine retribution.

Despite the separation of church and state in India, religion and politics in this country have long influenced one another in ways direct and indirect.

Contemporary analysts too frequently assume that the mutually fructifying influence between religion and politics either no longer exists or is deeply problematic. Their mistake is a result of focusing too narrowly on the recent constitutional trend toward strengthening the separation of church and state, rather than looking more broadly at the worlds of religion and politics as they actually intersect, and mutually flourish today. That church and state in India are in fact separate means that ours is a secular government—but it does not mean that ours is a secular society. It isn't now. It has never been.

In fact, the terrain on which religion and politics have most often met in Indian history is the realm of non-state institutions we call civil society. In every aspect of human endeavor, faith matters to people and to particular communities, and, when as citizens these people and communities participate in politics, to the nation at large.

These facts suggest a logic for religious engagement in the civic realm that clashes with a dominant strand of argument in academic philosophy that, although prominent in scholarly debates, has very little to do with how people actually talk and act. The academic philosophers insist that the convictions of the religious need to be translated into a purely secular idiom if the faithful are to join in political deliberation. If the religiously minded are not comfortable translating their convictions into such a secular idiom, they had best remain silent.

Some versions of this argument—for example, that associated with the late John Rawls—are subtle and complex. Others are much simpler. They assume that there is a single vocabulary for political discussion; if your speech lies out side the purview of a secular language of 'public deliberation,' it isn't legitimately public speech at all.

The draconian requirement that a purely secular mode of speech supplant all other ways of making public argument cuts against the grain of American political history and civic culture. In the real world of religion and politics as they actually coexist in America, citizens resort to 'god talk' at least as much as they use 'rights talk.' Faith informs the way America speaks and has always spoken. The U.S. Constitution never required that people give up the communal dimensions of their faith as the price for civic admission. Catholics, Lutherans, Jews—all built networks of schools and charitable institutions. Jews, in particular, distinguished themselves publicly through visible markers of their identity in dress and in dietary regulations. Even a cursory glance at our history shows the manner in which confessional pluralism and social pluralism have been linked in the American polity as religious differences were marked publicly through a variety of modes of communal identification. One reason that America's religious institutions are such an indispensable part of American civil society is that religion in America has never been compelled to privatize itself along the lines suggested by Rawls.

For the first 150 years of the American republic, primary responsibility for religious rights and liberties was lodged in the states. No federal law governing religious institutions in their relation to the government was ever passed. The federal government got into the act where religion is concerned—at least in a big way—only during the last half century.

In recent years, a constitutional position has emerged that might be called strong separationism. This position seeks to do on the level of law what a strict version of Rawlsian philosophy aims to do in the realm of discourse—namely, to strip public life of religious markers, emblems, and ceremony.

This position can be called as liberal monism, for its origins lie in certain strands of classical liberal political philosophy. This position holds that all institutions within a democratic society must conform to a single authority principle; a single standard of what counts as reason and deliberation; a single vocabulary of political discussion. Within this position, religion is routinely discounted-as the secularization hypothesis would have it—as irrationalism, or as a search for epistemological privilege.

Rather than asking how much religion can, or should, the polity tolerate, we might pose a different question instead: What sort of political arrangements "enable religion to play the constructive public role that religious commitments themselves demand?"

One enters political life as a citizen. But if one also has religious convictions, these convictions naturally will inform one's judgments as a citizen. My religious views help to determine who I am, how I think, and what I care about. This is as it should be. In India it makes no sense to ask people to bracket what they care about most deeply when they debate issues that are properly political.

Religion has served as a valuable anchor in the lives of millions of people since the founding of our republic. It is said that India is the most religious of the major industrializing states. We have religions that believe in the use of hallucinogens; religions that believe that your money should be theirs; many religions that believe that they are the chosen people and the rest of us are toast; religions that are proud of the objectification of women; religions that worship animals and others that worship plants.

We have Hindus, Muslims, Sikhs, Catholics, Methodists, Mormons, Presbyterians, Lutherans, Jews, Buddhists, Christian Scientists and many more. If you want to divine the future by reading the entrails of a liberal, knock yourself out. We have so many different religions in this country that if you can't find one that you like then you ain't trying! And if you don't find one, make up your own.

MORALITY AND POLITICS: WHOM TO BELIEVE?

A nation's political trends are governed by several factors—the state of the economy, the vested interests of politicians and bureaucrats, the attitudes of the media, and many others. But the fundamental factor is moral: the beliefs people have about right and wrong, good and bad; their aspirations for their lives; the virtues they practice and vices they denounce; the responsibilities and obligations they accept; the things they feel entitled to; the standards that govern their sense of fair play; the ideals that shape their sense of what is worthy.

The impact of morality on politics is obvious for many of the issues on the political front burner today, such as sex and violence in popular entertainment, or the alleged decline of "family values." But these are just the tip of the iceberg. To understand the broader and more pervasive impact of morality, consider another issue on the front burner: Social Security reform.

On its face, the plan to privatize the government retirement system is not a moral issue but an economic one. Advocates of the plan argue that because Social Security is a "pay as you go" system, in which current benefits are paid by current taxes rather than by returns on funds invested in the past, the system is headed for financial disaster as the number of retirees increases in proportion to the number of workers supporting them. Opponents claim that the problems can be fixed by relatively minor adjustments to the retirement age, payroll tax rates, and benefit levels.

Opponents of the privatization plan also claim that investing retirement funds in the stock market is too risky a proposition for most people; too many would end up destitute in old age. Advocates of privatization argue that the market trends upward over the long-term, and that the returns people get over an extended period will far exceed what they can expect from Social Security.

So where in the debate over Social Security does morality enter the picture? Everywhere.

Social Security was created in 1935 as the centerpiece of President Franklin Roosevelt's New Deal. Imagine that 150 years earlier, someone had proposed to the Founding Fathers, at the Constitutional Convention where they were creating a new federal government, that the government pay for every citizen's retirement by taxing a portion of every citizen's earnings. It would have been denounced as a system of universal dependence and universal slavery, an insulting attempt to treat

free men like the mob in ancient Rome. What made Social Security possible in 1935 was not economic change. It was not the Depression. There had been depressions before, and absolute standards of living were still much higher in the 1930s than in previous generations, despite the increase in relative poverty.

What made Social Security possible was the growth of collectivist thinking among intellectuals and cultural leaders during the preceding century. The ground was prepared by critics of individualism who taught that solidarity and equality are more important than freedom. As noted in book A Life of One's Own, thinkers like Thomas Hill Green and L.T. Hobhouse in England and John Dewey in America explicitly rejected the tenets of individualism. They attacked the pursuit of self-interest as selfish, insisting that individualists must be made to serve the public interest. They attacked the culture of self-reliance, insisting that individuals are creatures of their social environment. During the decades prior to the New Deal, advocates of the welfare state claimed that the poor are not responsible for their condition; they attacked private charity organizations for trying to teach "bourgeois" virtues to the poor. They argued that the old rights of life, liberty, and property had to be supplemented with new rights to economic security provided by the government.

Roosevelt was relying on this cultural background when he crowed that the New Deal represented "an appeal from the clamor of many private and selfish interests . . . to the ideal of the public interest," and when he spoke of "a second Bill of Rights under which a new basis of security and prosperity can be secured for all." These moral assumptions were essential to the creation of Social Security and other welfare state programs.

The same assumptions operate today. Critics of Social Security privatization appeal to the "solemn compact between the generations", that is, the moral ideal of solidarity. They argue that society has a moral obligation to provide for the essential needs of its members. They defend Social Security's massive transfers of wealth—from workers to retirees, from the wealthy to the poor, from men to women, from the able-bodied to the disabled-on the grounds of equality.

This is not to say that moral assumptions are the only relevant factors. Economists have shown the deleterious effects of the current system. The Cato Institute, the National Center for Policy Analysis, and other think tanks have worked out proposals showing in detail how a private system would work-and how to get there from here. José Piñera, architect of Chile's privatization, has been a tireless promoter of similar efforts worldwide. Without this massive evidence for the practicality of a private system, a purely moral argument would never get a hearing. The same is true for other efforts to get government out of our lives.

But without the moral argument, the practical arguments don't stand a chance, either. We have a mixed economy because we have a mixed culture. Our market society is saddled with government regulations and subsidies because our individualist culture is densely marbled with veins of altruist, egalitarian, and communitarian moral premises. Advocates of freedom have had great success in areas like deregulating the airlines and privatizing municipal services, where there is no strong moral sentiment to overcome. But we have had little success in cutting back the welfare state, which rests on an unchallenged altruist foundation. And we are losing ground in areas like civil rights and the environment, where the enemy's moral assumptions are in the ascendancy.

In economic terms, capitalism has won its century-long battle against socialism. But in moral terms, as Ayn Rand said, it remains an unknown ideal.

NOTA : STARTING POINT FOR A CLEAN-UP

With a view to bringing about purity in elections, the Supreme Court on September 27, 2013 held that a voter could exercise the option of negative voting and reject all candidates as unworthy of being elected. The voter could press the 'None of the Above' (NOTA) button in the electronic voting machine. The court directed the Election Commission to provide the NOTA button in the EVM.

Giving right to a voter not to vote for any candidate while protecting his right of secrecy is extremely important in a democracy. Such an option gives the voter the right to express his disapproval of the kind of candidates being put up by the parties. Gradually, there will be a systemic change and the parties will be forced to accept the will of the people and field candidates who are known for their integrity.

The NOTA option will accelerate effective political participation in the present state of the democratic system and the voters will in fact be empowered.

Not allowing a person to cast a negative vote would defeat the very freedom of expression and the right to liberty. Election Conduct Rules 41(2) and (3) and 49-0 of the Rules were ultra vires Section 128 of the Representation of the People Act and Article 19(1)(a) of the Constitution to the extent they violate secrecy of voting.

Civil liberties activists in India have had to fight long for, first, the right to cast a negative vote, and next, to protect the secrecy of this negative ballot. In the age of the Electronic Voting Machine (EVM), once the invalid vote ceased to exist, voters had only one option to show their dissatisfaction with the candidates seeking to represent them, and with the whole political system: staying away from the polling booth. The problem, of course, was that the activist-protesters got clubbed with those too lazy to stand in a queue and vote. Then came the recourse to 49-0, a rule in the Conduct of Election Rules, which allowed voters to not cast their vote after entering the polling booth and registering their electoral roll number in the register of electors in Form 17A. Under this rule, the voters had to record their decision to not vote in the remarks section of the form available with the presiding officer. This record of non-voting was necessary to ensure that the presiding officer was able to tally, after the voting came to an end, the total votes polled with the number of voters who had signed against their roll number in the register. But this effectively compromised the secrecy of the so-called negative vote. After a long legal battle, the Supreme Court on September 27, 2013 ordered the provision of a "None of the Above" (NOTA) option in EVMs and ballot papers at the end of the list of the contesting candidates.

Hard-won it might be, but NOTA can at best nudge the electoral system towards incremental changes. While delivering the judgement on this issue, the Supreme Court expressed hope that this would accelerate effective political participation of the people in the democratic system and empower the voters. In its immediate effect, however, a NOTA vote is not much more than an "invalid" vote on a ballot paper. The NOTA option cannot result in the rejection of the entire list of contestants, and even if a majority of the people press the NOTA panel on the EVM, the contestant with the largest number of votes would still win under the first-past-the-post system.

If the NOTA option holds not just some symbolic value, and is not a mere outlet for moral outrage, it is because of what is could do rather than because of what it is. Former Chief Election Commissioner N. Gopalaswami says, "a time will come with demands for fresh election with a fresh set of candidates if, in the first election, NOTA scores the highest votes." NOTA will gain political legitimacy when it outscores the contestants. Then, it is hoped, the option would not be allowed to remain impotent, and there will be a popular demand for the cancellation of the election.

But if the realisation of NOTA's potential is a desired goal, then the time to invest NOTA with more purpose is now and not later after an election in which NOTA outscores the winner. Indeed, if a NOTA vote that can reject all contestants is in place, political parties might pay more attention to who they are nominating as candidates.

In the NOTA judgement, the Supreme Court voiced this expectation of political parties: "When the political parties will realise that a large number of people are expressing their disapproval with the candidates being put up by them, gradually there will be a systemic change and the political parties will be forced to accept the will of the people and field candidates who are known for their integrity." But electoral reform in India has been slow, and often at the initiative of the judiciary. The NOTA plan has been lying with the centre for the 14 years. The Law Commission of India on May 29, 1999, had favoured NOTA in its 170 report to then law minister Ram Jethmalani. The Centre had sought the commission's view on the issue on November 2, 1995.

No doubt, NOTA would encourage voters, who shy away from voting process given the credentials of candidates, to cast their vote which would deter unscrupulous elements from casting vote on their behalf.

Comprehension

Comprehension is a very important part of English paper. The questions on comprehension lay particular stress on understanding a given passage. You are required to read a passage and answer a few questions based on it.

IMPORTANT TIPS

While answering comprehension questions, you must comply with the following important points:
1. First, read the whole passage attentively, carefully and quickly.
2. Read it for the second time, slowly but steadily.
3. Work out the meanings of new words, from the context in which they have been used.
4. Underline and look for transitional words and phrases as an aid to comprehension.
5. The process of elimination should be used while selecting the correct answer.
6. Your answers should be brief and to the point.

Direction: *Read each of the following passages and answer the questions that follow.*

PASSAGE - 1

We have witnessed several disasters in recent times, some natural, others man made. The frequency of such calamities has injured us and deadened our collective sensitivity, but that does not reduce the enormity of the personal tragedy of each victim's family and community. The economic loss is only secondary to the human suffering, but is also substantial. The Government whether State or Central has standardised its response. This consists of reacting late, blaming others, visits by VIPs announcing a relief package including compensation for those affected and then forgetting all about it. There seems to be little attempt at drawing lessons from each disaster, storing the knowledge for future use, long term planning for possible pre-emptive action. Preparedness for disasters thus falls short of what is possible using today's technologies.

Floods in many parts of India like the states of Bihar and Assam are a yearly phenomenon. Yet the government seems to be caught by surprise year after year. It is obvious that tarpaulins, vaccines, medicines, clothes, satellite phones, large numbers of doctors and paramedical staff etc. will be needed as will boats and buses for evacuation. This is known to all those who have combated emergencies yet the non-availability of these essential services and commodities occurs. Worse, the organisational structure and mechanisms for dealing with disasters are lethargic and ill defined. The National Disaster Management Agency, set up a short time ago being a central government agency has limitations relating to infringing the jurisdiction of states. It could have aggregated and disseminated experiences and knowledge, stocked many of the essential items required in an emergency or worked with agencies to ensure sufficient stocks, but hasn't.

While the reaction to major disasters is dismal, the response to emergencies like accident is equally sad. Victim lie unattended since passers by are wary of getting caught in a labyrinthine of police and legal systems. The resulting delay in treatment converts injuries into deaths. Of late, unique and free service to provide assistance in emergency cases is operational. Emergency Management and Research

57

Institute (EMRI) is a professionally managed operation-initiated by the vision and grant from a corporate house. The service, which is a successful example of public private partnership likely to become operational in a few states in the near future. Given the sad failure of conventional government organisations in handling disasters, it is time we looked at the PPP model as an alternative without the government seeking in any way to abdicate its responsibility. While the state provides the funding, private organisations will provide the drive, professionalism, competent management and output linked efficiency of a good corporate organisation. Combining the sensitivity and purpose of an NGO with private entrepreneurial drive to handle disasters together is thus a worthwhile challenge for both corporates and the government.

QUESTIONS

1. Why do bystanders not help accident victims?
2. What is the author's view on the government's current reaction to natural disasters?
3. Why is there a lack of medical care at disaster sites?
4. What does the author consider "a worthwhile challenge for both corporates and the government"?
5. Which will be the likely impact/s of the public private participation model of disaster management?

PASSAGE - 2

For months the old tanker, African Queen, lay turned over on her side, stuck fast in the sands off the coast of Maryland. She had run aground so badly that her owners had decided to leave her to her fate. It was considered impossible to refloat her and the ship began to rust and sink deeper and deeper into the sands. Men frequently came out in small boats and removed any parts that could be sold—until two men decided to attempt the impossible to float the African Queen once more. Both men were engineers and had no experience of ships. So, few people thought they could succeed.

The men began by studying the exact state of the African Queen and came to the conclusion that she would float again if air were pumped into the tanks which were now full of sea-water. A diver was sent down to examine the underside of the ship. In the cold, dark water he found an enormous hole in her side which had been torn when the ship ran aground. It was plain that nothing could be done until the hole was repaired. As no single sheet of steel would cover it, the men were obliged to order a great number of sheets which had to be joined together. For several weeks divers worked continually to close the hole. At times, the sea was so rough that it was difficult to go down; and on more than one occasion, they had to contend with sharks.

At last the hole was covered and the men began to pump the sea-water out of the ship's tanks. It seemed as if they were bound to succeed, for when the tanks were full of air, the African Queen began to stir in the water. The men could not understand why she still would not float until they discovered that her rudder was embedded in mud. Huge cranes were brought to haul the sunken rudder out and the ship was again afloat. By this time, the men were almost exhausted. They had worked ceaselessly for three months to save the African Queen and had succeeded when everyone thought they would fail. Now they stood on the bridge of the ship, tired but proud, as tugs brought the African Queen into the harbour.

QUESTIONS

1. Why did men frequently go out to the African Queen?
2. How did the two men propose to float the ship again?
3. What was the danger which the divers faced?
4. Due to which reason the two men felt proud?
5. What is the part of the ship used for steering?

PASSAGE - 3

Political ploys initially hailed as master-strokes often end up as flops. The ₹ 60,000 crore farm loan waiver announced in the budget writes off 100% of overdues of small and marginal farmers holding upto two hectares, and 25% of overdues of larger farmers. While India has enjoyed 8%-9% GDP growth for the past few years, the boom has bypassed many rural areas and farmer distress and suicides have made newspaper headlines. Various attempts to provide relief (employment guarantee scheme, public distribution system) have made little impact, thanks to huge leakages from the government's lousy delivery systems. So, many economists think the loan waiver is a worthwhile alternative to provide relief.

However, the poorest rural folk are landless labourers, who get neither farm loans nor waivers. Half of the small and marginal farmers get no loans from banks and depend entirely on moneylenders, and will not benefit. Besides rural India is full of the family holdings rather than individual holdings and family holdings will typically be much larger than two hectares even for dirtpoor farmers who will, therefore, be denied the 100% waiver. It will thus fail in both economic and political objectives. IRDP loans to the rural poor in the 1980s demonstrated that crooked bank officials demand bribes amounting to one-third the intended benefits. Very few of the intended beneficiaries who merited relief received it. After the last farm loan waiver will similarly slow down fresh loans to deserving farmers. While overdues to co-operatives may be higher, economist Surjit Bhalla says less than 5% of farmer loans, to banks are overdue *i.e.,* overdues exist for only 2.25 million out of 90 million farmers. If so, then the 95% who have repaid loans will not benefit. They will be angry at being penalised for honesty.

The budget thus grossly overestimates the number of beneficiaries. It also underestimates the negative effects of the waiver-encouraging wilful default in the future and discouraging fresh bank lending for some years. Instead of trying to reach the needy, through a plethora of leaky schemes we should transfer cash directly to the needy using new technology like biometric smart cards, which are now being used in many countries, and mobile phone bank accounts. Then benefits can go directly to phone accounts operable only by those with biometric cards, ending the massive leakages of current schemes.

The political benefits of the loan waiver have also been exaggerated since if only a small fraction of farm families benefit, and many of these have to pay bribes to get the actual benefit, will the waiver really be a massive vote-winner? Members of joint families will feel aggrieved that, despite having less than one hectare per head, their family holding is too large, to qualify for the 100% waiver. All finance ministers, of central or state governments, give away freebies in their last budgets hoping to win electoral regards . Yet, four-fifth of incumbent governments are voted out. This shows that beneficiaries of favours are not notably grateful, while those not so favoured may feel aggrieved, and vote for the opposition. That seems to be why election budgets constantly fail to win elections in India and the loan waiver will not change that pattern.

QUESTIONS

1. Why do economists feel that loan waivers will benefit farmers in distress?
2. What message will the loan waiver send to farmers who have repaid loans?
3. What is the author's suggestion to provide aid to farmers?
4. What was the outcome of IRDP loans to the rural poor?
5. What are the terms of the loan waiver?
6. What is the author's view of the loan waiver?
7. According to passage, who penalises deserving farmers?
8. Which will definitely be an impact of loan waivers?
9. What impact will the loan waiver have on banks?
10. According to the author what is the government's motive in sanctioning the loan waiver?

PASSAGE - 4

The strength of Indian Democracy lies in its tradition, in the fusion of the ideas of democracy and national independence which was the characteristic of the Indian Nationalist Movement long before independence. Although the British retained Supreme authority in India until 1947, the provincial elections of 1937 provided real exercise in democratic practice before national independence. During the Pacific war India was not overrun or seriously invaded by the Japanese and after the war was over, the transfer of power to a government of the Indian Congress Party was a peaceful one as far as Britain was concerned. By 1947 'Indianisation' had already gone far in the Indian Civil Service and Army, so that the new government could start with effective instruments of central control.

After Independence, however, India had faced two vast problems; the first, that of economic growth from a very low level of production, and the second was that of ethnic diversity and the aspirations of sub-nationalities. The Congress leadership was more aware of the former problem than of the second. As a new political elite which had rebelled not only against the British Raj but also against India's old social order they were conscious of the need to initiate economic development and undertake social reforms, but as nationalists who had led a struggle against the alien rule on behalf of all parts of India, they took the cohesion of the Indian nation too much for granted and underestimated the centrifugal forces of ethnic division, which were bound to be accentuated rather than diminished as the popular masses were more and more drawn into politics.

The Congress party was originally opposed to the idea of recognizing any division of India on a linguistic basis and preferred to retain the old provinces of British India which often cut across linguistic boundaries. However, this was later conceded as the basis for a federal 'Indian Union'. The rights granted to the States created new problems for the Central Government. The idea of making Hindi the national language of a united India was thwarted by the recalcitrance of the speakers of other important Indian languages, and the autonomy of the States rendered central economic planning extremely difficult. Land reforms remained under the control of the State and many large-scale economic projects required a degree of co-operation between the Central Government and one or more of the States which, it was found, was impossible to achieve. Co-ordination of policies was difficult even when the Congress Party was in power both in the States and at the Centre. When a Congress Government in Delhi was confronted with non-Congress parties in office in the States, it became much harder.

QUESTIONS

1. Why was central economic planning found to be difficult?
2. Which problems had India faced after Independence?
3. Why was the linguistic reorganization of the States accepted?
4. According to the passage, what can be cited as an exercise in democratic practice in India before Independence?
5. Which party was originally opposed to the idea of recognizing any division of India on a linguistic basis?
6. Where does the strength of the Indian Democracy lie?
7. What were the issues which appropriately realized by the Central Government?

PASSAGE - 5

It is difficult to imagine the extraordinary number of controls on Indian industry before 1991. Entrepreneurs needed permission to invest and could be penalized for exceeding production capacity. Even with the given investment capacity they had, entering certain areas was prohibited as these were reserved for the public sector. If they had to import anything, they required licences. To get these licences was tough, they had to persuade a bureaucrat that the item was required but even so permission was unavailable if somebody was already producing it in India. The impact of the reforms was not instantaneously and permanently wonderful. In India's case it began to show after about a year-and-a-half. After 1993 there came three years of rapid industrial growth of about 8% or so. But, in the second half of the 90s, there was a tapering of industrial growth and investment. After 1997 and the East Asian crisis there was global slowdown which had an impact on the Indian industry. But in the last few years there has been a tremendous upturn. With the rise of investment industrial growth has reached double digits or close.

However, even during the period when industrial growth was not that rapid, there is a lot of evidence that positive results of the reforms were seen. There were companies that didn't look at all internally but instead performed remarkably in the highly competitive global market. For instance, the software sector's performance was outstanding in an almost totally global market. Reliance built a world-class refinery. Tatas developed an indigenously designed car. The success of the software sector has created much higher expectations from and much higher confidence in what Indian industry can do. On the government's side it is a vindication that liberalization of both domestic and external policies, including the increased inflow of Foreign Direct Investment, has created an environment in which industry can do well, has done well and is preparing to do even better. What they need is not sops, but good quality infrastructure. For the 11th Plan an industrial growth rate of around 12% is projected. It will have methods of developing infrastructure, which will close the deficit. This can be done through increased investment in public sector for those infrastructure areas, which cannot attract private investment, and through efforts to improve private participation in different ways of public-private participation.

In the early stages of reforms, the liberalization of trade policies and a shift to a market-determined exchange rate had the effect of removing constraints on agriculture in 'terms of depressed prices. The removal of protection on industry helped to produce a more level playing field, because the earlier system was extremely unfair to agriculture. The lesson to be learnt from the reforms process is to persevere in reforming the strategic parts of the economy, which will lead to even higher growth rate. India has to do better than its current average growth rate of 8% and ensure that benefits from this higher growth go beyond industry and urban areas and extend to agriculture.

QUESTIONS

1. How did software companies deal with slow industrial growth in an open Indian economy?

2. Why did India experience a slow down in growth during the late 1990s?

3. According to the passage, what can be said about the reforms of 1991?

4. Which factor was responsible for the fall in India's growth rate in the late 1990s?

5. How did the economic reforms affect the agriculture sector?

6. What was the impact of the flourishing Indian Software Sector?

7. Mention any restriction on Indian industry which was prior to 1991?

8. What does the author recommend to ensure that the industrial sector continues to perform better?

9. Why was investment by private business disallowed in certain sectors?

10. What is the author's opinion about the government's decision to liberalise the economy is 1991?

PASSAGE - 6

Though it is commonplace to say we live in a globalised world, less well understood is that globalisation is taking place in stages. In the first stage as flows of capital and goods were liberated the benefits of globalisation *e.g.,* technological advancements, flowed primarily to the developed world. As we enter the current newer age of mobility, people have begun to move across borders in great numbers in pursuit of economic security and a better life for themselves and to keep their families out of poverty. At the turn of the 20th century the United Nations estimates that approximately three per cent of the world's population is on the move, a similar scale to that witnessed in earlier eras. Growing economic inequality together with natural and man made crises prompt emigration. But this mobility has the potential to chip away at the vast inequalities that characterise our time and accelerate progress throughout the developing world. To take an example, last year migrants sent home $264 billion triple all international aid combined. The freer movement of people helps to underwrite health care, education and grassroots entrepreneurship across the developing world.

It helps to oil the global economy. When industrialised nations need to recruit nurses or software programmers developing countries are often the source. Yet, rather than look at how these gains can be harnessed to reduce poverty, governments have been slow to adapt. The result is burgeoning illegal immigration, and trafficking, social tension and intolerance, loss of faith in the government and the empowerment of criminal networks. Until a few years ago, migrants were paying exorbitant fees to send money home losing about 20% in transaction costs. Today though migrants move freely and easily thanks to easy access to low cost transport and the internet, affordable and rapidly advancing telephony and satellite television which keep them in constant touch with home. Banks easily and wirelessly transmit hard won and sometimes meagre salaries instantly to their families. The flow of people until now mostly benefited richer countries and generated worries about brain drain and the violation of migrant rights in poorer ones. Global fora represent a step in the effort to harness the power of migration to advance development and increase our knowledge of how to make the migration equation work for all. Rather than focus on the negative consequences and recriminations of exploitation by developing countries such summits provide an opportunity for all nations to come together and address these issues in a comprehensive, logical and rational way so that the benefits of migration are fully realised in both developing and industrialised countries. Countries may examine how dual citizenship laws can ease the way for migrants to play a bigger role in development by bringing their capital, knowledge and networks back home. Such efforts will usher in the third stage of globalisation where everyone can share in the world's prosperity.

QUESTIONS

1. What is the author's main objective in writing the passage?

2. What does the fact that remittance exceeded international aid illustrate?

3. According to the author why do people migrate?

4. How does the author view migration?

5. What is the objective of international fora on migration?

6. According to the passage what has facilitated migrants access to their native countries?

7. 'Governments have not fully exploited the potential benefits of migration.' Is it true in the context of the passage?

8. Mention any two impacts of globalisation.

PASSAGE - 7

The US Senate's approval of an immigration Bill has been welcomed in India as well as in the IT industry in America because of the proposal to double HI-B visas for skilled foreign workers. However, the more important bit in the legislation, if approved by the House of Representatives, is the lifeline to millions of illegal immigrants in the US. Some of the key proposals in the Bill include allowing illegal immigrants, who have been in America for five years, to become legal residents by paying a certain amount in fines and back taxes. Those who have been in the country between two and five years can go to a point of entry at the US border and file an application. There is also provision for creating a guest worker programme especially meant for farm workers. These are welcome moves to recognise the huge presence— according to some estimates 12 to 15 million—of illegal immigrants in the US and legitimising their existence. But it must be understood that the US is not considering this legislation out of a sense of altruism. The truth is that the bulk of immigrants are doing jobs that Americans simply don't want to do. They are employed in jobs that pay minimum wages and entail long working hours. But giving illegal immigrants the opportunity to become legal residents will at least ensure that they are not exploited by employers and that they are covered by social security benefits.

American legislators, however, need to go beyond this. They must recognise that the US needs trained people in various fields, particularly in schools and hospitals. India with its vast population of educated youth is a natural source of such personnel. Instead of just targeting India for its best brains, the US should open up its labour market for more school teachers, nurses and technicians from India. Compared to Mexicans, the largest component of immigrants to the US, Indians have a natural advantage in that they know English. They would also be willing to work in America's inner cities and other supposedly 'hardship' stations, Along with nuclear deals and technology transfer, the two largest English-speaking democracies must realise that they could mutually benefit from bilateral employment agreements. India, with its one-billion plus and growing population, has the potential of supplying First World nations with declining birth rates much-needed labour.

QUESTIONS

1. What is provision for an illegal immigrants in the US, who has been in America for five years?

2. India can be an effective source of man power in which sectors of USA?

3. According to some estimates how many illegal immigrants are there in the US?

4. What is the main reason behind the bulk of emigrants in the US?

5. Which country contributes the largest number of immigrants to US?

6. In which types of jobs the illegal immigrants are employed mainly?

7. Name the immigrants country who enjoy an advantage of good communication skills in English.

8. What is the basic premise of the immigration Bill?

9. What will ensure the Bill by giving illegal immigrants the opportunity to become legal residents?

10. How can USA be benefitted by India in the author's opinion?

PASSAGE - 8

The art of effective presentation is the fruit of persistent efforts and practice. Your personality is reflected in your presentation. Adequate planning and preparation are essential for a successful presentation. A thorough preparation is the best antidote for nervousness. If a person is not successful in presenting his views and ideas then it will become the greatest obstacle in his career and life. People form a perception about how competent you are by how you present yourself when you stand and speak.

A successful presentation can help a person in winning orders for the company he works for. Most people who work in organizations find that their effectiveness and success depend on their ability to organize their ideas and present them effectively. Delivering your message in person provides immediate feedback that helps you clarify points and answer questions.

Oral presentations are often more persuasive. As far as possible, one should never read a presentation or memorize it. Then the presentation will lose flexibility and communication will suffer. The spoken word wields great power. Face-to-face interaction demands thinking and speaking. Anecdotes, quotations and humourous touches often make a presentation interesting. One may consult his notes frequently when he is making his presentation. This may create a feeling among listeners that the speaker has taken pains to prepare for the occasion. A positive response will be generated and the speaker will be heard with respect. Speaker's enthusiasm and confidence can influence people to accept or reject an idea in a way that a written document cannot. A presentation should be persuasive and should change the audience's attitude. The topic of the presentation must be interesting to the audience. The topic should be of interest to the speaker also otherwise he will go through the motions of making a presentation. No perfunctory approach should ever be resorted to while making a presentation. It is very important that the speaker is perceived by the audience as credible and qualified to speak about the topic. Speaker must adapt to intellectual level of the audience.

QUESTIONS

1. What is essential for a successful presentation?
2. What will happen if a person is not successful in presenting his views and ideas?
3. Which type of presentation is often more persuasive?
4. What does face-to-face interaction demand?
5. What makes a presentation interesting?
6. In author's view what is the best antidote for nervousness?
7. What can be countered by meticulous preparation of one's presentation?
8. In author's opinion which type of topic of the presentation must be?
9. What is reflected in a presentation?
10. When will the presentation lose flexibility and communication suffer?

PASSAGE - 9

Goldman Sachs predicted that crude oil price would hit $200 and just as it appeared that alternative renewable energy had a chance of becoming an economically viable option, the international price of oil fell by over 70%. After hitting the all-time high of $147 a barrel, a month ago, crude oil fell to less than $40 a barrel. What explains this sharp decline in the international price of oil? There has not been any major new discovery of a hitherto unknown source of oil or gas. The short answer is that the demand does not have to fall by a very sizeable quantity for the price of crude to respond as it did. In the short run, the price elasticity of demand for crude oil is very low. Conversely, in the short run, even a relatively big change in the price of oil does not immediately lower consumption. It takes months, or years, of high oil price to inculcate habits of energy conservation. World crude oil price had remained at over $60 a barrel for most of 2005-2007 without making any major dent in demand.

The long answer is more complex. The economic slowdown in the US, Europe and Asia along with dollar depreciation and commodity speculation have all had some role in the downward descent in the international price of oil. In recent years, the supply of oil has been rising but not enough to catch up with the rising demand, resulting in an almost vertical escalation in its price. The number of crude oil futures and options contracts have also increased manifold which has led to significant speculation in the oil market. In comparison, the role of the Organization of Petroleum Exporting Countries (OPEC) in fixing crude price has considerably weakened. OPEC is often accused of operating as a cartel restricting output thus keeping prices artificially high. It did succeed in setting the price of crude during the 1970s and the first half of the 80s. But, with increased futures trading and contracts, the control of crude pricing has moved from OPEC to banks and markets that deal with futures trading and contracts. It is true that most oil exporting regions of the world have remained politically unstable fuelling speculation over the price of crude. But there is little evidence that the geopolitical uncertainties in west Asia have improved to weaken the price of oil. Threatened by the downward slide of oil price, OPEC has, in fact, announced its decision to curtail output.

However, most oil importers will heave a sigh of relief as they find their oil import bills decline except for those who sought options to import oil at prices higher than market prices. Exporting nations, on the other hand, will see their economic prosperity slip. Relatively low price of crude is also bad news for investments in alternative renewable energy that cannot compete with cheaper and non-renewable sources of energy.

QUESTIONS

1. What factor is responsible for rise in speculation in crude oil markets?
2. Which is costlier, renewable energy sources or non-renewable energy sources?
3. What has been the impact of the drop in oil prices?
4. What did result in rise in demand for crude oil?
5. When was OPEC established?

6. What was the reason behind establishing the OPEC?

7. What is the function of OPEC?

8. Today who sets the oil prices to a large extent?

9. What led the alternative energy sources being considered economically feasible?

10. What does the author want to convey by citing the statistics of 2005-2007?

PASSAGE - 10

Politicians and generals talk of military strategies and manoeuvres but something completely different is needed. Stability will come only when economic opportunities exist, when youth can find jobs and support families rather than seeking their livelihood in violence. Peace can only be achieved with a withdrawal of foreign troops, sanctions and peacekeepers and the arrival of jobs, productive farms and factories, healthcare and schools. Repeatedly the fragile peace in impoverished countries has broken down because of the lack of economic follow-up. Despite promises of aid, the actual record of international aid to post war reconstruction is deficient.

Once the war ends, agencies involved in post war relief efforts fail to understand how to start or restart economic development in a low income setting. They squander time, surplus aid funds and opportunities because they are not familiar with local conditions and do not understand their point of view. There are distinct phases of outside help to end a conflict. In the first phase, focus is on providing food, water, shelter and medicine to refugees, *i.e.,* humanitarian. In the second, emphasis is on the refugees returning home while in the last phase long term investments and strengthening of courts is the main focus.

However, once a conflict is over, aid agencies sanctioned by the World Bank send study groups instead of requisite personnel. There is a gap of several years before moving from humanitarian relief to economic development. By the time such help arrives the war has restarted. It is possible to restart

economic development through targeted 'quick impact' initiatives. Most economies in post conflict countries are based on agriculture. Providing free packages of seeds, fertilizers and low cost equipment quickly will ensure that former soldiers will return to their farms and establish their livelihood. But the window of opportunity closes quickly and one has to implement these measures almost immediately.

QUESTIONS

1. According to author when will stability come?

2. What will happen when economic opportunities exist?

3. Why have post conflict reconstruction efforts failed?

4. Where does the problem lie in implementing post war relief measures?

5. According to author what will prevent wars?

6. Are sanctions a means to ensure peace?

7. Where is the focus in the first phase of a war?

8. How can economic development be restarted in an impoverished country?

PASSAGE - 11

Over the past few decades, many Asian nations transformed from poverty into global competitors. From 2003 to 2007, Asian economies expanded at an average annual rate of 8.1%, triple that of advanced economies. Over the same period, inflation in Asia averaged only about 3.5%. But Asia could be facing turbulent economic times. In May, the average inflation rate throughout the region reached nearly 7%, led by spikes in oil and food prices. In India, inflation jumped to an 11.6% annual rate in June, according to the latest government figures, the highest in 13 years.

Policymakers and central bankers are forced to raise interest rates and limit credit to get inflation under control. But these same measures suppress the investment and consumption that generates growth. The combination of slowing growth and soaring inflation makes economic policy-making tricky. Inflation stirs up the middle classes because it can quickly erase years of hard won personal gains. Inflation is cruel to the poor, because families have to spend a larger share of their meagre incomes on necessities. In the Philippines, farmers, unable to afford fuel for tractors, use water buffaloes to plough their fields.

But to avoid unrest, leaders cannot blindly adopt rigid anti-inflation measures. Voters won't hesitate to remove from office any politician who doesn't deliver the goods. So they cannot overreact to the inflation threat and scale down economic growth in the process. Developing nations need to grow quickly to create jobs and increase incomes for their large populations. With prices soaring, doing nothing is not an option. Most central banks in Asia have started raising interest rates. The Reserve Bank of India increased its benchmark rate twice last month to a six year high of 8.5%.

The challenge is especially difficult because currently, inflation is not of domestic origin. Prices are being driven higher by a global surge in oil and food prices, which individual governments can do little to control. Of course, inflation is not just a problem in Asia. World Bank President Robert Zoellick called rising food and oil prices a man-made 'catastrophe' that could quickly reverse the gains made in overcoming poverty over the past seven years. For now, though, there is more talk than action on the international front, so Asian governments are on their own.

Even though inflation throughout the region is likely to continue to rise in coming months, no one is expecting an economic calamity. According to the Asian Development Bank, Asian countries have large hard currency reserves and relatively healthy banks, and so are far better prepared to absorb external shocks than they were during the region's last recession ten years ago. Asian policymakers have learned their lessons and are more alert.

QUESTIONS

1. From 2003 to 2007, by what rate did the Asian economics expand?

2. What was the inflation rate in Asia over the same period?

3. In the context of passage, mention any one anti-inflation measure which in being used by Asian countries.

4. What makes it difficult for Asian countries to control inflation?

5. Why are experts not very concerned about the impact of inflation on Asian economies?

6. What in the author's advice to politicians regarding the handling of inflation?

7. What could the impact of stringent inflation measures be?

8. Why is high economic growth necessary for developing countries?

9. Why has inflation been referred to as a 'Catastrophe'?

10. Which factor was responsible for inflation in India?

PASSAGE - 12

If you cast a thoughtful glance around you, you will become conscious of God's infinite grace. God has given us firm earth to put our feet on; He has given us oxygen enough to inhale as much of it as we like; He has created the sun to give us light and heat to illumine and warm the world; He has given us water in plenty to quench our thirst with; He has given us space enough to fly into if we can; He has created so many animals to serve us in a variety of capacities; He has given us trees and plants to provide us food, fuel and medicines; and he has given us rich soil to grow crops in.

But what is of utmost importance is the fact that he has given us our existence. We are able to avail ourselves of the universe because we exist. Had we had no existence, the whole phenomenon would have had no meaning for us.

Yet, these rich gifts of God fail to satisfy us : we want more. And we want more because we feel others have more. We want God to do for us all that we wish to happen. Should we not thank God for what he has given us even without our asking for it? I would like everyone of us to say to God everyday "God! I thank you for bringing me and my near and dear ones into existence, giving me the capacity to dream, and providing me this universe to realize my dreams in."

QUESTIONS

1. When do we become conscious of God's unlimited grace?
2. What is the purpose of animals in the world?
3. In which situation would the whole world have been rendered meaningless for us?
4. Why is man not satisfied with what he has been given by God?
5. For what does the author want to feel grateful to God?

PASSAGE - 13

Micro finance institutions aim to provide credit to the poor who have no access to commercial banks. In general, these institutions receive financial support from western donors, NGOs or commercial banks, which lend to micro finance institutions, often against below market interest rates. The micro finance institutions in turn, lend this money to domestic small companies and poor agents. The size of the loan varies but is most often small.

According to the United Nations (UN), in 2002 almost one-fifth of the world's population was living in extreme poverty, earning less than one dollar a day. In recent public debates micro finance has been mentioned as an important instrument to combat poverty. The result has been that micro finance has received a lot of attention, both from policy makers as well as in academic circles. Especially during the past 10 years, micro finance programmes have been introduced in many developing economies. Well-known examples are the Grameen Bank in Bangladesh, Banco Sol in Bolivia and Bank Rakyat in Indonesia. The Grameen Bank system of group lending (established in 1976 by Muhammad Yunus, a Bangladesh banker and economist), in particular has been copied in other developing countries. Between December 1997 and December 2005 the number of micro finance institutions increased from 168 to 3,133. The number of people who received credit from these institutions rose from 13.5 million to 113.3 million during the same period.

To support the view that micro finance can be an important instrument to fight poverty, the UN declared 2005 to be the international Year of Micro credit. Recently, the attention for micro-finance and its role in reducing poverty was dramatically increased when Muhammad Yunus received the Nobel Peace prize. According to Nobel Committee, micro finance can help people to break out of poverty, which in turn is seen as an important prerequisite to establish long lasting peace. This has led to an almost euphoric attitude among policy makers and aid organizations about potential poverty reducing effects of micro credit.

QUESTIONS

1. What is the main purpose of micro finance institutions?
2. Why has micro finance been receiving a lot of consideration?
3. What is seen as a prior requirement for the establishment of long lasting peace?
4. From where do micro finance companies get their funds?
5. Why has the UN declared the year 2005 as the Year of Micro credit?
6. In which countries micro finance programmes have been introduced in the recent past?

PASSAGE - 14

Though the Cold War has ended, selective tactics are still continuing for ensuring the military and economic dominance of developed countries. Various types of technology denial regimes are still being enforced which are now being mainly targeted against developing countries like India.

Today, we in India encounter twin problems. On one side, there is a large scale strengthening of our neighbours through supply of arms and clandestine support to their nuclear and missile programmes, and on the other side, all efforts are being made to weaken our indigenous technology growth through control regimes and dumping of low-tech systems, accompanied with high commercial pitch in critical areas. Growth of indigenous technology and self-reliance are the only answer to the problem.

Thus in the environment around India, the number of missiles and nuclear powers are continuously increasing and destructive weapons continue to pile up around us, in spite of arms reduction treaties.

To understand the implications of various types of warfare that may affect us, we need to take a quick look at the evolution of war weaponry and the types of warfare. I am highlighting this point for the reason that in less than a century we could see change in the nature of warfare and its effects on society.

In early years of human history it was mostly direct human warfare. During the twentieth century up to about 1990, the warfare was weapon driven. The weapons used were guns, tanks, aircraft, ships, submarines and the nuclear weapons deployed on land/sea/air and also reconnaissance spacecraft. Proliferation of conventional nuclear and biological weapons was at a peak owing to the competition between the superpowers.

The next phase, in a new form, has just started from 1990 onwards. The world has graduated into economic warfare. The means used is control of market forces through high technology. The participating nations, apart from the USA, are Japan, the UK, France, Germany, certain South-East Asian countries and a few others. The driving force is the generation of wealth with certain types of economic doctrine.

The urgent issue we need to address collectively as a nation is, how do we handle the tactics of economic and military dominance in this new form coming from the backdoor? Today technology is the main driver of economic development at the national level. Therefore, we have to develop indigenous technologies to enhance our competitive edge and to generate national wealth in all segments of economy. Therefore, the need of the hour is *arm India with technology.*

QUESTIONS

1. Which are the issues of great concern that India is facing at present, according to the author?
2. Enforcement of technology denial regimes by developed countries implies which kind of tendency?
3. According to the author, is it necessary to examine how weaponry and warfare have evolved?
4. What is the most effective way to counter our major problems?
5. What, according to the author, is the solution to our problems in the international field?
6. What is the general outcome of arms reduction treaties as a whole according to the author?
7. What is the immediate problem to be collectively resolved by our country?

PASSAGE - 15

All men by nature, desire to know. An indication of this is the delight we take in our senses: for even apart from their usefulness they are loved for themselves; and above all others, the sense of sight. For not only with a view to action, but even when we are not going to do anything, we prefer seeing (one might say) to everything else. The reason is that this, most of all the senses, makes us know and brings to light many differences between things. By nature, animals are born with the faculty of sensation, and from sensation, memory is produced in some of them, though not in others. And therefore, the former are more intelligent and apt at learning than those which cannot remember; those which are incapable of hearing sounds are intelligent though they cannot be taught, *e.g.,* the bee, and any other race of animals that may be like it; and those which besides memory, have this sense of hearing can be taught. The animals other than man live by appearances and memories and have but little of connected experience; but the human race lives also by art and reasoning. Now from memory, experience is produced in men; for the several memories of the same thing produce finally the capacity for a single experience. And experience seems pretty much like science and art, but really, science and art come to men through experience; for 'experience made art', as Polus says, 'but inexperience luck.' Now art arises, when from many notions gained by experience, one universal judgement about a class of objects is produced. For, to have a judgement that when Callias was ill of this disease that did him good, and similarly, in the case of Socrates and in many individual cases, is a matter of experience; but to judge that it has done good to all persons of a certain constitution, marked off in one class, when they were ill of this disease, *e.g.*, to phlegmatic or bilious people when burning with fevers—this is a matter of art. With a view to action, experience seems in no 'respect inferior to art, and men of experience succeed even better than those who have theory without experience. (The reason is that experience is knowledge of individuals, art of universals, and actions and productions are all concerned with the individual; for the physician does not cure man, except in an incidental way, but Callias or Socrates or some other called by some such individual name, who happens to be a man. If, then, a man has the theory without the experience, and recognises the universal but does not know the individual included in this, he will often fail to cure; for it is the individual that is to be cured.) But yet we think that knowledge and understanding belong to art rather than to experience, and we suppose artists to be wiser than men of experience (which implies that wisdom depends in all cases rather on knowledge); and this because the former know the cause, but the latter do not. For men of experience know that the thing is so, but do not know why, while the others know the 'why' and the cause. Hence, we think also that the masterworkers in each craft are more honourable and know in a truer sense and are wiser than the manual workers, because they know the causes of the things that are done (we think the manual workers are like certain lifeless things which act indeed, but act without knowing what they do, as fire burns, but while the lifeless things perform each of their functions by a natural tendency, the labourers perform them through habit); thus we view them as being wiser not in virtue of being able to act, but of having the theory for themselves and knowing the causes. And in general, it is a sign of the man who knows and of the man who does not know, that the former can teach, and therefore, we think art, more truly knowledge than experience is; for artists can teach, and men of mere experience cannot. Again, we do not regard any of the senses as Wisdom; yet surely these give the most authoritative knowledge of particulars. But they do not tell us the 'why' of anything—*e.g.*, why fire is hot; they only say that it is hot. At first, he who invented any art whatever, that went beyond the common perceptions of man was naturally admired by men, not only because there was something useful in the inventions, but because he was thought wiser and superior to the rest. But as more arts were invented, and some were directed to the necessities of life, others to recreation, the inventors of the latter were naturally always regarded as wiser than the inventors of the former, because their branches of knowledge did not aim at utility. Hence, when all such inventions were already established, the sciences which do not aim at giving pleasure or at the necessities of life were discovered, and first in the places where men first began to have leisure. This is why the mathematical arts were founded in Egypt; for there the priestly caste was allowed to be at leisure. We have said in the Ethics what the difference is between art and science and the other kindred faculties; but the point of our present discussion is this, that all men suppose what is called wisdom to deal with the first causes and the principles of things; so that, as has been said before, the man of experience is thought to be wiser than the possessors of any sense-perception whatever, the artist wiser than the men of experience, the masterworker than the mechanic, and the theoretical kinds of knowledge to be more of the nature of wisdom than the productive. Clearly then, wisdom is knowledge about certain principles and causes.

1. What is the relationship between sensation and memory?
2. What is the difference between art and experience?
3. Why, according to the author, were the mathematical arts founded in Egypt?
4. What is the central idea of the passage?
5. What does experience reveal in this passage?
6. What is wisdom here?

PASSAGE - 16

We should recognise the indebtedness of the country to its farm families who toil to safeguard national food security. Loan waiver is the price we have to pay for the neglect of rural India over the past several decades. There has been a gradual decline in investment in key sectors related to agriculture such as infrastructure, marketing, post harvest technology etc. The four crore farmers whose debt is to be relieved will be eligible for institutional credit for their cultivation expenses during Kharif 2008. The challenge is to prevent them from getting into the debt trap again. For this purpose the Central and various State governments should set up an Indebted Farmers' Support Consortium, comprising scientists, Panchayat Raj officials and others relevant to assisting farmers to improve the profitability and productivity of their farms in an environmentally sustainable manner. The smaller the farm the greater is the need for marketable surplus to reduce indebtedness.

The Indebted Farmers Support Consortium should aim to get all the four crore farmers all the benefits of the government schemes such as the Rashtriya Krishi Vikas Yojana, Irrigation Benefit Programme and others. If this is done every farm family released from the debt trap should be able to produce at least an additional half tonne per hectare of food grains. This should help increase food production by about 20 million tonnes by 2008-10. At a time when global and national food stocks are dwindling and prices are rising, this will be a timely gain for our national food security. We need to ensure that the outcome of the debt waiver is enhanced farmers' income and production. The prevailing gap between potential and actual yields in the crops of rainfed areas such as pulses and oilseeds is over 200 per cent even with the necessary technologies on the shelf. We are now importing without duty large quantities of pulses and oilseeds. If helped, farmers can produce these at a lower cost.

Opportunities for assured and remunerative marketing are essential if loan waiver is not to become a recurring event leading to the destruction of the credit system. This is why the Minimum Support Price is necessary for all not just for a few crops which is the case at present. This is the single most effective step to make loan waivers history. There is another urgent step which needs to be taken. The loan waiver does not cover those who borrow from moneylenders. It will not be possible for the government to scrutinise the veracity of such private deals but steps can be taken such as giving them Smart Cards which will entitle them to essential inputs like seeds and fertilizers. The gram sabha can be entrusted with the task of identifying these farmers so that there is transparency in the process and elimination of the chances for falsification and corruption. Fear of occasional misuse should not come in the way of enabling millions of poor farmers who have borrowed from informal sources if we are to achieve the goal of four per cent growth in agriculture.

1. Why does the author feel that rural India has been overlooked in the past?
2. How can small farmers avoid debt?
3. What is the objective of the Indebted Farmer's Support Consortium?
4. What does the author mean by the phrase "indebtedness of the country to its farm families"?
5. Why does the loan waiver not cover credit taken from money lenders?
6. Why is there a vast gap in actual and potential yields of crops in rainfed areas?
7. What should be the aim of indebted Farmers' Support Consortium?

PASSAGE - 17

Planning in India has essentially been an effort to determine the overall direction of the economy by directing public investment accordingly. It was possible to conceive of outcomes on the basis of government spending between 1947 and 1985 when the public sector made up more than half the gross domestic product. Now that is neither possible nor desirable. The private sector accounts for three-fourths of the gross domestic product reducing the role of public expenditure in meeting growth targets. Besides, decades of the government occupying the commanding heights of the economy merely resulted in low rates of growth and nearly two-fifth of the population living below the poverty line till 1991.

How can planning contribute to today's economy? It should be reconceived as a think tank that works at maximising outcomes from investments in social and physical infrastructure by identifying problems of governance. Outcomes in health and education are crucial to realise the potential of our billion-plus population, while shortcomings in power and port handling facilities can hold up future growth. Where public-private partnerships involve a number of government agencies the Commission can work as a nodal body that takes a larger view of projects and ensures their smooth implementation.

Planners should aim at meeting growth targets by ensuring that markets function efficiently. They can advise the government on market-specific policies that address lack of access to information. They can identify sunrise areas in the next decade and promote research and innovation through public-private partnership. Simultaneously, planners should explore markets for products made by unskilled workers.

The Eleventh Plan aims at 9 per cent "inclusive" growth by raising investment in infrastructure from 5 per cent of GDP to 9 per cent. Of the $475 billion investment needed for infrastructure. $130-140 billion is expected to come from the private sector. Public sector enterprises are expected to raise resources internally, with the Plan proposing lower support for them. The Plan has got its priorities right by reducing support for PSEs and increasing social sector allocations. Education is a big-ticket item, with the Planning Commission earmarking ₹ 2,75,289 crores for it alone with a view to meeting the skills shortage. Sadly, health has not been given the same emphasis. But, generally speaking, we are on the right track.

QUESTIONS

1. According to author, what was the possibility during the first 38 years after India's independence?

2. Which factor is closely associated with the term 'planning' in India?

3. Which is a way to derive maximum outcome from investment?

4. What does the author expect planners to do about the products manufactured by unskilled workers?

5. "The area of health has been given a secondary treatment", is this statement appreciated by the author?

6. What is the best explanation of the term "Sunrise areas"?

PASSAGE - 18

Hiero, King of Syracus, had commissioned from a goldsmith of the town a crown of pure gold, but, having taken delivery of the finished article, he was suspicious. There was reason to believe that the craftsman had mixed with the gold a certain amount of other metal of inferior value. But how to find out? There was no direct evidence, and it was therefore obviously a case for the learned men of the city. And who was more learned than Archimedes?

The mathematician was therefore charged with the task which would nowadays be considered a simple one, but was then a matter for serious thought. Nothing known to science could be brought forward to prove fraud or otherwise on the part of the goldsmith.

It is more than probable that the human side of the problem interested Archimedes not at all, but the scientific puzzle worried him intensely. This worry pursued him everywhere he went for days, and persisted through the routine acts of his daily round.

In the normal course of that routine, he went to the public baths. We can imagine him standing at the edge of the bath tub as he prepares to enter it, absently allowing the water to flow until he cannot help noticing it. Suddenly, he splashed out of his tub shouting at the top of his voice: "Eureka! Eureka!" (I have found it! I have found it!). Without waiting, or even thinking of such a detail as clothes, he tore out of the building and rushed through the streets of Syracus, still shouting: "Eureka! Eureka!"

Arrived at his house, the mathematician put his newly found discovery to a practical test, and found indeed that a body plunged in a fluid loses an amount of its weight which is equal to the weight of the fluid displaced by it. With this as a starting point—as it was to prove the starting point of many subsequent discoveries of importance—Archimedes was able to tell his king how much pure gold was in his crown. Thus was the first fundamental law in hydrostatics enunciated.

Archimedes was by this time well known to his fellow townsmen, and his sometimes strange appearance and unusual actions probably met with indulgent smiles. He came from a good family; his father Pheidias was an astronomer; he was on intimate terms with, and—according to some—was even a kinsman of King Hiero himself.

QUESTIONS

1. Why could the king not punish the fraudulent goldsmith?
2. Why was Archimedes charged with the task of finding out if there was any impurity in the crown?
3. What was the king's suspicion?
4. Why was Archimedes curious when he was entrusted with the task?
5. Why did Archimedes utter "Eureka! Eureka!"?

PASSAGE - 19

On hearing the news of the massacre at Jallianwala Bagh, Udham Singh did not attend his school but took a train to Amritsar and visited the spot. There, he stood for several minutes in a trance, picked up the soil, rubbed it on his forehead and put some in a phial. He fasted that night. According to his family members he placed fresh flowers on the holy dust every morning, drawing inspiration from it. One early morning he went to the river Ravi and pledged that he would colour its waters with the colour of his blood to create what he called the freedom's flood. With this aim in view in 1921, he first landed in Africa. From there, he went to America to meet the Indian revolutionaries working for the liberation of the motherland.

In 1923, he landed in England. In 1928, he returned to India in response to an urgent call from Bhagat Singh. When he reached Lahore, he was detained for violation of the Arms Act. He was released after four years rigorous imprisonment. In 1935, he escaped from Germany by giving a slip to the police. From Berlin, he reached Paris and purchased a revolver. He kept it ready for action and managed to reach London again. Opportunity came on March 13, 1940 when Sir Michael O'Dwyer was to speak at a seminar in the Caxton Hall. As Sir Michael turned to resume his seat after the speech, Udham Singh pulled out his revolver and fired at him. Sir Michael died without a shriek. Udham Singh was arrested and produced before the court on April 2, 1940. The court passed death sentence on him and he was hanged at Pentonville Prison, London on July 3, 1940.

QUESTIONS

1. Why did Udham Singh go to America?
2. Where did Udham Singh buy the weapon which was used for killing Sir Michael?

3. What is the link between London and Sir Michael O'Dwyer?

4. Where was Udham Singh arrested and for what?

5. Why did Udham Singh return to India in 1928?

PASSAGE - 20

1. Music constitutes mood with variable notes of rhythm transformed from any corner to the destination with a view point of sowing seeds of mental relief with sensational pleasure. It allows generations to bear the pleasure of routing melody of listening lyrics challenging aweful ruckus of mental distress with sweet and melodious voice into individual ears.

   Renowned musicians have earned landmark, attribution to the theme of music therapy, woven with classical and orchestral beat of drum sound shakes beat with thrill and pleasure. Music allotes identity to host and listener with keen interest of sweeping away boring and stranded congestion of monotony.

2. A folk singer from Bengal who sings spiritual Baul songs, on hearing a snatch of Blues music remarked, 'That sounds so much like our kind of singing.' Indeed it is possible to hear Baul, Blues and folk rhythms one after another, without feeling any strangeness. Any kind of good music rejuvenates and moves a person and knows no geographical boundaries.

3. This is also the case with instrumental music. A person listening to a Latin American flute could easily be reminded of a plaintive raga composition. The guitar recital of the Latin American guitarist Paco de Lucia could be just as thrilling as a recital by an Indian sitarist playing in full flow. As for percussion, imagine the dance the gods would break into, if African drums were to play alongside the mridangam, tabla and the dholak!

4. There are scores of music lovers around the world who like Elvis Presley's singing as much as the singing of Subbalakshmi. Even in the very interior of India it would not be surprising if someone were to talk of the Las Vegas legend with as much feeling, for it is possible to feel comfortable with specific cultures and yet like the music one has been associated with.

5. Since music allows latitude, it encourages an exhilarating exchange of genres and people. In ancient days Muthuswamy Dikshitar introduced many North Indian ragas into Carnatic music. The late John Higgins 'Bhagavatar', an American, was a distinguished scholar of Carnatic music. Similarly, Kadri Gopalan, an exponent of Carnatic music, plays it on the western saxophone. The Beatles produced some wonderfully popular numbers, such as 'Norwegian Wood', and 'Girl', by infusing elements of Hindustani classical music. Suman Kabir uses the tabla to great effect with his trademark solo guitar. Indeed many Indian musicians and groups display comfort in playing a western melodic rhythm in their music. Bollywood has matured in the nineties to mix melodic traditions. A R Rahman pioneered this new trend. In most of his music he uses African beats and the tabla to good effect.

6. Music has promoted the fusion of genres without compromising the identity of any form. Really good musicians around the world like their creative counterparts in other fields to shuttle into each other's traditions while being rooted in their own. That is what the richness of music really means. That is the kind of music that elevates.

QUESTIONS

1. On the basis of your reading of the passage answer the following questions. Write your answers against the correct blank numbers.

   (i) List two qualities mentioned by the writer about good music.

(*ii*) What is unique about the music of John Higgins and Kadri Gopalan?

(*iii*) What is A R Rahman's contribution to Indian music?

2. Answer the following notes appropriately. Do not add extra information. Write your answers against the correct blank numbers.

(*i*) Folk music of Bengal __________

(*ii*) Las Vegas legend __________

(*iii*) Latin American guitarist __________

(*iv*) Norwegian wood __________

3. On the basis of your reading the passage answer the following. Write your answers against the correct blank numbers.

(*i*) Geographical boundaries refer to
(Para 2) __________

(*ii*) Latitude in this paragraph means
(Para 5) __________

(*iii*) A fusion of genres means
(Para 6) __________

PASSAGE - 21

1. Mind management is a way to control one's mind. To do this, we need to be cautious about our thinking process and also need a high level of understanding and meditation as well. Understanding is wisdom – 80 per cent of people are knowledgeable, while 20 per cent are wise. Knowledgeable men take sides without reason. They feel sad seeing deprived people but jealous when they see happy people. They work in the guidance of others' inspiration, take unnecessary responsibility to keep themselves disturbed.

2. A wise person does not stand for or against any idea without concrete reason. He works according to the situation and capacity. He looks at everything intellectually. To him, failure is a stepping stone for future success. So depression and conflict are not seen. Like the phrase 'Stop, Look, Go', first one should see, and this needs patience. Meditation is necessary to control and manage mind which then becomes an easy task.

3. Unless we control or manage our mind, it is difficult to achieve success and peace. Psychologists say every interest is first born in the mind as a seed. Then it continues to grow. Later it takes its real form which everybody can see. The interest that first appears in the mind remains weak for the first three minutes and it becomes strong within the next five minutes. All the negative aspects should be deleted within the first three minutes. If not taken out, they would become stronger later and you can never throw them out. After taking control over the mind, we can control passion, interest and unrest. Mind management is essential for a peaceful, successful and healthy life.

4. The age of computers has thrown us on the escalator of aspirations but has robbed us of simple charms like falling asleep. The compulsions of hectic schedules burden the mind and cause stress. However, the joys that elude us can be regained by practising power meditation. It creates tranquility, simplifies life and cleanses the mind. It helps control indolence, ego and anger and builds confidence and patience. With power meditation, negative thoughts get dissipated and a sense of happiness is achieved.

5. With happiness and spiritual knowledge, one can relearn the meaning of life. The picture of life's journey also becomes clearer. Osho said, "As science is not based on orthodox and blind beliefs and functions only on the principle of cause and effect, similarly power meditation doesn't function on age-old theories or communal thoughts but originates from rational and divine experience. It strives to make an individual free from the confining pressures of daily life".

6. The beauty of meditation is that it is independent of religion. According to modern medical science, combinations of factors like pollutants, imbalanced diet and high aspirations have rendered the human mind restless, thereby making the body perpetually ill.

7. Here is a meditation method, which will enable you to control stress. Sit in the padmasan or sukhasan, cross-legged and erect. Keep your back, spine and neck straight. Keep your eyes closed. Sit in this position for 10 minutes. The method has two stages: for the first five minutes, breathe in slowly, hold it and then release it very slowly. Again, for the next five minutes, breathe and release your breath slowly.

QUESTIONS

1. Answer the following questions briefly :
 (*i*) What is mind management?
 (*ii*) What are the character traits of wise person?
 (*iii*) Why should all negative aspects be deleted within the first three minutes?
 (*iv*) Why do we feel stress in this age of computers?

2. What do the following statement mean :
 (*i*) 'Failure is a stepping stone for future success'.
 (*ii*) 'Mind management is essential for a peaceful, successful and healthy life.'

3. Find words from the passage whose opposites are given below :
 (*i*) to let free   [para 1]
 (*ii*) peaceful and calm   [para 2]
 (*iii*) strong   [para 3]
 (*iv*) complex   [para 4]

PASSAGE - 22

1. A youngster quit Facebook in December after spending over three years on the social networking site. With that one act, he bid a silent adieu to more than 300 contacts that he had added to his account during the period. Like almost everyone from his "friends' circle," the 20-year-old was a regular on the service; visiting it everyday to post photos and status updates. But last week, a new feature on Facebook called Timeline forced him to reconsider the pros and cons of being on the networking site.

2. 'Everyone has some skeletons in their closet and I am just not comfortable with Facebook digging up and displaying all the facets of my life on a bulletin board,' says this youngster who joined the network in July 2007 while he was in Class 11.

3. Facebook, you see, had compressed the time he spent on the site and arranged it in chronological order. And while he initially liked the new, neatly organised scrapbook-like feature, he wasn't happy to reveal posts from the past, those that, until recently, were hidden under layers and layers of recent updates. Just clicking on a date on the timeline could transport his friend back in time and enable them to 'view every embarrassing comment, link or photo he had posted on his profile'.

4. "I think it's a recipe for disaster," he says. "In 2007, I had some wall posts, which seemed appropriate at the time, but now after a lapse of four years, I have moved on and don't want them to be openly displayed for all to see."

5. And he is not alone. Many users, worried about how Facebook activity could possibly affect their offline lives, are choosing to commit 'Facebook suicide'. While some have privacy concerns, others feel that the site that was meant to bring them closer to their friends actually does the opposite – it reduces their friendship to something superficial.

6. "Poking and liking are not enough to keep a friendship going," says a business analyst. Having quit Facebook three years ago, she prefers meeting her 'real' friends face-to-face, instead of reading their trite posts online.

7. "On Facebook, people hype everyday issues including what they ate and where they went on a daily basis," says this analyst who continues to use Twitter.

8. Similarly, an engineering student, quit Facebook last December four years after joining it. One fine day, he exported all the data from his account into a little zip file and hit the delete button.

9. "I realised that when it came to my friends who really mattered, I could actually keep in touch with them over the phone or by meeting them in real life," he wrote on his blog.

10. "Facebook had become a time sink and it could not justify the time I spent on it," he says, "I spend more time calling up friends or relatives over the phone now.... I also go out and meet people whenever possible and have a good offline life. I do not regret the change." Today, Facebook has 800 million users of which 37 million are Indian. The site has become an online identity for most, and many of those who decide to quit cannot overcome the withdrawal symptoms and return. Facebook, fully aware of its addictive powers, facilitates this return by allowing users to 'deactivate' their accounts. The option allows members to temporarily disable their accounts, but continues to store their information on its servers so that they can return from their 'break', whenever they wish.

QUESTIONS

1. Answer the following questions briefly :
   (i) What did this youngster do with his Facebook account and why?
   (ii) What was this youngster upset about?
   (iii) Why are people generally not comfortable about their past being revealed?

2. Complete the statements given below :
   (i) In a period of four years people ________ on.
   (ii) Facebook suicide means __________.
   (iii) Instead of bringing friends closer it ___________.
   (iv) We generally keep __________ who matter to us.

3. Find words from the passage which mean the same as :
   (i) the advantages and disadvantages [Para 1]
   (ii) various aspects of one's life. [Para 2]
   (iii) complete details of a person [Para 3]
   (iv) to remove [Pare 4]

ANSWERS

PASSAGE-1

1. They are wary of cumbersome police formalities and legal systems, so bystanders do not help accident victims.

2. The author's view on the government's current reaction to natural disasters is apathetic and it has not managed to handle disasters effectively.

3. Improper medical care at disaster sites is due to lack of disaster management training for medical staff.

4. Their working together to manage disasters completely keeping public interests in mind.

5. Two things are crucial—(a) aid will be effectively deployed (b) professional approach to disaster management efforts, for the public-private participation model of disaster management.

PASSAGE-2

1. They wanted to take part of the ship and sell them.

2. The two men proposed to float the ship again by pumping air into the tanks.

3. Having to contend with sharks, was the danger which the divers faced.

4. The two men felt proud because they had succeeded when everyone thought they would fail.

5. Rudder is the part of the ship used for steering.

PASSAGE-3

1. As other government relief measures have proved ineffective so economists feel that loan waivers will benefit farmers in distress.

2. They will be angry at being penalised for honesty.

3. Loan should be disbursed directly into bank accounts of the farmers using the latest technology.

4. Corrupt bank officials were the unintended beneficiaries of the loans.

5. The ₹ 60,000 crore loan waiver has been sanctioned for 2.25 million marginal farmers.

6. It will have an adverse psychological impact on those who cannot avail of the waiver.

7. The loan waiver penalises deserving farmers.

8. Opposition will definitely win the election.

9. Farmers will make it a habit to default on loans.

10. To ensure they will be re-elected.

PASSAGE-4

1. The central economic planning was found to be difficult because autonomy was given to the states in certain matters.

2. After Independence, India faced with two problems increasing the production from a very low level and ethnic diversity and the aspirations of sub-nationalities.

3. Because the States were not co-operating with the Central Government.

4. The handing over of power by the British to India.

5. The Congress Party.

6. The strength of the Indian Democracy lies in its tradition, in the fusion of the ideas of democracy.

7. The issues were :
   (a) Implementation of the formulated policies
   (b) A national language for the country
   (c) Centre-State relations
   (d) Ethnic diversity of the people

PASSAGE-5

1. They campaigned for infrastructure development.

2. Because, initially the economic growth rate of the country was too rapid.

3. They encouraged foreign direct investment in India.

4. There was a slowdown in the global economy.

5. A system of market determined exchange rate was introduced.

6. Other companies were unable to be competitive in the global market.

7. Industrial growth had to be maintained at a certain percentage fixed by the government.

8. Ensure a combination of public and private sector involvement in developing infrastructure.

9. To protect the interests of the public sector in these sectors.

10. It was beneficial because it created confidence in the Indian economy.

PASSAGE-6

1. To exhort nations to make a collective effort to ensure migration results in development of all countries.

2. Migrants misuse concessions granted to them by the countries where they earn their livelihood.

3. To get very well paid jobs in developed countries and to provide for their families.

4. As a means to reduce economic inequality.

5. Devise practical steps to optimise the benefits of migration.

6. Readily available technology, advances in telecommunication, economical means of transport, affordable means of communication etc.

7. Yes. The statement is true.

8. Increased job opportunities in developed countries and encouraging movement of citizens away from their native country.

PASSAGE-7

1. To become a legal resident by paying a certain amount in fines and back taxes.

2. In the health and education sectors.

3. 12 to 15 million.

4. Opportunity and availability of jobs in bulk.

5. India.

6. They are doing jobs that Americans simply don't want to do. They are employed in jobs that pay minimum wages and entail long working hours.

7. Mexico and India.

8. It is a concern of the Federal Government of the USA for welfare of the mankind.

9. It will ensure that they are not exploited by employers and that they are covered by social security benefits.

10. Both the countries should make a bilateral employment agreement.

PASSAGE-8

1. Adequate planning and preparation are essential for a successful presentation.

2. It will become the greatest obstacle in his career and life.

3. Oral presentation.

4. It demands thinking and speaking.

5. Anecdotes, quotations and humourous touches often make a presentation interesting.

6. A thorough preparation.

7. Innate stage fright of a speaker.

8. It must be of relevant interest to the audience to induce their responses.

9. Personality of a person.

10. Reading or memorizing a presentation.

PASSAGE-9

1. Existence of large number of oil futures and oil contracts.

2. Renewable energy sources are costlier than non-renewable ones.

3. OPEC has decided to restrict its production of oil.

4. Lack of availability of alternative renewable energy resulted in rise in demand for crude oil.

5. OPEC was established in 1970.

6. To protect the interests of oil importing countries.

7. Determining prices of crude oil.

8. Today futures trading markets set the oil prices to a large extent.

9. Exorbitant crude oil prices made alternative energy sources and attractive option.

10. If the price of oil is high for a short time it does not necessarily result in a drop in consumption.

PASSAGE-10

1. Stability will come only when economic opportunities exist.

2. Youth can find jobs and support their families rather than seeking their livelihood in violence.

3. Aid organizations do not understand issues from the perspective of the poor.

4. Aid agencies fail to study the situation.

5. Providing employments to the younger generation will prevent wars.

6. No, sanctions are not a means to ensure peace.

7. On providing humanitarian aid.

8. By means of focusing on agricultural initiatives.

PASSAGE-11

1. At an average annual rate of 8.1%.

2. Only about 3.5%.

3. Checks on lending.

4. The problem is global in nature, not restricted to their individual countries.

5. Because the condition of Asian banks is currently both stable and strong.

6. They must focus on maintaining high economic growth rate as inflation will taper off on its own.

7. Politicians may be voted out of power.

8. To sustain their economies despite the ill effects of inflation.

9. Because our past efforts to reduce poverty will be nullified.

10. Sudden rise in prices of oil worldwide.

PASSAGE-12

1. When we look around thoughtfully, we become conscious of God's unlimited grace.

2. The purpose of animals in the world is to serve mankind.

3. If there had been no human being, the whole world would have been rendered meaningless for us.

4. The reason of dissatisfaction was his more desire.

5. For bringing him into existence, for giving him capacity to dream and for creating the universe for him to live in, is the important reason.

PASSAGE-13

1. To provide money to small-scale companies and poor agents who have no direct access to commercial banks.

2. It is considered as an important instrument to alleviate poverty.

3. Enabling the poor to break out of poverty by providing them with access to credit.

4. Microfinance companies get their funds from the many banks of western countries such as Commercial banks, Non-Government organisation and donors of the same countries.

5. Micro finance has become a crucial means for combating poverty.

6. Micro finance programmes have been introduced in many developing economies. Best examples are the Grameen Bank in Bangladesh, Banco Sol in Bolivia and Bank Rakyat in Indonesia.

PASSAGE-14

1. The role of other countries is the main concern in the form of supplying high-tech weaponry, nuclear assistance and others anti Indian activity to Indian's neighbours.

2. Exploitation of developing nations by the mightier ones.

3. To understand their implications for us.

4. The most effective way is the development of indigenous technologies to counter our major problems.

5. The solution is to eliminate dependence on developed countries and enhancement of in-house technology.

6. They seem to have become totally defunct.

7. Eradication of poverty and become economically self reliant.

PASSAGE-15

1. When sensation is remembered, it becomes memory experience and this leads to connected experience, which in turn gives rise to reasoning.

2. Art explains the cause of things together with its effect, whereas experience gives us just the effect of things, not the cause.

3. Because the sciences which do not cater to necessities or pleasures develop only after the previous two have been invented and only then, men have time for themselves. So, was the case in Egypt where the priestly caste had ample leisure time.

4. The central idea of the passage is "What actually is 'Wisdom'?"

5. Experience seems pretty much like science and art, but really, science and art come to men through experience.

6. Wisdom is knowledge about certain principles and causes.

PASSAGE-16

1. Due to drop in investment in central areas related to agriculture.

2. They have to ensure that a sufficient amount of their farm product is sold.

3. It has to track farmers eligible for government schemes.

4. Citizens should be grateful to farmers and their families for the hardships borne by them to cultivate crops.

5. It is difficult to verify these contracts between farmers and money lenders.

6. The government prefers to import these crops at a lower rate.

7. The aim should be to get all the four crore farmers all the benefits of the govt. schemes such as the Rashtriya Krishi Vikas Yojana, Irrigation Benefit Programme, and others.

PASSAGE-17

1. As per author, the only possibility during the first 38 years after India's independence was to envision the result of economic growth with the help of Government spending.

2. An attempt to mobilise public investment to give a proper direction to economy.

3. The most effective way to derive maximum outcome from investment is by exploring and recognising problems of governance.

4. The author expects planners to explore the market for products made by unskilled workers.

5. The given statement is not appreciated by the author in Eleventh Plan.

6. Research and innovation are the best explanation of the term "Sunrise areas".

PASSAGE-18

1. The king did not have concrete evidence to prove the fraud that's why he could not punish the fraudulent goldsmith.

2. Archimedes was famous as the most learned man as well as mathematician. So, he was charged with the task of finding out if there was any impurity in the crown.

3. The king's suspicion was that the goldsmith had mixed a cheaper metal with gold in the crown.

4. It was a challenge to unearth scientific fact.

5. It was a spontaneous reaction of excitement due to a discovery.

PASSAGE-19

1. Udham Singh went to America to meet fellow citizens working for the same cause.

2. Udham Singh bought the weapon in Paris which was used for killing Sir Michael.

3. Udham Singh shot at Sir Michael O'Dwyer in London.

4. Udham Singh was arrested in Lahore as he was charged for possessing unlicensed arms and ammunition.

5. Udham Singh returned to India in 1928 because he was called by Bhagat Singh in India.

PASSAGE-20

1. (*i*) Good music has mood with variable notes of rhythm and provides mental relief with sensational pleasure.

(*ii*) Both of them practised Carnatic music.

(*iii*) He pioneered the use of African beats and tabla in his music.

2. (*i*) Baul songs   (ii) Elvis Presley

(*iii*) Paco de Lucia   (iv) The Beatles

3. (*i*) limits   (ii) freedom

(*iii*) mixing of styles

PASSAGE-21

1. (*i*) Mind management is a method to control one's mind.

(*ii*) A wise person does not accept or oppose any idea without valid reason. He works as per the situation and his capacity. He is always optimistic.

(*iii*) Because if kept any longer in mind they become stronger and difficult to remove later.

(*iv*) Because our aspirations are raised. The compulsions of hectic work-schedules burden the mind and cause stress.

2. (*i*) When one fails, he works hard and strives to achieve success with increased vigour. Hence, his failure acts as stepping stone for future success.

(*ii*) When we manage our mind, we have patience, peace and calmness which pave the way to success, and a successful and peaceful life is a healthy life.

3. (*i*) control

(*ii*) disturbed, unrest

(*iii*) weak

(*iv*) easy

PASSAGE-22

1. (*i*) The youngster closed his Facebook account after using it for three years. He did not like the Timeline feature of the Facebook that was recently introduced.

(*ii*) He was upset because his friends will be able to see his old posts on Facebook easily with the help of the new feature. Until now those were buried under heaps of recent posts.

(*iii*) Every one commits some mistake or foolishness while posting online comments or photos which are almost forgotten by the time but if the same is easily accessible to all. The situation will be embarrassing and may cause more harm than good.

2. (*i*) moved   (*ii*) deactivating it

(*iii*) separates   (*iv*) friends

3. (*i*) pros and cons   (*ii*) facets of life

(*iii*) profile   (*iv*) to delete

Precis Writing

The word 'Precis' has been derived from the Latin word 'Precidere' which means to cut short and the French word 'Precis' through which it has been introduced into English language and means precise, exact and definite. From these derivations, it is clear that precis-writing means the art to cutting short a composition in such a way as to make it precise, exact and definite.

Success in precis-writing, depends upon two things: (a) command over the language, i.e., knowledge of and ability to use the language; and (b) power of discrimination, i.e., to be able to sift chaff from grain.

IMPORTANT TIPS

1. Read the passage very carefully and sufficiently to ascertain clearly its main theme or general meaning.
2. Find a proper title, indicating in it the main topic or the central theme.
3. Go through the passage again in greater detail to make sure of the meaning of each sentence, phrase and word. Underline the important points and relevant facts to be included in your final precis.
4. Prepare brief-notes on the points in your own words. Do not copy the language of the original.
5. Put aside the original passage and write out the first draft by referring to your notes only. Ensure that precis is: (*i*) continuous; (*ii*) coherent; (*iii*) grammatically correct; (*iv*) simple; (*v*) straight-forward; (*vi*) clear; (*vii*) self-contained; (*viii*) in the indirect form of speech and in the past tense.
6. Count the number of words in this draft precis. Adjust the length if necessary.
7. Now, compare this draft precis with the original to make sure that you have correctly rendered its meaning.
8. Write out a fair copy of your precis under the title you have selected.
9. Read the fair copy critically. You should ensure: (*i*) that it would be easily understood even by a reader who has never seen the original; (*ii*) that it is in readable English; and (*iii*) that the grammar and punctuation are correct.
10. Append at the foot of the fair copy of the precis the number of words it contains (excluding those of the title). (Normally one-third of original)

Common Faults to be Avoided
1. Writing your precis in a very small hand in order to give the impression of conciseness.
2. Comments of your own and other irrelevancies like quotations, ornamental phraseology, figurative language, etc.
3. Stealing phrases from the original.
4. Emphasis on wrong and irrelevant points.
5. Exceeding, or falling short of, the prescribed length by more or less than about five words.
6. Bad style, lack of unity, detached ideas, illogical sequence, etc.

Special Techniques
To write a good precis, the following special techniques are adopted:
1. **Precis of Words:** It is mere reduction of the length of a passage. This can be done by: (*i*) substitution; and (*ii*) economy of words.

2. **Precis of Arrangement:** It involves the careful selection of the important facts in the original passage and their proper arrangement. This requires two techniques:

   (i) Omission; and

   (ii) Synthesis.

3. **Precis of Ideas and Arrangements:** It refers to the gathering together, in logical sequence, of the scattered portions of an argument or piece of description.

4. **Precis of Direct Speech by its Conversion into Indirect Speech:** While making a precis, all direct speech in the original must be turned into indirect speech.

EXERCISE

Ex. 1

Moreover in its relationship to the rest of the world the United States is in a healthier state than it has been for many years. For years, the United States and the Soviet Union were locked in an all-out confrontational Cold War. That policy, if indefinitely continued, could have led only war too fearsome to both nations.

The two countries have concluded in recent years that those results are in the interests of neither, that machinery for crisis management must be built, and that efforts must be undertaken to limit the arms race.

The stance of the United States toward the developing world has also undergone an improving change that is in some ways analogous. Since the end of the Second World War, United States' policy towards the unindustrialized world has been the product of a mixture of motives, objectives, and perceptions. In part, the developing countries were perceived by Americans as objects of pity and compassion, to be guided along to political and economic maturity in the democratic free-market image of the United States itself. In part, the industrially undeveloped areas have been seen by the United States, and its private companies, as sources of raw materials and, to some degree, markets. And, in part, these countries have been seen by the United States as battle grounds for the Cold War and as political pieces to be lined up and voted on Cold War issues in accordance with our wishes.

These American perceptions have led to disappointment for the United States. The countries of the developing world have not generally followed our free-market, liberal democratic example. They have demonstrated little disposition to play the role of grateful recipients of charity. They have become increasingly inclined to follow their own perception of their political interests and preferences. And now, shifts in world power relations and economic bargaining power have increasingly made it possible for developing countries, or a group of them, to make themselves heard, to bargain for their own objective, and to act independently.

Yet another adjustment toward reality that has been made by the United States in recent years is the successful accommodation of its international military and political commitments to accord with the reality of its military power. One way to view the Vietnam experience is as a lesson to this country—and to all countries—that, short of all-out nuclear destruction, there are distinct limits to the ability of any nation to achieve political results through military means, especially at long distance. Commitments that outrun credible performance are dangerous and destabilizing. We can expect that henceforth the scope and scale of United States' international political commitments will be more closely aligned with the actuality of our military capacity—a most salutary development.

Finally, the United States has in the past few years avoided a yawning pitfall into which we might easily have fallen. We did not recoil into neo-isolationism in reaction to Vietnam and to the reduction of our global leverage. The United States remain the most powerful single polity and economy in the world, deeply interlocked with the interests, problems, hopes, and fears of other nations. For the United States, a policy of withdrawal from the world is not a realistic or workable policy option.

Granting that the United States today is better focused and closer to reality than before, what of the rest of the world? Astonishingly the same generalization holds. *(Words: 567)*

ANALYSIS WITH COMMENTS

- **Para I.** *Main Point:* USA's comparatively better relationship with the rest of the world. *Supporting Points*: (i) Earlier Cold War between USA and Soviet Union (ii) More possibilities of War (iii) Realization of the countries to limit the arms race.
- **Para II.** *Main Point.* Change for the better in USA's policy towards developing countries. *Supporting Point*: Earlier, since World War II, American policy directed by own selfish economic and political aims.
- **Para III.** *Main Point:* USA's disillusionment with its earlier policy. *Supporting Points:* (i) Developing countries safeguard their own national interests (ii) They have become independent, more aware and powerful
- **Para IV.** *Main Point:* American's more realistic approach to military capability for achieving political ends. *Supporting Point:* Example of Vietnam War.
- **Para V.** *Main Point:* USA knows its important role and position in international affairs and has not fallen back on the unrealistic policy of non-participation and non-involvement in world affairs. This attitude true of the rest of the world also.

PRECIS

America's Dynamic Foreign Policy

The Unites States of America now enjoys comparatively better relations with the other countries of the world than it did in the past. For years it was involved in a cold war with the Soviet Union. This could have led to disastrous consequences for both the countries. They however realized the importance of limiting the arms race. America's attitude towards the developing and unindustrialized countries has similarly improved. Since the Second World War America's policy towards such countries had been based on vested interests as she sought raw material and markets for her finished products. Politically, they were made battle grounds for the cold war. America became disillusioned with its earlier policy as the developing countries envisaged her designs of economic and political exploitation and realized their own national interests. They have grown independent and formed their own powerful group which is strong enough to bargain for its objectives. America has also realized the limitations of military power in achieving political ends, especially at long distance, as the Vietnam War showed. America's international political commitments will now be more appropriate to its military capacity. However, aware of its vital role in the international scene, America has not adopted the unrealistic policy of withdrawing from international affairs. The rest of the world too has shown a change towards a better focused and realistic policy. *(Words: 223)*

Ex. 2

Little babies are fun; in fact, they are absolutely adorable. I hope this opening statement will absolve me of the guilt the following words are going to drown me in. So, babies are sweet little things, but why do most parents the world over make out that their babies are the sweetest? The most common and prodigious phenomenon of nature continues to be the world's greatest event every time there is a new entry into the parents' ranks.

Creation is wonderful and there are few who can refute that, but certain laws of nature don't allow for improvisations and such laws apply to little babies. Every baby, if he is a normal little bounder, just has to cry when his little food bag is empty. There is nothing particularly intelligent about that, but there are parents who go poetic on this attribute of the little one.

Then comes a stage where a baby just has to roll over on to her stomach periodically. Every baby does it. But try explaining that to a fanatic parent. "Oh but she does it all by herself. It's just marvellous. You should watch her, you really should. Come on Baby boo, on your stomach". Much does "Babyboo" care for parental pride at that stage. While the bored parent of four shuffles her feet waiting for the demonstration the new parent is totally engrossed in repeating the request.

After a while Baby seems to oblige but not because she has some Mohammed Ali complex of Pam the Greatest but because her little body wants to. This act is promptly interpreted as the corroboration of the parental statement that Baby is so intelligent and look how she did it on request!

There is something extremely appealing about babies, and little detours in conversation now and then centred around a sudden gurgle or cooing is perfectly normal. What is vexing is one has one's attention constantly dragged away from some very absorbing discussion to a perpetual refrain of "My baby now..."

Babies, left to themselves are charming creatures; even in their tantrum-prone state. Add a dash of parental pride by all means, but when it increases beyond proportion, the compound is unpalatable. A state of extreme pathos presents itself when an unmarried person visits friends who have just acquired parental status. The new Papa and Mama might be slightly sensitive about fitting into the gushing new mould initially. But when Baby suddenly gurgles and the visiting friend responds impulsively, it is completely out of hand.

Another interesting transformation in many fresh parents is from I-love-babies to I-love-only-my-babies. Two sets of new parents get together and after the cursory chucking of chins of each other's baby there is a very compulsive game set in motion called i-vaguely-know-you-are-talking-about-your-kid-but-what-I-have-to say-about-mine is far more interesting. It is confounding how the love for babies gets concentrated into a concentric point once one becomes a parent.

There are exceptions to every generality but sometimes one wishes the exceptions would become the generality and vice versa. This would be a nice state of affairs in the meet-my-baby context or should it be contest? *(Words: 519)*

ANALYSIS WITH COMMENTS

- **Para I.** *Main Point:* Babies are a great joy. *Supporting Points*: (i) They are adorable (ii) Parents always claim their babies to be the sweetest. (iii) Birth of a baby marks the greatest event in the parents' lives.
- **Para II.** *Main Point:* Babies are a wonderful creation but they are the same everywhere. *Supporting Points*: (i) They cry in hunger (ii) Some parents attribute it to their intelligence and become even poetic on the subject.
- **Para III.** *Main Point:* At a particular stage, every baby rolls on its stomach. *Supporting Points*: (i) Parents take pride in this activity of their baby. (ii) Parents already having children are not amused by such activities. (iii) The baby's parents ask it to repeat the action.
- **Para IV.** *Main Point:* The parents consider their baby intelligent if it repeats the action.
- **Para V.** *Main Point:* It is very irritating if one's attention is constantly directed from something interesting to the other's baby. *Supporting Point*: Sometimes a reference to a baby's antics is quite appealing.
- **Para VI.** *Main Point:* Babies are very charming when left to their own world. *Supporting Points*: (i) Parents should limit their pride in their babies (ii) An unmarried person does not find himself very happy in the company of new parents.
- **Para VII.** *Main Point:* Parents love only their own babies.
- **Para VIII.** *Main Points:* Exceptions are always there. *Supporting Point:* (i) Exceptions should become the generalities and *vice versa*.

PRECIS

Babies—Everyone's Joy

Babies are a source of great joy and pleasure. They are loved and doted upon by their parents. The birth of a baby is a momentous event in the lives of the parents. Babies are a wonderful creation but are the same everywhere. Hunger makes them cry but the parents consider their baby very intelligent and tend to become poetical. Every baby rolls on its belly at a certain stage but the parents pride this achievement. The new parents ask their baby to repeat the act while parents already having children do not get amused by such demonstrations. The baby may repeat the act to meet its physical need but the parents attribute it to the baby's intelligence and understanding. Although the antics of babies are quite enjoyable sometimes, is irritating when an interesting conversation is regularly disturbed by baby talk. Babies should be left to themselves in their own world. The extreme pride of parents in their baby can make a bachelor visitor feel sorry and out of place. Besides, new parents are usually much more fond of their own babies than of others'. But exceptions are always there. The author wishes that exceptions in such cases would become generalities and vice versa. That would be acceptable in the 'meet my baby context' or, more appropriately, contest. ***(Words: 218)***

Ex. 3 ________________________________

The most have neglected the careful study of the cinema. When they think of the cinema they think only of sex and immorality, they do not think of the good things about the cinema. Many of them seem to have a closed mind on the subject. They are suffering under a complex, caused by the age-old prejudice of the so called genteel folk towards any kind of show business and the men engaged in it. Even in countries like England and America which are certainly more advanced than India, they look down upon actors and actresses with an air of superiority. The main reason for this prejudice is perhaps that members of this profession always depend on public support and patronage for their very existence. The showman, like a politician, exists only at the pleasure of the public. He is always dispensable, not indispensable. He is always to bow down to the whims and fancies of his public. Here the public becomes superior to the showman and the showman accepts the position of superiority assumed by publicmen because publicmen like showmen depend on the same public. If publicmen work for the good of the public, showmen do, as a matter of fact, work for the pleasure of the public, the two are different spheres of activity. That is all the difference.

Another reason for the inhibited growth of the cinema is the confused thinking about its use, its scope and its purpose. It can be and is, as a matter of fad, to a very large extent, used as a means of propaganda, publicity and advertisement. It can be developed as one of the fine arts in its own right. It can be used as a medium for the enlightenment of other nations about our own culture, customs and manners. It has often been said that one of the potent causes of international misunderstanding, hot and cold wars, is the people of different countries do not have the means to appreciate and understand each other adequately. We are all familiar nowadays with the international exchange of students and professors, permanent culture establishments in foreign countries, tourist information bureaus, and hundreds of goodwill missions. There can be no gainsaying that the cumulative effect of all these activities in establishing mutual international understanding and paving the way for permanent world peace is very great. No wonder, therefore, that all modern States consider the film industry as a 'key' industry which has to be preserved and fostered at all costs.

The scope of cinema being so wide, and the purpose for which it can be applied so varied, it is obvious that the agencies employing the medium of screen for various specific purposes must also be necessarily as varied. Its use as a medium of advertisement, for instance, can be sponsored only by commercial interest.

Its use as a medium of mass education is pre-eminently the domain of National and State Governments. It is, indeed, a great pity that our educational institutions have not begun to exploit the immense potentiality of the film for educational purposes. A careful consideration of the different agencies which can exploit motion picture for specific purposes leads to the inevitable conclusion that the only scope for private enterprise is the field of public entertainment. I take it that it is agreed on all hands that recreation and entertainment are almost as important as food, clothing and shelter.

Apart from recreation, being good of the people themselves, it is in the interest of the State itself to keep the people contented and well provided with wholesome pastimes during the time when they have no work. The idle man's brain is indeed the devil's workshop. That is why all successful governments, from time immemorial, have made it a policy of high statecraft to keep the people away from mischief and discontent by means of State-sponsored recreation. *(Words: 646)*

ANALYSIS WITH COMMENTS

- **Para I.** *Main Point:* Leaders and intellectuals have not paid careful attention to the impact of cinema. *Supporting Points*: (i) They associate cinema only with sex and immorality (ii) Gentry have an old prejudice against actors and actresses who are looked down upon. (iii) Show business is based on public support and patronage. (iv) Whereas public men work for people's welfare, showmen work for people's pleasure.

- **Para II.** *Main point:* Due to lack of clarity about its use, scope, purpose, cinema has not grown fully; yet, film industry is considered very important for its tremendous impact and role by all modern countries. *Supporting Points*: (i) It can be very useful in the spheres of education, propaganda, advertisement, publicity. (ii) It can be a source of enlightenment about different cultures. (iii) It can bring about better understanding among the peoples of the world and help the cause of world peace.

- **Para III.** *Main point:* As the scope of cinema is very wide, the agencies using the medium of cinema must also be varied and cinema as a means of entertainment must be patronized by the state. *Supporting Points:* (i) Commercial interests sponsor it as a medium of advertisement (ii) It can be used effectively for mass education by national and state governments. (iii) It has great scope for private

enterprises in the sphere of public entertainment but the government must ensure healthy recreation and entertainment.

PRECIS

Cinema : Role and Potential

It may be said that public men and intellectuals have not paid careful attention and importance to the influence of cinema. They generally associate cinema with sex and immorality and overlook its advantages. The gentry has an old prejudice against showmen who are not respected mainly because they live on public support and patronage. Both publicmen and showmen are dependent upon the public. But they differ in their sphere of activity. The former work for public welfare and the latter for public entertainment. Lack of clarity about the purpose, scope and use of cinema has obstructed its growth. Modern countries, however, consider film-industry essential for its tremendous impact and role in different spheres of education, entertainment, propaganda, commerce, in the spreading of culture and even as an art. Cinema can bring about better understanding among the peoples of the world and help the cause of world peace. Its scope is very wide and varied. Hence, the agencies using it as a communication media for specific purposes should be many and varied. Unfortunately, the great potential of cinema for educational purposes remains untapped although its use as a medium of mass education falls in the sphere of the government. The government must patronize cinema and ensure healthy entertainment and recreation for the masses. *(Words: 212)*

Ex. 4

That without a free Press there can be no free people is a thing that all free people take for granted: we need not discuss it. Nor will we at this moment discuss the restrictions placed upon the Press in time of war. At such times all liberties have to be restricted; a free people must see to it that when peace comes full freedom is restored. In the meantime, it may be wholesome to consider what that freedom is and how far it is truly desirable. It may turn out to be no freedom at all, or even a mere freedom to tyrannize; for tyranny is, in fact, the uncontrolled freedom of one man, or one gang, to impose its will on the world.

When we speak of the freedom of the Press, we usually mean freedom in every technical and restricted sense—namely freedom from direction or censorship by the Government. In this respect, the British Press is under ordinary conditions, singularly free. It can attack the policy and political character of ministers, interfere in the machinery of foreign diplomacy, conduct campaigns to subvert the Constitution, and generally harry and belabour public servants with almost perfect liberty. It can even become a weapon to coerce the Government to conform to what it asserts to be the will of the people. Generally speaking, this freedom works to secure and sustain that central doctrine of democracy that the State is not the master but the servant of the people. The Press, as a whole, is free in Britain in peace time; there is no shade of political opinion that does not somehow contrive to express itself. But if we go on to imagine that every particular organ of the Press enjoys the larger liberty of being a forum of public opinion, we shall be gravely mistaken. Livery newspaper is shackled to its own set of overlords and in its turn, exercises a powerful bondage upon its readers and on the public generally. The editorial policy of a popular daily is controlled by two chief factors. The first is the interest of the advertisers from whom it gets the money which enables it to keep up its large circulation. No widely circulated newspaper dare support a public policy, however much in the national interest, that might conflict with the vested interest of the advertisers. Every newspaper lives in a perpetual precarious balance: it must increase its sales to justify its advertising rates, and to increase its sales, it must sell itself far below the cost of production; but if it sells more copies than its advertising will pay for, it faces financial disaster. Consequently, the more widespread and powerful the organ, the more closely it has to subserve vested interests.

The second chief source of a newspapers' revenue is the wealth of the man or company that owns it; accordingly, its policy is largely determined by the personal spites and political ambitions of its proprietor. The failure, for example, of a newspaper magnate to secure a government appointment may be the signal for the unleashing of a virulent campaign, in every organ which he controls, against the minister or the party which has disappointed his ambitions. The public, knowing nothing of the personal bias behind the attack and little of the vast network of control which ties up whole groups of newspapers in the hands of a single man or combine, sees only that great numbers of (what appear to him to be) independent organs are united in a single, savage, and persistent condemnation. Unless he is exceptionally shrewd, exceptionally cynical or of exceptionally resolute and independent mind, he can scarcely help being influenced;, and having his vote 'influenced; and it is odds that he will ever realise the nature of the pressure brought to bear upon him.

But still more serious, because more subtle, than the control applied to individual papers by various kinds of interest is the control and censorship exercised by the Press upon the news and opinions which it disseminates. This control exploits two basic assumptions about the public: (a) that they have not the wit to distinguish truth from falsehood; (b) that they do not care at all that a statement is false, provided it is titillating. According to both assumptions, the readers can be made to believe anything. The result is that accurate reporting, which used to be the pride of the old-fashioned independent newspaper, has largely given place to reporting which at best is slipshod and at worst tendentious.　　　　　*(Words: 755)*

ANALYSIS WITH COMMENTS

- **Para I.** *Main point* : Free Press is an essential pre-requisite of a free nation. *Supporting Points* : (i) Although during war the freedom of the Press is curbed, it must be restored soon after the war is over (ii) This freedom must not degenerate into absolute freedom for oppressing the people.

- **Para II.** *Main point :* Freedom of the Press implies absence of government control and censorship, yet the Press has its limitations as a forum of public opinion. *Supporting Points*: *(i)* The British Press enjoys, this freedom completely. *(it)* But every organ of the Press functions under restrictions and limits *(iii)* Newspapers are influenced by advertisers. *(iv)* The different organs of the Press serve vested interests.

- **Para III.** *Main points :* Policies of newspapers are largely determined by proprietors and greatly influence masses and voting behaviour. *Supporting Points*: *(i)* Newspaper magnates may indulge in malignant campaigning against a minister, party or government if they fail to find favour with them. *(ii)* The masses are prejudiced in a subtle manner through the Press *(iii)* People never suspect any influence upon them and this leads to indirect bias.

- **Para IV.** *Main points:* More than individual papers, censorship exercised by the Press upon its news and opinions is more subtle and hence, more serious. *Supporting Points* : (i) Press assumes people's inability to discern truth from falsehood (ii) Press assumes people's fallibility to titillation (iii) Accurate and independent reporting as in the past is rare.

PRECIS

Plea for a Free and Enlightened Press

Free press is an essential pre-requisite of a free nation. Although during war the freedom of the press is curbed, it must be restored as soon as the war is over. It's freedom must not vitiate into license to oppress the people. Freedom of the press implies absence of censorship, governmental direction, influence and control. The British press best symbolizes this freedom, for it can criticise, comment upon and discuss the conduct of ministers, the foreign policy, constitutional matters and public opinion. The British press embodies the democratic ideal that the people are sovereign and the State is for their welfare. However, the press—a forum of public opinion functions under certain restrictions and limitations.

Every newspaper is greatly influenced by advertisers for its popularity and existence. As newspapers sell below their production cost and advertisers meet the losses, the newspapers support government policies which are in keeping with the advertiser's interests. Similarly, their policies are influenced by their proprietors who may launch a malicious campaign against State policies when they fail to find favour with the government. Propaganda thorough newspapers may be profound and subtle to bias the unsuspecting masses and influence their voting behaviour. More than the newspapers, the press may bias its news and opinions which have harmful effects. It may assume people's inability to discern truth from falsehood and their susceptibility to sensationalism. This only leads to degeneration in independent and accurate reporting.

(Words: 237)

Ex. 5

Coal has a nickname. It is called "Black Diamond", not because, like diamonds, it is mostly carbon, but because it is as valuable as diamonds. We could easily do without diamonds, but we could not do without coal.

The industrial prosperity of Britain was built on coal. She has always been rich in coal and iron, and as they are found near each other it costs little to bring one to the other. This was a great advantage when Britain began her industrial development. She soon became the workshop of the world. She produced more coal than she could use and had a good surplus for export. This surplus brought in money from overseas and increased the national wealth. Some of the best coal in the world, anthracite, that burns hotly with little smoke, is mined in Wales. It finds a ready market all over the world.

But British mines are not what they were. They are old. When a mine is new, the coal is near the surface and its extraction is fairly easy and cheap. The deeper the mine, the higher the cost of mining. Coal is found in layers called seams. If the seam of coal runs a mile below the surface of the ground, then the mine must be a mile deep. The passage underground, usually called galleries, may run for miles. In one mine, in the north of England, where a recent disastrous explosion caused the loss of more than a hundred lives, the galleries run out for six miles under the sea. Thus, the miner often has to travel long distances underground before reaching the coal face, which is the name given to the place where the coal is cut. A little railway carries him to the coal face, but even so, mining in these circumstances is difficult and expensive. In many mines much of the work of cutting the coal is done by machinery, but in Britain local difficulties often prevent the full use of cutting machinery. For this reason the output of the American miner is greater than that of the British one. For the first time in her history, Britain, whose wealth was largely founded on coal, had to import some herself in 1947, and again in 1950.

To try to restore mining to its old place in Britain's economy, new laws have been passed. All the private owners of mines have been bought out, and the mines are now national property; they have been nationalized. The miner no longer works for a private owner; he works for the country. The hours of labour have been decreased and a five-day working week has been introduced. Those who absent themselves from work on frequent occasions without just cause are being dismissed. Wages have been raised and up-to-date machinery is being brought into the pits. Young miners are given periods of free training to fit them for their work.

Nevertheless, one may wonder why anyone in his right senses becomes a coal miner. Yet, it is the natural occupation of most boys born near the coalfields, just as farm work is the natural occupation of those born in an agricultural district. Ordinary people have little choice of occupation. When they leave school, they look for work that will enable them to live at home. The natural fate of a miner's son is to be a miner. We cannot choose our parents; if we could, most of us would probably prefer them to be millionaires or ministers. Fate and luck plays a great part in our lives.

We should, however, remember that the miner does not live a life of perpetual dirt, work and danger. When he comes to the surface at the end of a day's work, he is certainly tired and dirty. The whites of his eyes shine strangely from a face blackened with coal dust. But after a bath, change of clothing, a meal and a rest, he is a different man, and ready for a visit to his club, the football field or the cinema. Miners are fond of all kinds of sports. It they do not play themselves, they eagerly follow the fortunes of those who do. They are fond of betting, too, and every horse-race that is run takes money out of some pockets and puts it into others. In good times they live cheerful, ordinary lives. They are accustomed to the ever-present danger in the mines, and accept it as a natural part of their existence.   *(Words: 749)*

ANALYSIS WITH COMMENTS

- **Para I.** *Main Point:* Coal is perhaps of even greater use than diamonds. *Supporting Point:* (i) Coal is given the name of 'Black Diamond'.
- **Para II.** *Main Point:* Britain owes its industrial development and prosperity to coal. *Supporting Points*: (i) Britain has large iron and coal mines. (ii) She has prospered even by exporting her surplus coal.
- **Para III.** *Main Point:* British coal mines have now been exhausted and she even had to import coal. *Supporting Points*: (i) Coal extraction is easy and cheap if coal is near the surface as in a new mine but it is otherwise in an old mine. (ii) The miner often has to travel long distances underground before reaching the coal face. (iii) coal-cutting is done by machines but in Britain local difficulties do not enable it. (iv) The output of any American miner is greater than the British one due to the use of machinery.
- **Para IV.** *Main Point:* Britain has nationalized its coal mines. *Supporting Points*: (i) Miners no longer work for a private owner but for the government. (ii) They have better facilities, wages, machinery and training.
- **Para V.** *Main Point:* People born in the neighbourhood of coal mines take to coal-mining as it enables them to live at home.

Supporting Point: It becomes a hereditary occupation.

- **Para IV.** *Main Point:* The coal miners have their own active, cheerful and normal life like any other people once they are out of the mines. *Supporting Point*: They accept the risks of a mining life as a natural part of their lives.

PRECIS

The Miners of Black Diamond

Coal is often called 'Black Diamond' and is indispensable for its greater utility value than even diamonds. Britain owes its industrial development and prosperity to coal. She has large coal and iron mines and has prospered even by exporting surplus coal. However, British coal mines have nearly been exhausted. In a new mine, coal extraction is easier and cheaper than an old mine because the coal is nearer to the surface. Coal has to be dug now from very deep layers, miles below the surface of the earth. The coal-miners are carried to the coal-face by little railways. Local limitations in Britain's coal-mines hamper the use of cutting machinery. Hence, coal-mining in England is no more economical. She had to even resort to import of coal. In order to revitalize the industry and its economic output, Britain has nationalized its coal-mines. The miners are encouraged by way of better facilities, higher wages, lesser hours of work, free training and the latest coal-cutting equipment and machines. Usually people born in the neighbourhood of coal mines take to coal mining as it enables them to live at home. It becomes a hereditary occupation with them. Despite a hard, hazardous and dirty occupation, the coal miners have their own active, cheerful and normal lives like any other people once they are out of the mines. They enjoy sports and various other forms of entertainment. They accept the risks of a mining life as a natural part of their lives. ***(Words: 246)***

Ex. 6 ___________________

It is proved beyond doubt that women in modern India can be good administrators. Women rulers like Chand Bibi, Elizabeth and Rani of Jhansi proved to the world their solid worth. They ruled most efficiently and brought glory to their nations. Women are intelligent and hard-working. They are not frivolous and light. They take up work very honestly, sincerely and earnestly and they put heart and soul in their work. It is very fortunate that we have in India educated ladies who are very keen to take up administrative work. We are amazed to see what wonderful work they are doing in offices of Central Secretariat as Reception officers. It has been observed that they are very quick to understand and very efficient in work. They have won an applause from the bureaucracy. Moreover, they cheer up others; with a sweet smile, they can win over others to their point of view. All important services have been thrown open to women. They are competing for the Indian Administrative Service, Indian Foreign Service, and many other important fields of life. Very soon we will be seeing women as magistrates, judges, revenue officers, income-tax officers, and so on. Women are cool-headed and they ponder over important issues. They are dispassionate. Objective and impartial and never see things in another light. Their minds are unbiased and unprejudiced and they can be generous even to the extent of forgiveness. It will be seen that women will be good arbitrators in serious disputes and they would like to avoid bloodshed and acrimony. By means of peaceful discussion and negotiation, they will be able to solve their problems. Mrs. Pandit has been a very successful ambassador and she has raised the prestige of India very high in foreign countries. Women are good diplomats and they can display their diplomacy in important key posts in the Indian Foreign Service.

In modern India, women have played an important role as doctors. Lady doctors have relieved much human suffering and pain. Women can work as trained nurses, efficient midwives, doctors and surgeons. The maternity cases are taken up by lady doctors. They can be of great service to women and children. Florence Nightingale made nursing popular among the women of upper class. Thus, in India, women of the upper class can work in villages and small towns where disease takes heavy toll of human lives.

Educated women have to play the role of teachers. An educated lady can serve the country in the humble capacity of teacher. The education of children mainly depends upon women. Women can build up the character of children. Women can instruct as well as please; they can teach as well as amuse. "Human soul is, without education like marble in a quarry." Women can do research work and they are winning laurels in art, literature, philosophy music and painting. We are fortunate in having very intelligent girls who are anxious to have training in foreign countries. They are being given scholarship by the government of India and many of them have proceeded to the U.S.A., the U.K. and Western countries and have made their mark as educationists. Women in modern India do not want to lag behind in any activity.

Women can also render social service whenever there is flood, famine, earthquake or some natural calamity. They can render social service. It is also during war that they can be of utmost utility to the nation. Knitting, sewing, embroidery, dressing, etc. can be done by the ladies. In free India, ladies are being given training in First Aid, use of rifles and guns and some ladies are getting training as drivers and pilots. The defence of the country is a matter of great importance to all and women should share the burden with men. In case of war, women might be asked to offer their service in theatres of war.

Women, surely, have a very important role to play in modern India. They have shown their worth as leaders and administrators and that time is not far off when India will have at the helm of affairs women who will lead the country from strength to strength. As legislators, they have distinguished themselves and their speeches in the Parliament are carefully heard and listened to. As musicians and singers, they have the admiration of men.

(Words: 721)

COMMENTS

The ideas to be emphasized are: Women's accomplishment and excellence in every sphere of life—Women's vital role in the development of free and independent India—Their achievements and potential as administrators, diplomats, doctors, nurses, etc—Their role as teachers and in the character formation of children—their dynamic role in India's progress and their tremendous potential of the future.

PRECIS

Women in Modern India

Women have made their presence felt in every field of activity and are playing a vital role in the development of free and modern India. They have proved their intellectual and administrative qualities through their honest, sincere and painstaking efforts and efficient accomplishments. Women have proved their skill in every sphere of administration and management. They are objective and impartial in their approach. Women have also enhanced India's prestige in the world as diplomats. Women in modern India have achieved great success in the role of doctors and nurses. They have relieved human suffering and are an asset to work in rural areas. Nursing has also become very popular now. Educated women are an asset as teachers and even pursue research work in different areas of human knowledge. Women have a pivotal role in teaching and guiding the children and building a strong foundation for the future of the country. They have a great role in the character formation of children. They are very intelligent and have made their mark as educationists. Women can contribute immensely to the social welfare of the people. They can render social service both during times of peace and during war. They are receiving training even in the use of arms to enable them to serve in the country's defence in case of an emergency. They have excelled in every sphere and in future, they will prove their worth to the country's progress.   *(Words: 238)*

Ex. 7

It is necessary to understand what we mean when we talk of regeneration of women. It presupposes degeneration, and if that is so, we should further consider what led to it and how. It is our primary duty to have some very hard thinking on these points. In travelling all over India I have come to realise that all the existing agitation is confined to an infinitesimal section of our people, who are really a mere speck in the vast firmament. Crores of people of both sexes live in absolute ignorance of this agitation. Full eighty-five per cent of the people of this country pass their innocent days in a state of total detachment from what is going on around them. These men and women, ignorant as they are, do their bit in life well and properly. Both have the same education or rather the absence of education. Both are helping each other, as they ought to do. If their lives are in any sense incomplete, the cause can be traced to the incompleteness of the lives of the remaining fifteen per cent.

In the observations that I am going to make, I will confine myself to the fifteen per cent above mentioned, and even then it would be out of place to discuss the disabilities that are common to both men and women. The point for us to consider is the regeneration of our women relatively to our men. Legislation has been mostly the handiwork of men; and man has not always been fair and discriminate in performing that self-appointed task. The largest part of our effort, in promoting the regeneration of women, should be directed towards removing those blemishes which are represented in our Shastras as the necessary and ingrained characteristics of women. Who will attempt this and how? In my humble opinion, in order to make the attempt, we will have to produce women pure, firm and self controlled as Sita, Damayanti and Draupadi. If we do produce them, such modern sisters will receive the same homage from Hindu society as is being paid to their prototypes of yore. Their words will have the same authority as the Shastras. We will feel ashamed of the stray reflections on them in our Smiritis, and will soon forget them. Such revolutions have occurred in Hinduism in the past, and will still take place in the future, leading to the stability of our faith.

We have now discussed the root cause of degeneration of our women, and have considered the ideals by the realisation of which the present conditions of our women can be improved. The number of women who can realise those ideals will be necessarily very few, and, therefore, we will now consider what ordinary women can accomplish if

they would try. Their first attempt should be directed towards awakening in the minds of as many women as possible a proper sense of their present condition. I am not among those who believe that such an effort can be made through literary education only.

(Words: 506)

☐ **PRECIS**

Women's Emancipation in India

The cause of women's emancipation presupposes their degradation at present. The matter requires serious thought. During the course of his travels all over India the author realized that the movement for women's upliftment was limited to a very small minority of people. An overwhelming multitude of eighty-five percent of people was absolutely ignorant of any such campaign. The author, confining his observations to the minority of fifteen per cent of people, holds that any sense of incompleteness in the lives of the majority is traceable to the incompleteness of the lives of the minority. Women's regeneration requires more consideration, relatively, than men's. Women's welfare has for long been in the hands of men. The image of women as characterized by the scriptures needs radical change. Women of great character and will, as in the past, are required. This will revitalize their image in the scriptures. Such transformations have occurred in Hinduism and they will hopefully occur in future too, to bring stability in the faith of the people. For the regeneration of each woman it is essential to instill among all women a consciousness of their present deplorable state. The author does not believe that only literary education can arouse such a consciousness.

(Words: 203)

Ex. 8

Capitalism, Socialism, Central planning are means not ends. In themselves, they are neither moral not immoral, human nor inhuman. We have to ask what are their results. We have to look at what are the consequences of adopting one or another system of organization. From that point of view, the crucial thing is to look beneath the surface. Don't look at what the proponents of one system or another say about their intentions, but look at what the actual results are.

Socialism, which means government ownership and operation of means of production, has appealed to right-minded, fine people, to people of idealistic views, because of the supposed objectives of socialism, especially because of the supposed objectives of equality and social justice. These are fine objectives, and it is a tribute to people of goodwill that those objectives should appeal to them.

But you have to ask the question: does the system—no matter what its proponents say—produce those results? Once you look at the results, it is crystal clear that they do not. Where are social injustices greatest? Social injustices are clearly greatest where you have central control. The degree of social injustice, torture, and incarceration in a place like Russia is of a different order of magnitude than it is in those Western countries in which most of us have grown up and in which we have been accustomed to regarding freedom as our natural heritage.

Again, look at the question of equality. Where is there the greatest degree of inequality? In the socialist states of the world. I remember about 15 years ago my wife and I were in Russia for a couple of weeks. We were in Moscow with our tourist guide and I happened to see some of the fancy Russian limousines, the Zivs, that were sort of a take-off of the 1938 American Packard. I asked our tourist guide out of amusement how much those sell for. "Oh" she said. "those aren't for sale. Those are only for the members of the Politburo."

In a country like the Soviet Union there is an enormous inequality in the immediate literal sense that a small select group has all of the services and amenities of life, and large masses have a very low standard of living. Indeed, more directly, the wage rate of foremen is much higher relative to the wage rate of ordinary workers in the Soviet Union than it is in the United States.

Capitalism, on the other hand, is a system of organization that relies on private property and voluntary exchange. It has repelled people, it has driven them away from supporting it, because they

have thought it emphasized self-interest in a narrow way. They were repelled by the idea of people pursuing their own interests rather than some broader interest.

Yet it is clear that the results go the other way around. Only those countries in which capitalism has prevailed over long periods have experienced both freedom and prosperity. Of course, there is not perfect freedom—we all have our defects. Yet, in those mostly Western countries that have had capitalism there has been far more freedom, far more social justice, and less inequality than in the centrally controlled countries.

The question that you have to ask is, has socialism failed because its good qualities were perverted by evil men who were in charge? Was it simply because Stalin took over from Lenin that communism went the way it did? Has capitalism succeeded despite the immoral values that pervade it? I believe that the answers to both questions are in the negative. The results have occurred because each system has been true to the values it encourages, supports, and develops in the people who live under that system.

In discussing moral values here, we are concerned with those that have to do with the relations between people. In judging relations between people, I do not believe that the fundamental value is to do good to others whether they want you to or not. The fundamental value is not to do good to others as you see their good. Neither is it to force them to do good.

I believe that the fundamental value in relations among people is to respect the dignity and the individuality of fellow men to treat them not as objects to be manipulated for our purposes or in accordance with our values but as persons with their owns values—as persons to be persuaded not coerced, not forced, not bulldozed, not brain-washed. That seems to me to be the fundamental value in social relations. *(Words: 766)*

| PRECIS |

Capitalism Versus Socialism

Capitalism or Socialism and Central planning are not ends in themselves. They are the means to achieve certain cherished goals in life. No values can be attached to them. It is the results and not the intentions that matter. Socialism aims at equality and social justice through government ownership and control over the means of production. Yet, no socialist country has been able to realise these aims. Even in Russia which is the pioneer of Socialism, much injustice, oppression and inequality prevails. There are glaring disparities between the elite and the masses. On the contrary, the Capitalist system is based on private property and voluntary exchange. People have disliked it on the presumption that it serves narrow and vested interests only. However, Capitalist countries have shown better results as people there enjoy comparatively more freedom and prosperity, and less injustice and inequality. It would be incorrect to say that socialism or communism was made corrupt by wicked and incompetent rulers or that capitalism has been successful in spite of the prevalence of immoral values in it. No political system can succeed unless its good and moral qualities are sustained. However idealistic any particular system may be, it can be upheld only by ensuring respect for the dignity and individuality of each person, his rights and values, and by guaranteeing his personal freedom. Compulsion and the use of force, or exertion of psychological pressure should give way to gentle urging, reasoning and convincing. This is the fundamental value in inter-personal human relationships in society.

(Words: 253)

Ex. 9

Doing housework, taking care of children, and carrying but assorted jobs of husbands are work just as much as is performing paid employment in an office or factory. To ignore this is to do a disservice to women in the labour force. The reality of housework is that women's work in the home averages 56 hours per week for the full-time homemaker, and 26 hours per week for the employed wife/mother. Husbands and children barely increase their contribution to housework and child care when the wife/mother is in the labour force. As a result, the employed woman with family responsibilities gives up most of her leisure to carry out the responsibilities of family life.

We realize that it may sound strange to hear women's activities in the home called work. Since women who do house work and take care of children receive no salary or wages, home making is not considered "work". Economists have finally helped us to recognize the importance of women's work in the family by estimating the monetary value of homemaking. These estimate range from $4,705 (1968) through $8,200 (1972) to over $13,000 per year (1973), depending on whether the work of the homemaker is considered equivalent to an unskilled, skilled, or a professional worker, respectively. For example, is child care comparable to baby sitting at $0.75 per hour, to a nursery school aid at $03 per hour or to the care of a child psychologist at $30 per hour?

Some people have proposed that the solution to the problems of the employed housewife would be simply to pay women for being housewives; hence, women with heavy family responsibilities would not have to enter the labour force in order to gain income for themselves and/or their families. This is not a solution for many reasons.

Wages provide income, but they do not remedy the isolating nature of the work itself, nor the negative attitudes housewives themselves have towards housework but not towards child care.

Wages for housework would reinforce occupational stereotyping by freezing women into their traditional roles. Unless women and men are paid equally in the labour force and there is no division of labour by sex, women's work in the home will have no value.

Since it is not clear what constitutes housework and we know that housework standards vary greatly, it would be difficult to know how to reward it.

Pay for housework might place homemakers (mainly wives) in the difficult position of having their work assessed by their husbands, while in the case of single homemakers it is not clear who would do the assessing.

Wages for housework, derived from spouse payments, overlook the contribution women make to the society (e.g. by training children to be good citizens), and assume that their work is only beneficial to their own families.

Finally, payment for housework does not address itself to the basic reason women with family responsibilities work: to increase family income over that which the employed husband/father makes. Also, single women with family responsibilities work because they are the family breadwinners.

It may seem puzzling that the hours of US women's home activities have not declined because of the availability of many appliances (washing machines, gas and electric ranges, blenders, etc.) and convenience products (prepared soaps, frozen foods, mixes, dried food, etc.), the truth is that appliances tend to be energy-saving rather than time-saving, and the convenience of appliances has encouraged a rise in the standards of housekeeping. Hence, women today spend more time than their grandmothers doing laundry, since family members demand more frequent changes of clothing today than in earlier generations. Husbands and children expect more varied meals. Advertising encourages women to devote an inordinate amount of time and money to waxing floors, creating rooms free of "odour causing" germs, and seeking to meet other extraordinary standards of cleanliness. Furthermore, the increasing concern with good nutrition means that many homemakers are spending more time preparing foods that are not available in the market place, or which are only available at great costs.

(Words: 671)

PRECIS

Should Housewives be Paid?

The amount of household work carried out by women in different capacities is equivalent to paid employment in an office or factory. Employed women work even more to look after the family life and its responsibilities. Women's housework however, is never considered work at all. Economists have finally calculated the monetary value of women's housework in the family and have made us realize its great importance. It has been suggested that women should be paid for their household duties and responsibilities. However, it does not sound to be a very practical and satisfactory solution to the problem for several reasons. Women's work in the home has no value unless men and women are treated at par with each other for payment in the labour force. It would also be difficult to assess the housework for the purpose of payment. Household duties like care and training of children would not be covered by the salary paid for housework. Besides, women may be employed in offices or factories to increase the family income or may themselves be the bread-winners of the family. The US women's household activities do not occupy less time because of modem gadgets and scientific appliances which are energy-saving rather than time-saving. Furthermore, women have to meet higher standards of cleanliness and greater demands like daily washed clothes and new and nutritious dishes.

(Words: 224)

Ex. 10

Members of both sexes should be represented as whole human beings with human strengths and weaknesses, not masculine or feminine ones. Women and girls should be shown as having the same abilities, interests and ambitions as men and boys. Characteristics, that have been traditionally praised in males such as boldness, initiative, and assertiveness should also be praised in females. Characteristics praised in females such as gentleness, compassion, and sensitivity should also be praised in males.

Like men and boys, women and girls should be portrayed as independent, active, strong, courageous, competent, decisive, persistent, serious-minded, and successful. They should appear as logical thinkers, problem solvers, and decision makers. They should be shown as interested in their work, pursuing a variety of career goals, and both deserving of and receiving public recognition for their accomplishments.

Sometimes men should be shown as quiet and passive, or fearful, indecisive, or illogical or immature. Similarly, women should sometimes be shown as tough, aggressive and intensive. Stereotypes of the logical, objective males and the emotional, subjective females are to be avoided. In descriptions, the smarter, braver, or more successful person should be a woman or girl as often as a man or boy. In illustrations, the taller, stronger person should not always be male, especially when children are portrayed.

Women and men should be treated with the same respect, dignity, and seriousness. Neither should be trivialized or stereotyped, either in text or in illustrations. Women should not be described by physical attributes when men are being described by mental attributes or professional position. Instead, both sexes should be dealt with in the same terms. Reference to a man's or a woman's appearance, charm, or intuition should be avoided when irrelevant.

In descriptions of women, a patronizing or girl-watching tone should be avoided, as should sexual innuendoes, jokes, and puns. Examples of practices to be avoided: focusing on physical appearance (a buxom blonde); using special female-gender word forms (poetess, aviatrix, usherette); treating women as sex objects or portraying the typical woman as weak, helpless, or hysterical; making women figures of fun or objects of scorn and treating their issues as humorous or unimportant.

In descriptions of men, especially men at the home, references to general ineptness should be avoided. Men should not be characterized as dependent on women for meals, or clumsy in household maintenance, or as foolish in self-care.

To be avoided: characterizations that stress men's dependence on women for advice on what to wear and what to eat, inability of men to care for themselves in times of illness, and men as objects of fun (the henpecked husband)

Women should be treated as part of the rule, not as the exception. Generic terms, such as doctors and nurses, should be assumed to include both men and women, and modified titles such as "woman doctor" or "male nurse" should be avoided. Work should never be stereotyped as "women's work" or "a man-sized job". Writers should avoid showing a "gee-whiz" attitude toward women who perform competently. ("Though a woman, she ran the business as well as any man.")

Women should be spoken of as participants in the action, not as possessions of the man. Terms such as pioneer and settler should not be used as though they applied only to adult males.

(Words: 545)

PRECIS

Equality of the Sexes

Men and women should be depicted as whole and individual human beings. They should not be characterized by traditional attributes of their sexes. Women should be shown to have the same practical, positive and objective attitudes as men. Similarly, men should also be represented as having unreasonable, subjective and negative attitudes. In the portrayal of children, girls should often be shown as strong and even domineering. Both men and women should be treated with equal respect and dignity. While the outworn traditional attributes of each sex should end, their physical attributes should be avoided as far as possible. The sexist approach of viewing women as sex objects, cracking jokes at their expense and satirizing their issues, should be avoided. Likewise, men should not be characterized and ridiculed as overdependent on, and dominated by women. The various spheres of activity should not be characterized by sexist demarcations but should include both men and women. Writers should avoid an attitude of disbelieving surprise at women's competence and efficacy. Women should be spoken of as active participants and not as men's possessions. Besides, women are as much initiators and originators as men.

(Words: 189)

Ex. 11 ______________________________

The advance of science and technology makes it definitely possible to solve most of the economic problems of the world and in particular, to provide the primary necessities of life to everyone all over the world. It holds the promise of higher standards and avenues of cultural development opening out. Today the Welfare State and even a classless society are not the ideals of socialism only, but are accepted by capitalist countries also, even though the approaches are different. Thus, the basic ideals come nearer to each other and there is a possibility of approaching those objectives even though the methods might be different. These methods will not only be based on some logical theories, but will have to depend upon the background and cultural development of a community of a country—geographical, historical, religious, economic and social. Any real change cannot easily be imposed. It has to grow. A country, especially one with an old civilization, has deep roots in the past, which cannot be pulled out without great harm, even though many weeds in the form of harmful or out-of-date customs and institutions can and should be pulled out. Even as Nature establishes some kind of an equilibrium which cannot be disturbed suddenly without untoward results appearing, so also in a community or a country, it is not easy or desirable to upset old ways of living too suddenly. The attempt to solve a problem in this way might well lead to graver and more difficult problems.

This applies to the external world we live in; much more so does it apply to the inner life of human beings. In dealing with tribal and somewhat primitive societies, it is well known that an attempt at too rapid a change has led to disastrous consequences. The more developed societies may not suffer so much from rapid change, but in the jet age and the coming age of space travel no one knows what biological and other changes may take place.

If that is so externally, then surely even greater changes would take place in the mind, emotions and spirit of man. Man today, as never before in human history, has to live with change as a permanent partner, in his activities and his institutions. Indeed, he cannot keep pace with this change and though he uses the products of science and technology, he seldom understands them. Education is supposed to develop an integrated human being and to prepare young people to perform useful functions for society and to take part in collective life. But when that society is changing from day to day, it is difficult to know how to prepare and what to aim at. There is a lack of harmony between a highly technical civilization and the older forms of social life and the philosophy underlying them. The relationship to Nature changes, and even the relationship to one's own personality diminishes in a mechanical society. The individual loses himself in the mass and tends to become merely an instrument in a complex setup which is constantly aiming at social and economic improvements of the group as a whole.

Many of us attach great value to the development and the freedom of the individual. Ideological backgrounds help or hinder in this process. But perhaps the most potent factor in diminishing the value of individual personality is mechanisation and automation.   *(Words: 561)*

PRECIS

Man and the Machine Age

Scientific and technological progress has realized the possibility of providing basic amenities of life to the whole of mankind. It has given hope for the people. The goals of establishing a Welfare State and a classless society are identical in Socialist and Capitalist systems although their approaches may be different. Their realization will require an over-all, wide-ranging cultural and environmental change as change has to be evolutionary. A country, especially with a glorious past and an ancient civilization, cannot be divested of its old traditions, practices and institutions by one stroke, howsoever outworn, or even harmful, they may be. Any such effort to bring sweeping changes in a comparatively backward and undeveloped society would be catastrophic. Besides, sudden changes would affect human consciousness. The modern age is characterized by constant, rapid changes. Although education seeks to develop an all-round and sociable human personal—or the welfare of the society, rapid social changes involve confusion and vagueness. There is a conflict between the technical civilization of today and the old social values and principles. Individuality suffers from mechanization as it is made to subserve the larger interests of the society and common good. The cherished value of individual liberty for human development may be controlled or promoted by a particular ideology. But, materialism tends to subvert the individual personality by treating human beings as robots or machines.   *(Words: 226)*

Ex. 12 _______________________________

Treasure hunting is almost as old as man; scientific archeology is a modern development, but in its short life of about seventy years it has done marvels. Thanks to excavation, thousands of years of human history are now familiar which a hundred years ago were a total blank; but this is not all, perhaps not even the most important part. The old histories, resting principally on written documents, were largely confined to those events which at every age writers thought most fit to record—wars, political happenings, the chronicles of kings—with such side lights as could be gleaned from the literature of the time. The digger may produce more written records, but he also brings to light a mass of objects illustrating the arts and handicrafts of the past, the temples in which men worshipped, the houses in which they lived, the setting in which their lives were spent; he supplies the material for a social history of a sort that could never have been undertaken before.

A single excavation is not likely to yield a complete or a continuous record, but by the time a number of sites have been dug the sum of the results worked out by the field archaeologist and his collaborators will be a genuine addition to history. Today we can read, as our grandfathers could not, the story, vivid and circumstantial of civilization newly unearthed and epochs in man's experience which until recently were literally 'dark ages', and, realising that of all this we have perhaps no contemporary written evidence, or virtually none, some may have been inclined to doubt its value, mistrusting the imagination which seems to base so much on a few potsherds. There must be imagination if life is to be breathed into the dry bones of a dead civilization, but imagination which has not been allowed to run riot: the value of the few potsherds as documents for the building up of history depends on the scientific methods which the archaeologist employs in his work: accurate observation and faithful record are preliminary to any reconstruction.

The prime duty of the field archaeologist is to collect and set in order material not all of which he can himself deal with at first hand. In no case will the last word be with him; and just because that is so his publication of the material must be minutely detailed, so that from it others may draw not only corroboration of his views but fresh conclusions and more light. Should he not then stop at this?

It might be urged that the man who is admirably equipped to observe and record does not necessarily possess the powers of synthesis and interpretation, the creative spirit and the literary gift which will make of him a historian. But no record can ever be exhaustive. As his work in the field goes on. The excavator is constantly exposed to impressions too subjective and too intangible to be communicated, and out of these, by no exact logical process, there arise theories which he can state, can perhaps support, but cannot prove: their proof will depend ultimately on his own calibre, but in any case they have their value as a summing up of experiences which no student of his objects and his notes can ever share. Granted that the excavator is adequate to his task, the conclusions which he draws from his own work ought to carry weight, and he is bound to put them forward; if they are palpably wrong then his observations also may justly be held suspect.

Between archaeology and history there is not a fenced frontier, and the digger who will best observe and record his discoveries is precisely he who sees them as historical material and rightly appraises them: if he has not the power of synthesis and interpretation he has mistaken his calling. It is sure that he may not possess any literary gifts and that, therefore, the formal presentation of results to the public may be better made by others; but it is the field archaeologist who, directly or indirectly, has opened up for the general reader new chapters in the history of civilized man. By recovering from the earth such documented relics of the past as strike the imagination through the eye, he makes real and modern what otherwise might seem a far off tale.   *(Words: 727)*

PRECIS

Archaeology's Contribution to History

Although treasure hunting has fascinated man from earliest times, archaeology in its more sophisticated form has developed recently. It has enabled an insight into the human past, totally unknown till very recently. Whereas history gives written accounts of very important events and the lives of kings, along with some incidental knowledge from the literature of those times, archaeological excavations unravel the various faces of the society and culture of an age. Excavations of numerous sites throw more light on history. The momentous events in newly-found out civilizations are authentically known to us unlike our ancestors. However, for want of written evidence, some people pass off information from mere excavations of potsherds as attributes of the digger's imagination. But, if assumptions on the basis of broken pottery are based on scientific methods, precise observation and unbiased accounts of the archaeologist, they can be of immense value to history. Archaeologists should collect all the relevant material in a systematic manner. However, his accounts cannot be taken as authoritative for there may not be a unanimity among experts about them, and more knowledge, opinions, and decisions could be coming. No account can be comprehensive and sometimes the excavator's subjective ideas too may carry weight. But, if he is unable to prove his views, his observations may be considered questionable. Archaeology and history are not entirely separate subjects. Although he may lack literary talents, an excavator's precision in his observations and annotations, proper synthesis, interpretation and critical examination could be a great asset in the cause of history for providing evidence and enlightenment of the past.

(Words: 262)

Ex. 13 _______________________

During the nineteenth century—at any rate in this country—there grew up a curious prejudice in favour of a native form of realistic art. It was an art, or rather a technique, which we call naturalistic, and we may describe any prejudice in its favour as curious because, if you examine the history of art from the earliest times, you will find that this kind of art is extremely rare. It is only at long intervals and usually in somewhat luxurious and decadent periods, that artists have tried to give in their paintings and sculpture an exact representation of what the eye sees. Now that we have photography—even coloured photography—there is no longer the excuse of recording the appearances of things, which was one of the functions of the artist in the past. But in the past that function was always considered a minor one, and the most exact artists, like the Dutch painters of flower pieces, have never been great artists. Great artists have always had what we rightly regard as a higher aim. They have always desired not merely to make a record, but to express an idea, even a point of view or judgement, and to do this with the proper materials of their art Thus the great masters of European art—Giotto Michelangelo, Rembrandt, Rubens, El Greco—such artists do not give you exact pictures of the natural world—they create a world of their own which is an imaginary world, bearing little or no relation to the appearance of nature.

Modern art is essentially an insistence on that freedom of artistic creation. In that sense it is merely a return to well established traditions.

That is all very well, it might be said, but there are limits. Liberty is not licence: the old masters, however free in their compositions, did at any rate base their art on realistic elements. However, imaginative their scenes and subjects, a man is always recognisably a man, a tree a tree, and so on. In your modern picture we never know whether we are looking at a man or a tree.

The truth is that art has no limits. Art is anything that can be imagined, and expressed. But living as we do in particular circumstances and with particular desires and experiences, the art of our time is not so indeterminate. It is something determined by our social and economic conditions, and by the ideas and habits we inherit from the past.

Those conditions are continually changing. Just as our social and economic conditions change, so do our habits and ideas. We change our houses and our clothes, our food and our morals. We change our art. But just as there are people who cling on to old fashions in houses and clothes, food and customs, so there are people who want to retain old fashions in painting and sculpture. And if we belong to a younger generation we say of such people that they are old-fashioned prejudiced.

I should like to suggest that the prevalent misunderstanding of modern art is due, not so much to a lack of sensibility, not even to blank ignorance of the aims of the modern artist, but simply to this sort of prejudice. We go about with a certain preconception of what art ought to be like; it is a narrow conception derived from our environment, from the education we have had, and from the economic limitations imposed on our mode of life. I do not say this in any kind of snobbish spirit. Indeed, the most limited people may be those who have enjoyed all the privileges of wealth and rank— who are, so to speak, heirs to a particular tradition. They inherit their culture along with the rest of their heirlooms, and it is they who most strenuously resist change and dispossession.

Surely these people, who inherit their culture and preserve it unchanged, are not the true traditionalists. Tradition is not a heritage; it is rather an active principle, a principle we apply to solve particular problems; and since the problems change with every age, so must the solutions. From this point of view, modern art is not fundamentally revolutionary or subversive. It only seems to be revolutionary because it insists on developing the central tradition of art. And it is not only in art that the return to tradition, or the maintenance of a tradition, takes on the outward appearances of a revolution; we might find plenty of examples in the history of religion and science. *(Words: 758)*

PRECIS

Art and Tradition

An unsophisticated and more realistic form of art came to be favoured during the nineteenth century. It aroused interest for its quite unusual and naturalistic technique. From time to time, artists portrayed and etched out true to life images, which has now been replaced by the modern medium of photography. Unlike the artists who were exact copiers, artists acknowledged as great depicted things based on their own imagination and not on nature. Modern art too emphasises imaginative creations which, in a way, is a return to tradition. However, an artist's creative freedom is not absolute and is based on reality so far as the basic forms of life and nature remain unchanged. Art is based on imagination and personal expression but is determined by socio-economic conditions and cultural heritage which are ever changing. Every sphere of life changes and the youth decries the bias towards the old system. The prevailing misunderstanding of modern art is mainly because of the prejudiced concept of art formed by our education, environment and status. Perhaps the most narrow-minded people in this regard are from the affluent and privileged classes who seek possessive inheritance of tradition and oppose change. But tradition is not heritage, it is a force that helps in finding solutions to specific problems which themselves keep changing. Thus, modern art does not seek to overthrow but only improve and develop the very tradition of art. This gives it a revolutionary appearance; as is also the case of tradition in religion and science. *(Words: 250)*

Interview

An interview is a conversation with a purpose. It involves the selector and the candidate. No doubt calibre and suitability of the candidate is very important, but equally important is the performance at an interview.

Interview is really face-to-face situation. A complete knowledge and plus-points of candidates are of paramount importance. A candidate must reveal his very best and most accurate aspects. He must tell interviewing officer about his qualification, experience and other particulars in a lucid, concise, confident and precise manner. A candidate, while being interviewed must always be polite, never lose temper and never be arrogant.

The way a candidate presents himself goes a long way to impress the interviewer. Pre-interview preparation is the key to a good interview. Nervousness often leads to poor performance.

Though the situation and atmosphere are tense-enough for the candidate, yet you should keep cool and normal as this is the grand-finale of the whole show and any mistake on your part due to tension or nervousness may spoil the whole show. Just have confidence in your knowledge and ability, and answer truly and logically whatever is asked from you. Keep in mind that you present yourself in the best possible manner and they are there only to select the best ones!

It must be remembered that being good at interview is a skill, which is quite different from work-skill. Be prepared and be positive about yourself.

A successful interview means a bright career. It has become an integral part of almost all competitive examinations. Interview is more revealing and important than a written test. It depicts candidate's power of expression, initiative, drive, tact, alertness and self-confidence. Interviewer judges through interview as to whether the candidates has the quality of critical appreciation, clear and logical exposition, balanced judgement, ability for social cohension, leadership qualities, moral integrity and social adaptability. An interview can make or mar your career.

Aim of an Interview

Aim of an interview is to create an opportunity for meeting and talking directly with the candidate. Interviewer and candidate are the real participants in an interview, former asks questions to explore while the latter answers to impress. A successful interview cannot be a one way traffic. It is an occasion for discussion and discovery of inner traits of candidate.

However, interviews do not end with your selection process. They continue throughout your life; whether in official capacity or in your social life. Always try to influence others with your strong points.

Interview Process

In the interview the interviewing officer is either the President or Vice-President of the Selection Board. He assesses the personality of the aspiring candidates. Interviewer has a certain set pattern which he follows while interviewing the candidates. They should be thus fully prepared and conduct themselves properly. They should also be abreast of important world affairs, in addition to national matters.

Remember, the interviewer is a senior officer and President of the Board. Hence, he expects that the interview must be 'productive'. He has to make a right selection. Hence no bluff or fluke will yield any trait. A successful interview is based on a series of question-answers and sense of mutuality between the interviewing officer and the prospective candidate.

During the interview, a candidate must make it a point that he is polite, pleasant to everyone who comes in contact, before, during and after the interview. The nicer you are the more they cooperate with you. You must fit in the group and extend full assistance, when called-upon.

IMPORTANT TIPS

1. Arrive at the place of interview in time and wait for your turn to be called.
2. Greet the staff members present there.
3. Put yourself at ease and establish rapport with those present.
4. Tell truly about your educational qualification and background when asked.
5. Tell the truth and don't bluff. The interviewers are highly educated, fully trained, experienced and well prepared to reveal the truth about you.
6. Your replies should be brief but meaningful, concise and precise.
7. Don't get trapped in over-formality of the interviewers. Take them seriously.
8. Lay stress on :
   (a) principal qualities and skill
   (b) experience/expertise
   (c) profession/occupation.
9. Display confidence, initiative, drive and resourcefulness.
10. Display ability to solve ticklish problems.
11. Display capacity to work under pressure.
12. Display determination and plenty of drive.
13. Avoid giving lengthy and vague answers to questions put by interviewer otherwise interviewer will lose interest in you. Don't talk too much.
14. Make every possible endeavour to avoid the 'pitfalls'.
15. Don't learn by heart any particular answers. You cannot expect exactly the same questions at interview which you have prepared.
16. Act naturally, by showing artificiality you create bad impression in the mind of interviewers.
17. Don't ever feel nervous/awkward. Behave like a genius.
18. Remember that you are giving 'Best' of yourself, hence present yourself in a confident manner without boasting.

Most Frequent Questions Asked at Interviews

1. What are the names of schools/colleges you studied?
2. Which subjects have you studied?
3. What are your educational achievements?
4. What are your most favourite/least favourable subjects?
5. What is the reason for choosing particular course of study?
6. Any training you have undertaken?
7. Tell something about yourself and :
   (a) Your strong points   (b) Your weakness
8. Tell us about your family background.
9. What is your hobby?
10. What are your leisure activities?
11. Which newspaper/periodicals/magazines etc. you read?
12. Which TV programme you like most?
13. Whether you held any appointment in your school/college time?
14. What do you feel if any responsibility devolves upon you?

15. What do you enjoy most?
16. What is your greatest achievement in life?
17. Whether you work with computers?
18. Whether you displayed any drive and initiative? If so explain.
19. Whether you got ability to adjust and get along well with people of different tastes?
20. Whether your present job gives you satisfaction?
21. Explain your working experience.
22. Why do you think you are better than others?
23. How do you get on with your superior?
24. How do you get on with your junior?
25. Tell us about your failure in any walk of life.
26. Tell us about your happiest day in life.
27. Tell us about your saddest day in life.
28. Tell us about your adventurous day in life.
29. Tell us about your funniest day in life.
30. Tell us about the most memorable event in your life.
31. In matter of money and power; which one of the two you prefer and why?
32. Type of people you like to mix-up?
33. How do you justify that you are a competent person for the post?
34. Tell us about the name of the places of interest you have visited?
35. Tell whether you are ambitious or otherwise.
36. Tell us about the place where you were born.
37. Tell us about the machineries, tools, equipments you are familiar with.
38. Why do you want to join the service?
39. Describe any events where you showed act of bravery?
40. Tell us something about your social, cultural, economical and educational status.
41. What is your ambition in life?
42. What will you do if you are not selected?

Positive & Useful Points to Enlist

The following points are of utmost importance while answering at the time an interview :

1. To tell about your skills, potentials and achievements.
2. To tell about your co-curricular activities during school or service career.
3. To tell about your initiative, drive, organising ability, communication ability, energy, sense of responsibilities, skill, resourcefulness, discipline etc. These positive points will go a long way for a successful candidate. Do not expose your failure and disappointment.
4. Maintain an up-to-date scrap-book containing the undermentioned details:
   (i) Name of school/college (where you studied)
   (ii) Examination passed, marks obtained and subjects studied
   (iii) Educational achievements
   (iv) Best subject you excelled
   (v) Co-curricular activities and prizes etc. you have won
   (vi) Any particular training you have received
   (vii) Extra skill to your credit
   (viii) Work which you found most satisfying
   (ix) Any appreciation you received for your performance
   (x) Name of Papers/Magazine/Periodical you read
   (xi) Your hobbies
   (xii) Your favourite game
5. To tell about your leadership qualities like initiative, drive, stamina etc.
6. To tell about your quality to get well with your colleagues.

Dress, Appearance, Behaviour & Etiquettes

1. Dress of a person is certainly a pointer to his personality. Your dress should be properly fitted and nicely ironed. Hair should be cut. Clothes need not be gaudy and expensive. Your shoes must be polished and cleaned.
2. Before entering the interview room just knock at the door. When called-in greet the interviewing officer. Don't offer your hand first for handshake.
3. Don't take seat unless you are asked by the officer and thank him after taking seat.

4. Be natural and sit-comfortably and do not be stiff.

5. When asked a question, pause for a while, think out answer and then reply.

6. If you have not understood the question, get it clarified.

7. Your speech should be natural (neither loud nor slow). Speak clearly and confidently.

8. Give due respect to interviewing officer. Be polite and clear in your language.

9. Your answers should be brief and to the point.

10. Be careful about your mannerism. Don't fiddle with any part of your body.

11. Don't bluff the interviewer. You should be straight forward and truthful. If you don't know the answer, say, 'sorry sir, I don't know'.

12. If you make a false statement or apply 'fluke', you lose your point.

13. Don't get irritated or become arrogant. Give answer politely. Remain cool.

14. Behave nicely and don't be assertive. Don't bear gloomy/serious look, while being interviewed. Always have a smiling face.

15. After the interview is finished, say thanks and good-bye and then leave the room keeping the chair properly.

Do's and Don'ts at Interview

Important Do's

A Day Before the Interview:

1. Select the dress or outfit you are going to wear and make sure that it is clean, well-ironed and without any missing buttons. Make sure that your outfit suits the occasion.

2. Ensure that your shoes are well-polished and that you have a matching pair of socks.

3. If you wear a turban, make sure that it is clean, matches your outfit and neatly tied.

4. Collect all your certificates, marksheets, and other relevant papers and file them in chronological order in a neat folder.

5. Go through your resume, marksheets and certificates and mentally prepare yourself to answer questions on your bio-data.

6. Brush up your general knowledge and collect important facts on current events especially those about your own state, India and the world.

7. Ensure that you have a pocket comb and your wrist watch is showing correct time.

8. Take your interview call letter (if any) and put it on the top of your folder containing your marksheets and certificates.

9. Listen to/view the late night news bulletin and take note of any important news items.

On the Day of the Interview:

1. Read the morning newspapers and note important headlines.

2. Listen to/view the latest news bulletin.

3. Get ready a little before time so that you have sufficient time available for collecting your folder and other things to avoid a last minute panic.

4. Try to reach the venue of the interview before time.

5. While you are waiting to be called in, converse with other candidates and discuss with them, without making noise, important current affairs and news items of the day.

6. Before entering the interview room make sure to switch-off your mobile phone.

During the Interview:

1. Enter the room after seeking permission and close the door after you. Make sure that you are courteous throughout. Wish the interviewers appropriately. Remember to say "Please" "Thank you" etc, as often as you can.

2. Be comfortable and relaxed. You have no reason to suffer from any inferiority complex. You want to be selected and interviewers before you have the task of finding a suitable candidate. Therefore, you must meet equals.

3. If confronted with odd or confusing questions don't become nervous. Instead try to answer with clarity and confidence.

4. Be attentive and alert throughout the interview.

5. Speak in clear voice and make sure each word is audible to board members.

6. Be a good listener so that you know what is being asked. If you are unable to understand any question, request the interviewer to repeat it saying "I beg your pardon." Don't start your answer until you have understood what is being asked.

7. Give well-thought out and balanced answers but be prompt so that the interviewers are able to ask as many questions as they like to have a proper judgement. You can do that only by giving your best.

8. Be relaxed throughout without showing any sign of anxiety and nervousness. Try to give the impression of being an ambitious young person willing to take on any challenge.

9. Look at all members one by one while addressing your answers. Do not stare all the time at the president or any particular member of the board.

10. When you are replying to a question asked by any particular member, look at him directly and address your answer to him.

11. Maintain a pleasant expression throughout. You should not look ill at ease, anxious or bored.

12. While discussing a serious problem, you should adopt a serious expression. You cannot continue to smile when a grave or tragic situation is being discussed.

13. If the president or any member appreciates your approach or the point you have made, take opportunity to immediately thank him for the compliment.

After the Interview:

1. Keep sitting calmly. Get up only when someone asks you to do so.

2. Thank the president and members of the board while getting up.

3. After the interview, if the interviewer extends his hand, shake hands with him confidently and thank him while holding his hand firmly. Do not take a feeble grip as it shows that you have an inferiority complex and lack of self-confidence. A firm grip, on the other hand indicates your confidence.

4. Put your chair in its proper place with grace and confidence.

5. Turn and move out of the room confidently gently closing the door behind you.

Important Don'ts

On the Day of the Interview:

1. Don't study late at night before the interview. A full night sleep is must before the interview to remain fresh and fit during the course of the day.

2. Don't eat a heavy breakfast on the day of your interview as it might make you feel uncomfortable, drowsy or heavy.

During the Interview:

1. Don't forget to close the door after you while entering the interview hall.

2. Don't forget to seek permission before coming in—Ask "May I come in Please".

3. Don't forget timely situation when you have reached near the table of the selectors. Greet them appropriately.

4. Don't sit down on your own. Wait for their instruction to take a seat then you should say "Thank you Sir."

5. Don't start on your own. Let them initiate the interview proceeding..

6. Don't speak too fast. Let every word you speak be clear and audible to all the members.

7. Don't have artificial or excessive gesticulation. Try to be as normal and relaxed as possible.

8. Don't be emotional on any particular point just to win the favour of the interview board.

9. Don't interrupt the selectors. Let the interviewer complete his question. Only after he has finished speaking, in case you have not followed, you may request him to repeat.

10. Don't enter into any arguments with the president or any member of the board.

11. Don't try to avoid questions. If consecutively two or more members have put their questions, reply to each one in the same order.

12. Don't give evasive or confusing answers. If you are not sure of something, be frank and politely and say "Sir, I am not aware of such a thing", or "I am sorry I do not know" or, "Excuse me Sir".

13. Don't fiddle around with your buttons, your hair or anything else as it shows your nervousness.

14. Don't change your stand and be consistent in the line of argument you have chosen. Do not give self-contradictory or conflicting answers.

15. Don't readily agree with everything the interviewer says if you have valid arguments to support your point of view. In case of disagreement, be polite and say "I beg to differ Sir", and try to convince him of your own view point.

16. Don't try to gain favour of the president or any of the members by giving a biased opinion which you think might please him. This will not show your maturity or integrity.

17. Don't enter into any political controversy. Never try to gain the favour of the interviewers by speaking against or in favour of any particular community.

18. While arguing a point, don't give up until the topic is changed by the interviewer.

19. Don't miss any opportunity to compliment the interviewer.

After the Interview:

1. Don't extend your hand for a handshake with any interviewer yourself. Let him offer his hand first if he wants.

2. While leaving the room don't turn back to look at the members. Don't forget your manner of leaving the hall because it is being observed by the interview board.

3. Don't forget to gently close the door behind you.

THE INTERVIEW PATTERN

The interview pattern is a four step process usually followed at all Selection Boards. The candidates are asked various type of questions with several questions intertwined in each question to check their grasp, mental alertness, knowledge and confidence level, and their qualities are assessed based on their responses. The candidate must listen to the questions very attentively and try to answer them in the sequence they are asked.

Types of Interview Questions:

1. Introduction Questions
2. Probing Questions
3. General Knowledge Questions
4. Practical Knowledge Questions

Let us now discuss in detail about the type of questions and way of approach to these questions.

1. Introduction Questions:

Usually this type of questions are put to the candidates in the beginning on their entry into the panel. The Interviewing Officer (IO) asks some basic questions which can be easily answered by the candidate so that the candidate feels at ease with the IO.

The questions may be like :
1. Tell something about your name and why you are named so?
2. Which place you are coming from and tell us something about that place?
3. Tell five things about your native place and which one you like most?

The first question is quite easy to answer for all.

For the second question, answer should be like this for a candidate from Delhi.

Sir I am from Delhi, a northern city of India which is also the capital of India. The population is about .... and the main occupations of people are .... The speciality is .... and the special things are ...., etc.

This way, the answer should cover over all aspects of Delhi. This gives a broad approach of your answer and it shows your knowledge also.

The answer given to the IO should be crystal clear, positive and truthful. It is easy to answer most of the introduction questions.

2. Probing Questions:

This part plays a major role in the process and occupies most of the time of the interview. This part carries two types of questions :

• Stress Questions • Rapid Fire Questions

Stress Questions : The stress questions reveal the original personality of the candidate. Normally it is easy to answer all the questions without losing temper if we have good communication skills, but answering stress questions is the real success and only the candidate with real officers like qualities will cross this hurdle easily.

They test whether under stressful and hard situations the candidate maintains his originality and keeps his position with good decision-making and solution-finding abilities.

They keep on asking more questions on the same area until you lose your temper or you exhaust your knowledge on that. They continue and try to break the ground of the candidate. In such situations the candidate has to keep smiling and answer the questions by showing his knowledge without bluffing. If you don't know the answer, better tell the IO, "Sorry sir, I don't know".

This is the way the IO checks the pulse and the truthfulness of the candidate being interviewed.

Rapid Fire Questions : These are a set of several questions which are asked in one go. These nearly ten to fifteen questions will be triggered out by the IO to check how many questions are followed by the candidate and answered well and how truthful he is with his replies.

These questions may start from your educational background, views about parents, teachers, friends' view about you and your view over them. Your hobbies and interests at free time, checking leadership qualities by asking your extra-curricular activities and how you will organize a task or situation, games and sports etc. you like and play.

Rapid Fire Questions are mostly raised from the Bio Data only. So prepare a Bio Data of your own, frame a set of questions and prepare the answers. Also check the answers critically.

Following questions may be raised from the Bio Data in the Rapid Fire Questions round:

From Educational Background:

- How much did you score in your tenth, twelfth and graduation exam?
- Why there is decrease in the marks level and what have you done to overcome the difficulty?
- Tell us about your achievements in the study.
- Which subject you like most and why?
- Which subject you don't like and why?
- Tell us about speciality of your school and college.

- Which teacher you liked most and why?
- Which teacher you didn't like and why?
- Why have you chosen to study this branch?
- Whether you have chosen the particular branch of study by self or by others' compulsion?
- Why there is a gap in studies between twelfth class and graduation?
- How you improved the percentage from tenth to twefth and what steps you have taken to achieve this?
- If you have scored less marks in twelfth than in tenth, the questions is—what are the steps you have taken to overcome this in graduation?
- What do your friends and teachers think about you?
- What do you think about your friends and teachers?

From Family Background:

- How much you like your father and mother?
- You are close to your father or mother and why?
- How do you help your father?
- How do you help your mother in your free time?
- How much pocket money you got in your school/college days and how did you utilize it?
- How responsible you are a person to your family?
- Tell us about your brother and sister.
- Whom do you like most in your family and why?
- With whom you play more?
- Which person, other than in your family and friends, you like most and why?
- What is your father/mother's rank in the working place and income they are getting?
- How are they utilizing their income and are you satisfied with that, if not, why?
- If your family becomes totally dependent on you tomorrow, how you will you run the family?

From Friendship:

- How many friends do you have?
- Which type of friends you like?
- How will you get new friends?
- Out of friends, how many are close to you?
- In your friends with whom you share the personal things?
- What do you like in your best friend and what does he like in you?
- What do your friends say about you?
- What do you say about your friends?
- Which thing do you like in your close friend and why?
- How will you help your friend or helped your friend in the past?
- What do you and your friends do in your free time or in holidays?

For Working People:

- Tell something about your company or organization?
- What do you say about your boss?
- What does your boss say about you?
- What do your co-workers say about you?
- What do you like most in your job?
- What you don't like in your job?
- What difficulty you faced in your job and what are the steps you have taken to overcome that difficulty?
- Why are you leaving your present job?

From Hobbies and Interests:

- What is your hobby?
- Why have you chosen this hobby?
- Since when you are having this hobby?
- What are the things you have learnt from your hobby?
- What are the new things you have implemented in your hobby?
- What was your childhood hobby and what are you doing now?
- Why have you changed the childhood hobby to this hobby?

They expect good knowedge of your hobby since everyone has a hobby, but only a candidate with good attitude has detailed information about his hobbies. The different types of hobbies are reading, photography, music, singing, philately, blogging, trekking etc. Form questions based on your hobby and prepare answers of expected questions for interview.

Interests:

- Which news channels, TV shows you see and which newspapers and magazines you read and why?
- Who is the author, publisher, editor, etc of the book/magazine you read?

From Games and Sports:

- Which player do you like most, and why?
- Which game do you like to play, and why?
- Which one would you like more if we say cricket and chess?
- Why have you chosen an outdoor game rather than an indoor game?
- Why have you chosen an indoor game rather than an outdoor game?
- What is your position in the team *i.e.* as a team member or captain?
- Depth of knowledge in the games or sports. *i.e.* questions from size of the play ground/court, rules of the game and recent world records in the game etc may be asked.
- What do you want to improve or suggest for the team in the game/sports you play?

A young person is expected to play a game in his spare time. So every candidate must have a game to play. If you still don't have a game to play, just join a club of your interest and start playing. It also helps you inculcate more OLQs. Also get thorough knowledge of the game which you like, play or used to play in the past.

Checking the Leadership and Organizing Ability:

Leadership and organizing ability is the most important quality of an officer. So this part of the process is very important. They may pose a situation to check your organizing ability and also may ask questions from the CV in the fields of extra-curricular and co-curricular

activities such as N.C.C. and N.S.S. etc. They may pose different situations and ask questions over them.

Co-curricular and Extra-curricular Activities:

The co-curricular and extra-curricular activities include N.C.C., N.S.S. etc.

- When did you join N.C.C./N.S.S. and why?
- Who motivated you to join N.C.C./N.S.S.?
- Which positions were held there by you?
- Which certificate you got, A, B or C?
- What have you achieved there?
- What have you learnt there?

3. General Knowledge Questions:

In this part the IO may ask questions on national issues, world issues and your solution to those issues. Also he checks the depth of your knowledge and approach to solve the issues.

e.g., He may ask for your views on corruption and then ask for your solution to this.

General Knowledge and Current Affairs: They may also ask some questions on General Knowledge, Defence Matters, History and Current Affairs of India and the World.

e.g., Tell us three news you recently read in newspaper. Tell in detail about a particular news.

4. Practical Knowledge Questions:

If you are from technical background, they may ask some basic technical questions relating to day to day life.

e.g., if you say that you play Cricket, he may ask, "How you will apply Physics Law to the swing bowling?" Also you may have to apply the Pythagoras theorem to the Table tennis service.

Note: You will find many important interview question-answers in the coming pages in various "Model Interviews". You need not learn the answers by heart but study and understand the manner in which questions are asked and answered.

MODEL INTERVIEWS

MODEL INTERVIEW NO. 1

Mr. Arpan is a young man five feet nine inch tall. He is well-built but looks slim if not lean for his tall stature. He is fair complexioned with a pink shining glow on his cheeks. He has an oval face and on his head his pitch black hair glistens brightly in the bright light of the fluorescent tube. He has medium sized black moustaches. In his white shirt and black pants he looks like a real hero. He wears a powerful red tie which seems to daze one's eyes if one chooses to stare at it continuously for a few moments. The brass buckle with which he ties his pants gives a shining glitter. He wears highly shining well-polished black shoes with a sharp tip which make his feet prominently touching the floor as he walks towards the panel table.

Mr. Arpan stands for a moment beside the empty chair and with a half smile in his eyes and an expanding glow on his cheeks, wishes the President and other five members of the panel in one go. He bows slightly while wishing. His right hand twitches slightly unobserved by the members of the panel as if he were going to salute them.

President : Mr. Arpan, please take your seat. (The President starts looking intently at the papers lying under his nose.)

Arpan : Thank you, Sir. (He slightly but very softly pushes the chair a little backwards and adjusts it to its normal position after sitting down in it. He hardly let make any audible sound while doing so.)

President : Mr. Arpan, you have cleared the written test. Will you please tell us for how many months did you prepare for it?

Arpan : Sir, preparation for an examination is, in fact, a long process. Even in my childhood, I used to play the role of an intelligence officer or police in my games. Right from my primary classes, I made up my mind to be in the intelligence service. However, for this particular test. I worked hard day and night for about six months.

President : Don't you think, Mr. Arpan, that getting through an examination is just a chance?

Arpan : No Sir, I don't think so. There is no doubt that the written test was quite hard but I was thoroughly prepared for it. I had already made myself conversant with the syllabus and collected the information regarding tests which were put to the students during past few years. So I had well planned my examination strategy.

President : By the way, what is the real meaning of the word 'strategy'.

Arpan : Sir, the literal meaning of the word 'strategy' is the art of planning operations in war especially of the movement of armies and navies into favourable positions for fighting. However, in real life, the word is used in connection with the skill in managing any affair.

President : You have just mentioned war and movement of armies and navies. Can you please say briefly what the army is constituted of?

Arpan : Sir, the Army is constituted of the Infantry, Armoured Corps, Artillery, Engineers, Communication, Medical Corps, and other support troops who take care of clothing, food,

President : What is the main function of the Armed troops and how is it carried out?

Arpan : Sir, the troops guard the country's borders and are trained for combat in all kinds of weather and terrains. Military bases are located all along the front line of control and across the mainland, where troops are maintained and combat exercises are carried out. Continuous training and exercises keep the troops ready for combat. While the Army relies to a great extent on its trained infantry and on guerrilla warfare, it has over the past few years, built upon its strength in equipment, armoured personnel carriers, tanks, missiles, helicopters, airborne artillery, mobile field guns, as well as nuclear power.

President : Mr. Arpan, why do you want to become an intelligence officer?

Arpan : Sir, I have already talked of my interest in it since my childhood. I have a great desire to do some heroic deeds for my country.

President : Would you like to say a few words about the bravery of our Kargil heroes and our duty in this respect?

Arpan : Sir, our jawans gave proof of their matchless valour there. The bravery displayed by our jawans and by daring young officers during the Kargil conflict should serve as an example to us all. Fighting in inhospitable conditions, and often engaging in hand-to-hand combat with an enemy who had a strategic advantage, our soldiers ejected the Pakistani-backed intruders in the face of odds that were almost insurmo-untable. Sir, all of us must learn a lesson from their sacrifices. We should be imbued with the spirit of patriotism and we must note once for all that freedom and security of the country can be safeguarded only by being ready to make any sacrifice any time in case of a surprise attack. Even the President of India said in his Independence Address to the nation that we must ever be ready for a surprise attack.

President : Do you think there were indications of Taliban's agenda for Kashmir even before the Kargil conflict?

Arpan : Sir, it was in October, 1998 that it was revealed in an article in the Hindustan Times that in an interview to daily *Jassarat*, Karachi, Osama Bin Laden said that after the exit of Soviet forces from Afghanistan, he wanted to cross over to Kashmir but was prevented by the Pakistan establishment from doing so. In a recent statement, Harkat-ul-Maujahideen claimed that Taliban were already in Kashmir and many more would be coming to join them soon.

President : Can you quote any other proof?

Arpan : Sir, in the U.S. missile strikes on Taliban training camps in Khost, Afghanistan, as also mentioned in the said article, about two dozen people who died in one of the targeted facilities were being trained for terrorist actions in Jammu and Kashmir.

President : Can you mention any presence of militants from Pakistan?

Arpan : Sir, the presence of militants from Pakistan, Afghanistan and Arab Afghans had been earlier verified from their casualties in the encounters with the security forces.

President : What do you think about the attitude of the Kashmiri people regarding Taliban brand of culture?

Arpan : Sir, the Kashmiris are nurtured in the liberal Sufi-Pandit culture which comprises Hindu-Muslim unity and communal harmony. So they cannot accept the rigid Taliban culture which is based on a narrow interpretation of Islamic canons.

President : Wasn't it that the prototypes of the Taliban had much earlier tried to impose such an ideology on the Kashmiris with the avowed aim of the ultimate arrival of the Taliban?

Arpan : Sir, in retrospect, with the onset of militancy in early 1990, the sponsors and managers of Taliban employed dreadful coercive methods to impose their ideology on Kashmir. Among other things, women were sought to be targeted under the influence of this ideology. The initiatives were also made to blur the ethno-cultural identity of Kashmir known as Kashmiriyat and substitute the Islamic identity enveloped in Rishi (analogous to Sufi order) traditions with a militant and violent Muslim identity. The objective was to create a social base for the future arrival and operations of Taliban in Kashmir.

President : How have the people of Kashmir reacted to the situation in Kashmir?

Arpan : Sir, right from the days of militancy, rather I should say, even during the 1948 Pakistan attack on Kashmir, the Kashmiris have all along been Indians first and last. They have regularly participated in all national and state elections. During the Kargil conflict, they rose as one man to drive away the enemy. Their overwhelming participation in 1999 Parliamentary elections is another pointer in regard to their Indianism, secularism and patriotism.

President : Mr. Arpan, will you please tell us what is Shimla Agreement and what does it say about the Line of Control?

Arpan : Indo Pakistan war of 1971 ended in the cease-fire of December 17, 1971. An agreement known as Shimla Agreement was signed. The Agreement is quite clear about the Line of Control. It says in unambiguous terms that "neither side shall seek to alter it irrespective of mutual differences and legal interpretations."

President : How did the Kargil conflict start?

Arpan : Sir, Pakistan, ever a transgressor, chose to alter the Line of Control and this is how the Kargil conflict started.

President : How did Pakistan plan the venture?

Arpan : As per reports available, in January, 1999, that is about two months before the Lahore Declaration, Pakistan Army Generals had a meeting with Lashkar-i-Toiba mercenaries. A joint plan was drawn out which was to be extended by Inter Services Intelligence of Pakistan, Pakistan Army and Mujahiddin. The plan was to capture mountain heights in Kargil, Batalik and Drass sectors during winter and give a surprise to the Indian army personal as they returned to those peaks on the onset of summer.

President : What was the purpose of this adventure?

Arpan : The purpose of this venture or misadventure as I would like to call it, was to capture the main highway No. 1 running from Leh to Srinagar to cut off Siachin and Ladakh from the rest of India.

President : Who are these Mujahiddin?

Arpan : These Mujahiddin are mercenaries from Afganistan, Arab and Pakistan with small mix of Kashmiri youth who mainly work as porters.

President : Why were the Mujahiddin involved in the venture or misadventure as you have called it?

Arpan : The Mujahiddin were highly motivated young men who had been indoctrinated to start Jehad or holy war in Kashmir. So, it was known that they would fight like a suicide squad. Secondly, and more prominently, as the Pakistan army regulars were to participate in the war on a large scale in the garb of mercenaries, the real inclusion of mercenaries to some extent would give the colouring of Mujahiddin's holy war for liberation of Kashmir rather than Pakistan's aggression against it, in case the plan got unshielded.

President : Can you quote any of Pakistan's worst barbaric actions in the Kargil conflict.

Arpan : Pakistan is a known rogue state and as such the record of its barbaric acts is aplenty in diabolical ink. However, it put itself to shame by brutally murdering Indian soldiers after keeping them as hostages for more than three weeks. A repulsive chapter of barbarism was opened before the world when six bodies were handed over to the Indian Army at Post Number 43 near Kargil. The victims' eyes were gouged out and their facial features, besides other vital organs, were mutilated. At the very worst, the barbarians could have called them "Prisoners of War."

President : What does the term "Prisoners of War" mean and how should such prisoners be treated?

Arpan : The term is commonly used to mean "any person captured or interned by a belligerent power during war". The updated Geneva Convention (1949) gave them clear basic human rights. They were to be removed from the combat zone and humanely treated. The Convention says that physical mutilation is "expressly forbidden". The PoWs are obliged to give no information under duress other than their names, dates of birth, service numbers and ranks. The flouting of the normative rights amounts to war crime.

President : How did the plan get uncovered?

Arpan : Perhaps the entire operation would have gone unnoticed but for the chance discovery of the presence of Pakistani positions by Indian reconnaissance groups in early May. They were surprised to see the bunkers vacated by them during the winter occupied by the enemy troops deep inside the LoC.

President : Can you please say a few words regarding India's beam weapon project?

Arpan : India's beam weapons project was mooted in 1985 by Mr. Chidambram, the then director of Bhabha Atomic Research Corporation, but the actual work started in 1989. The original purpose was industrial, but now it may be defence-oriented. The project comprises the assemblage of a powerful electron accelerating machine which is nicknamed "Kali-5000".

President : How is this beam weapon different from a laser weapon?

Arpan : Bursts of microwave packed with gigawatts of power (one gigawatt is 1,000 million watts) produced by this machine, when aimed at enemy missiles and aircraft will cripple their electronics systems and computer chips and bring them down. According to scientists, "soft killing" by high power microwaves has advantages over the so-called laser weapon which destroys by drilling holes through metal.

President : Can you mention any other rare weapon Indian scientists are capable of manufacturing?

Arpan : Sir, Indian scientists are capable of manufacturing the neutron bomb which can immobilise armies but does not destroy property.

President : You just talked of elections in Kashmir. Can you please mention a few of the electoral reforms suggested by the Law Commission?

Arpan : Sir, the Law Commission has finally given valuable suggestions for reducing the number of parties and independent candidates as contestants for the Lok Sabha or State Assemblies. The formal conversion into a 2-party or a maximum 3-party system now depends on the government. The Commission has also suggested that pre-election alliances should file a declaration with the Election Commission confirming continuance of alliance during full term of Parliament/ Assembly. These reforms were essential prior to declaration of general election.

President : Will you please mention a few other suggestions made by the Commission?

Arpan : Sir, other reforms suggested by this Forum related to a crime-free record of the candidate, party nominating a candidate to be responsible for his/her behaviour, declaration of assets along with nomination papers, educational background, record of service to society, permanent residence of the person during last 10 years in that area from where seeking elections and proper schooling and training to candidates seeking elections.

President : All right, Mr. Arpan you can go now.

Arapn : Thank you, Sir.
(Arpan rises from his chair softly smiling with a beaming face and leaves the room gently.)
(**Comments :** Certainly Mr. Arpan has played his cards well and is most likely to be selected.)

MODEL INTERVIEW NO. 2

Mr Ajay Arora has come for the interview. He is quite a fair complexioned young man from Punjab. He is slim and very cheerful by nature.

Ajay wishes the panel consisting of five members besides the President.

President : Take your seat, Mr Ajay.

Ajay : Thank you, Sir. (He pulls back the chair softly without creating disturbance and occupies the chair).

President : Ajay, you have passed your M.A. Political Science in the 1st division. I presume you must be having a lot of interest in politics.

Ajay : Sir, Politics is not quite the same thing as Political Science which is only an academic subject.

President : Do you mean that politics is the practical form of political science which is theoretical in nature?

Ajay : Sir you may take it like this, but I think there is a lot of difference between the two.

President : What exactly do you want to say, Ajay?

Ajay : Sir, I mean to say that political science is a study of several political theories and "isms" ancient, medieval and modern. As such, it studies the political theories of different political thinkers over the ages. It also has within its purview the emergence, existence and future of the state, its different organs, its present state and its future possibilities. As such it also studies different constitutions of the world.

President : Is political science a branch of science?

Ajay : No Sir, it has its separate identity.

President : Then why is the word 'science' attached to it?

Ajay : Sir, actually political science comes under the heading humanities or arts. But practically this subject is both an art and a science. It is so because it is very close to other humanities subjects like history, civics, sociology, anthropology etc. But in ancient times particularly as established by Aristotle, every subject was studied with exactness and analytically as a science subject. So there are certain set rules in political science.

President : Can you give any particular example?

Ajay : Sir, the simplest example can be the organs of a state.

President : What are those organs?

Ajay : They are :
    1. Sovereignty,
    2. Population,
    3. Territory,
    4. A System of Government.

President : But in science research is always going on and old theories are being replaced by the new ones. Is it so in political science also?

Ajay : It is exactly so in political science also. In the history of mankind there have been several political thinkers who have offered political theories and then there have emerged new thinkers who have changed or reversed the old theories.

President : Can you give any concrete example?

Ajay : Sir, about four thousand years ago, Plato presented his theory of the State. His own disciple Aristotle later changed Plato's theory to a great extent. In recent times Karl Marx topsy-turvied Hegel's Dialectical Spiritualism into Dialectical Materialism.

President : Did Marx himself say anything in this connection?

Ajay : Sir, Marx said, "Hegel's theory was standing on its head; I have made it stand on its feet."

President : Can you give any example in this connection from Indian History?

Ajay : Sir, there is a clear-cut example of M.K. Gandhi and J.L. Nehru. Nehru was the disciple of Gandhi and Gandhi himself practically projected him as his successor. It is true that Nehru propagated or pronunciated to a great extent Gandhi's idea, or what is known as Gandhism but in doing so he brought about several changes in application thereof as he became the first Prime Minister of India.

President : Can you give any concrete example in this connection?

Ajay : Sir, for example Gandhi laid stress on cottage and small scale industries but Nehru went ahead for the setup of heavy industry.

President : Who in ancient Indian history first conceived of heavy industry?

Ajay : Long long ago, Chanakya was the first to think of heavy industry as he wanted to see Chandragupta Maurya to head a world government.

President : What do you think about Alexander?

Ajay : Sir, he wanted to conquer the whole world. Actually, even at that time when the means of communication were not so advanced, the idea of world government was in the air.

President : Who is said to have inspired Alaxander for it?

Ajay : Sir, as history books tell us, it was Aristotle.

President : What did Gandhiji believe about the British colonisation?

Ajay : Sir, Gandhiji firmly believed that British colonisation was the major cause of Indian impoverishment since the transport of Indian cotton, other agricultural raw materials and also ores and other minerals led to the destruction of Indian home industries, a direct cause for massive poverty and unemployment. He was convinced that a return to the large scale revival of home or cottage industries was most essential for reviving Indian economy.

President : Can you quote a few of Gandhiji's own words in this connection ?

Ajay : Once Gandhiji said, "I have found it impossible to soothe suffering patients with a song. The hungry millions ask for one poem—invigorating food!" Another time he stated : "When all around me people are dying for want of food, the only occupation permissible for me is to feed the hungry....To a people famishing and idle, the only acceptable form in which God can dare appear is work and promise of food as wages!"

President : Apart from national security, what in your opinion are the two biggest problems faced by India and how in your opinion can they be solved?

Ajay : Two of the biggest problems faced by India, are, no doubt, mass unemployment and mass migration of people from rural to urban areas. For solving these, there ought to be a combination of efforts in high (usually imported) and low (usually indigenous) technology industries in both urban and rural sectors. But more attention on low technology industries and rural sectors is essential because the large majority of the people live in the rural sectors and the employment potential in low-technology industries is higher.

President : What were Gandhiji's views regarding charity vis-a-vis work?

Ajay : Sir, it is a well known fact of history that during the Swadeshi movement foreign goods were boycotted, foreign cloths were burnt and shops selling foreign goods were picketed. Once when Rabindranath Tagore reproached Gandhiji for not having distributed the valuable clothes among the poor instead of burning them, he replied:
"I must refuse to insult the naked by giving them clothes they do not need instead of giving them the work they

sorely need. The ill-clad or the naked millions of India need no charity, but work."

President : What conclusion do you draw from this about Gandhiji's views?

Ajay : Sir, I infer that :
1. Gandhiji was against charity
2. He was for work
3. He preferred work to charity

President : Can you quote a few words of Gandhiji regarding his attitude to machinery?

Ajay : Gandhiji was not opposed to machinery as such but he was opposed to the fact that it was liable to put innumerable men out of work. Once he told one of his disciples, D. Ramachandran :

"I am not fighting machinery as such, but the madness of thinking that machinery saves labour. Men save labour until thousands of them are without work and die of hunger on the streets. I want to secure employment and livelihood not only to part of the human race, but for all. I will not have the enrichment of a few at the expense of the many. At present the machine is helping a small minority to live on the exploitation of the masses. The motive force of this minority is not humanity and love of their kind, but greed and avarice. This state of things I am attacking with all my might."

President : Gandhiji wished that the Indian capitalists should hold wealth in trust for the welfare of common people of India. Have they come upto Gandhiji's expectations?

Ajay : No, sir, they haven't.

President : What instead do you see?

Ajay : I see an unending sea of hungry and unemployed people and luxury cars fuming petrol, plying on the precarious roads of big cities. Cars in which blind people travel who can't see the vast endless sea all around them.

President : Do you think in India the Parliamentary form of Government should be replaced by the Presidential form?

Ajay : Sir, I think, the main point is that of vision and moral standards in our political and social life. The presidential system is no substitute for national character. It does not afford any alternative to vision, knowledge and moral standards in political life. Moral standards can be attained only after we have begun to impart value-based education to all strata of society. We should remember that in Philippines, the presidential system degenerated into dictatorship of the worst type and this can happen even in India. In America and France, the system is successful because of high morality of the political leaders. I mean high morality as far as political ethics are concerned. Sir, I don't think our political leaders with their moral stature in politics being abysmally low, can be relied upon in the matter of this vital issue.

President : Then what is your firm view?

Ajay : Sir, I am of the firm opinion that instead of taking a fresh look at the working of our Constitution, we must focus attention on building up a sound moral base and devising an ethical code, the absence of which has shaken our faith in the country's political system. The fault lies not in the Constitution, but with the individuals, who have been entrusted with the task of implementing it. If we ourselves are insincere, why should we blame the Constitution in vain?

President : Can you mention any specifically acute problem to which, in your opinion, proper attention is not being given?

Ajay : In my opinion, such a problem is the water problem. India is facing an acute water crisis, with some estimates showing that almost its entire economic growth gets wiped out by the health costs of water pollution. Inaugurating a three day national conference on "The potential of water harvesting", the President of India said leading experts had warned that the world was heading towards "a water shock" which might dwarf the oil crisis.

For India, the shortage of water and its growing pollution has acquired the proportion of a crisis for the people, specially the poorest of the poor. The health costs of water pollution did not get factored into our economic calculations, he added. Stating that historically, Indians had been the world's greatest water harvesters. Mr. President said a people's movement was needed to meet the growing water needs and to protect the water sources. Unfortunately, there is not much noise to air this problem as mainly it concerns the poor. The rich have means to drink costly bottled mineral and other pure water. Scarcity of water can hit even our irrigational projects and finally our food production which means starvation which hangs like a sword of Damocles over the teeming poor.

President : All right Mr Ajay, you can go now.

Ajay : Thank you, Sir. (He gets up slowly with an infectious smile spread across his face and leaves the room in a state of high expectation.)

(**Comments :** There seems not much necessity for explaining that Mr Ajay Arora has covered his interview time in a most useful and impressive way. His manner of speech has been audible, lucid and most convincing. He has been able to set a chain of catechism in a most shrewd and intelligent way which must pay him rich dividends.)

MODEL INTERVIEW NO. 3

Mr. Vijay is a young man with golden hair and bright golden eyes. He wears a pair spectacles. He is tall and lanky.

He has a fair complexion but there is a tinge of pallor on his cheeks. There is a sort of sprightliness in his limbs as he walks with swinging left arm and clinched fist. Before entering the room, he passes his hand first on his face and then through his hair and then walks to the table before the panel.

Although there is a seeming air of artificiality in the mannerism and demeamour of Mr. Vijay, yet his steady and well-measured steps and a straight look towards the members of the Board evinces an abundance of self-confidence in his heart. There is not the least sign of nervousness on his face and his heart seems to be running with its normal rhythm.

Mr. Vijay stands up in front of the President for a moment, greeting him and other members in a very pleasant though semi-serious manner with a half smile which brings a tinge of mild rosiness on his cheeks. Certainly it is not a blush but a natural tinge which betrays an amicability arising out of some deep insight and pondering in the heart.

President : Be seated Mr. Vijay.

Vijay : Thank you, Sir. (He slightly moves back the chair and sits in it. He puts his large long fingered hands on his crossed knees and waits expectantly for some pioneering query.)

President : Mr. Vijay, I find from your Bio-data that all along you have been a good student of literature, you have got fairly high marks in M.A. English. I wonder why you didn't opt for the job of a university or college lecturer? Are you not eligible for the post?

Vijay : Sir, I am quite eligible for the post, as I have got more than fifty five per cent marks in M.A. English and I have also had a good academic record. I do not think it would have been very difficult for me to clear the UGC-NET test.

President : Then why have you opted for an intelligence officer's job instead?

Vijay : Sir, I am fond of adventure and not the job of a teacher; and if I am appointed I can still pursue it in my spare time as a hobby.

President : Mr. Vijay, I do not feel my question is fully answered. What I actually mean is that young brilliant persons like you are much needed in the teaching profession which is the basis of all our sciences and arts. What specifically do you feel wrong about the teaching profession?

Vijay : Sir, I feel in the modern materialistic world the teachers have been greatly downgraded in society and I am by nature very sensitive and am a person of self respect.

President : But you know that even in this job you have to deal with all kinds of people some of whom may show little respect to you?

Vijay : I am sir, aware of this fact. For example the politicians care there hoots for even the highest government personnels. But all the same, I know that an honest man of integrity can keep the politicians and the so-called *dadas* at bay.

President : But is that not possible in the teaching profession also?

Vijay : That may be possible to some extent but I do not feel it can be done with so much effectiveness.

President : How is it so?

Vijay : Sir, there are a number of factors concerning this problem. I shall mention only a few of them:

1. Comparatively low salaries and perks

2. Lack of promotional avenues

3. Lack of post retiral benefits

4. Interference from managements, political parties and bureaucrats

5. An arduous affair of dealing with young mature minds; un-controlled by their parents and additionally misguided by political bosses, Bollywood films, T.V. serials and so on.

6. A virtual cessation of furtherance in knowledge because of lack of incentives and promotional avenues.

7. Lack of discipline in educational institutions which show only a sort of *mela* atmosphere than any sign of seriousness.

8. Irresponsiveness of the student community to the travails of a really hard-working, sincere and

conscientious teacher to show them the right path.

9. General callousness and indifference of society and authorities.

10. A general commercialisation of education not only in private academies but also in government institutions and even in universities.

President : So Mr. Vijay we realise, you do not feel inclined to think of the teaching profession. Will you please tell us how as a government officer you will be able to deliver the goods better?

Vijay : Sir, I am fond of working hard not only for myself but also for the society and for my country. I am aware of the fact that a teacher is nick-named a nation-builder. I think that is a misnomer now. When the society does not provide him proper facilities, it cannot expect of him to build the nation. Previously the teachers were held in high esteem but now it is money that matters. But as they do not have so much money as others they lost their place in society which now pays only lip service to them. As a government officer, if I am appointed at some key post in some key sector I think I can bring some very useful drastic changes in the set-up. (**Comment :** Now probably there was no necessity for talking about the teaching profession again).

President : Well, Mr. Vijay, we are glad to hear all this. From what you have said you seem to be a practical man. But lovers of literature are often men of imagination. Are these two aspects of your nature not contrary to each other?

Vijay : Not at all, Sir. Sir, it is well-known about Napoleon that he had divided his mind into sections and when one section worked, the others remained passive as in the case with various drawers in a chest—a fact which J.L. Nehru has also mentioned in one of his books. So, if you fear that my two apparently contrary aspects will clash against each other, I can say your fears are unfounded, Sir.

President : Mr. Vijay you have been an ardent student of literature and I suppose you must be a great lover of poetry. Poetry is related to nature. Will you like to say something about the seeming "imperfection" of nature?

Vijay : Sir, nature is "natural" rather than symmetrical or perfect. The imperfect arrangement of the heavenly bodies, the petals in the flower or the cells in the bee-hive, often considered a model of creativeness for the greatest poetry, amply demonstrates this fact. But behind this "apparent imperfection" in nature there must exist a "mysterious perfection" which must be "scientific" at the root. One can perceive that poetry must emanate from that "mysterious perfection" and pass through the layer of "apparent imperfection."

President : What is the role of a poet's mind?

Vijay : Sir, the poet's mind, the mirror of all-pervading nature, must reflect both these layers. Hence the reader has to penetrate the poet's mind to understand poetry. But a poem is not a shot from a sling or an arrow from a quiver, nor is it a display of a spectrum from a glass prism. It is a guided missile operating from a dynamic mind in a parabolic curve. But to look for even that symmetry or perfection in poetry is in vain.

However, it is here that the "objectivity" and the "subjectivity" have to balance themselves in poetry.

President : How does poetry operate?

Vijay : Sir, poetry, being the "language of the soul", operates as the "language of silence", where all turbulence ceases and eternal calm prevails. Shelley's words (in A Defence of Poetry) have not, indeed, grown stale yet: poetry "strips the veil of familiarity from the world and lays bare the naked and sleeping beauty which is the spirit of its forms." Thus if "Beauty is eternity gazing at itself in a mirror" as says Khalil Gibran, poetry is the mirror. While the essence of poetry remains the same, its form and structure change with the change of times. It , being analogous to life and nature, can "never be off the rails", as said Mr. Pottle long ago.

President : What does generally happen if we disturb the delicate balance between different seemingly contrary ingredients and literary "isms"?

Vijay : Intrinsically, any preference for or hostility to Romanticism or classicism or realism (or any other "ism") is futile, since we can ignore with impunity neither the fast changing "outer world" we live in nor the pulsating "inner world" which is no less real and alive. Then whenever we disturb this delicate balance between feeling and thought, emotion and intellect, between the subjective and the objective, between the primeval human affections and ratiocinational faculties, between the individual and the social, as often we do, the consequences are usually disastrous.

President : How can we have poetry serve the purpose of life at the present moment?

Vijay : We should endeavour to utilise our energies to have the ancient Indian balanced "inner" and "outer" attitude and enjoy the life as a "whole"—and experience the *"joie de vivre"*, to create in poetry a unison of the "twinkling stars" and the "throbbing heart", feel and realize the past and the future in the immediacy of the present moment, to perceive the nature of distant cosmic galaxies in the soil of our own familiar planet— to bring down to earth the "universal brotherhood" of all men, undistinguished by any "narrow domestic walls".

President : Can you name some great pre-Independence Indian poets who wrote in English?

Vijay : Sir, the most famous among them were Sri Aurobindo and Sarojini Naidu. Tagore is not straightaway an Indo-Anglian poet, but he can be regarded as such, as he himself translated many of his own works, including the Gitanjali, into English.

President : What is common among them?

Vijay : Sir, all three were great poets, patriots and statespersons. Additionally Sri Aurobindo was a great philosopher.

President : Can you name some great post-Independence Indo-Anglian-poets ?

Vijay : Sir, I can name Nissim Ezekiel, Jayanta Mahapatra, Kamala Das, Keki, N. Daruwallah, Shiv. K. Kumar, Vikram Seth, K.S. Gill, R.K. Singh, I.H. Rizvi, D.C. Chambial, O.P. Bhatnagar, T.V. Reddy, I.K. Sharma, Baldev Mirza and some others.

President : What have you to say about the condition of women in the world with particular reference to India?

Vijay : Sir, women have been discriminated against since earliest times. But in

India they were often held in high esteem.

President : How can you substantiate this latter fact?

Vijay : Sir, I can substantiate it from the fact that
1. Number of vedic hymns are said to have been written by women.
2. The names of women scholars and philosophers like Savitri, Gargi, Sita, Draupadi etc. are well-known.
3. A hymn in Sanskrit says that Gods live at the place where women are respected.
4. The women in Aryan times had all kinds of freedom, including choice of their match by themselves through the custom of "Swayamvar."
5. No Vedic Yajna was considered complete without the presence of a woman.

President : How does the modern world treat women?

Vijay : Not quite well, I can say. Nearly 30 countries have not ratified the Convention on the Elimination of All Forms of Discrimination Against Women. One-third of the signatories have substantive reservations. Article 16 of the Convention guarantees equality between men and women in marriage and family life. Twenty-four nations have lodged reservation against the article. Malaysia, Maldives, Morocco, Pakistan and Tunisia oppose sections that conflict with existing national, customary or religious laws. The United States is among the countries that have not ratified the convention.

President : What is the condition of women in India today?

Vijay : There is a double picture, Sir. On the one hand there are :
1. Women who roll in luxury, socialities and others.
2. There are great women entrepreneurs, professionals and public servants—pilots, engineers, doctors, nurses, judges, lawyers, teachers and others. Many of the women of the high society are highly educated.

President : What about the second picture?

Vijay : Sir the women of the lower strata are a miserable lot. They wallow in poverty, misery, over work, disease, illiteracy and so on.

President : Why is the general ratio showing so much disparity in India?

Vijay : It is because of negligence of women's health, female foeticide etc.

President : What can you say about abuse of women?

Vijay : Broad estimates indicate that women are abused on a large scale.

President : Can you say something about abuse of women on international level ?

Vijay : Sir, The World Health Organisation (WHO) believes that at least one in every five women in the world has been physically or sexually abused by a man at some time in her life. As many as 25 to 50 per cent of all women have been physically assaulted by an intimate partner. In a study in Chile, 80 per cent of assaults by spouses resulted in injury. Justice system statistics in Peru, Malaysia and the United States suggest that 60 to 80 per cent of rapists are known to their victims.

President : Can you, Mr. Vijay, visualise why Pakistan embarked upon the Kargil campaign?

Vijay : It's all very mysterious, Sir, since, Pakistan seems to have gained nothing thereby. All one can say that for Pakistan it was a "tragedy of miscalculations".

President : Can you please mention a few of such miscalculations?

Vijay : Sir, I can explain a few of them :

1. Pakistan probably believed that India wouldn't discover the campaign till late summer of 1999.
2. Pakistan thought that in view of a caretaker government, India was weak at the centre.
3. Pakistan miscalculated that India was a divided house because of multiplicity of parties, religions etc.
4. She thought that because of terrorism spread by ISI in different parts of India, the latter had become internally hollow and weak.
5. She thought the Muslims, particularly the Kashmiri Muslims, wouldn't side with the Indian government.
6. She felt that because of steep height of Kargil, Drass and Batalik peaks on the Indian side, the Indian forces would find it difficult to dislodge the Pakistani regulars from them.
7. Pakistan probably couldn't gauge the strength of the Indian army and determination and patriotism of the Indian soldiers.
8. It was Pakistan's perception that India wouldn't press in the air force.
9. Pakistan probably expected help from China.
10. She never thought that the world opinion would go against her.

President : All right, Mr. Vijay, You can go now.

Vijay : Thank you, Sir.

(He rises confidently and moves out of the room with a beaming face.)

(**Comment :** Vijay's performance speaks volumes of itself. He has confidently answered all type of questions.)

MODEL INTERVIEW NO. 4

Mr. Vikas is a medium statured dark brown complexioned young man. He has sandy black hair which somewhat match his complexion. His ears and nose are large in comparsion to his round face which is medium sized. He has large black eyes which have the habit of peering on all sides. He has chubby cheeks which give a black sheen. His brow is also broad in comparison to the total circumference of his face. He has thick black eyebrows and he also has thick black bristling moustache. His chin is too short. He is dressed in blue black suit. He wears a dark blue neck-tie on his sky blue coloured shirt. His black shoes look dull as if they had been carelessly polished. He looks a little nervous or thievish as he looks on all sides while entering the room with his short slightly staggering steps. He seems to walk with heavy steps as if he were tired or as if his shoes were pinching. As he reaches the panel table, he moves the chair aside with a bang and wishes the President and other members in a somewhat stammering voice.

President : Will you please sit down Mr. Vikas? (The candidate is already half bent to occupy the chair which looks awkward.)

Vikas : (In a slightly stammering voice) Thank you, Sir.

President : Mr. Vikas when did you do your graduation?

Vikas : Sir, I did it last year.

President : Why didn't you go in for post-graduation?

Vikas : Sir, even a graduate is qualified for appearing in this examination. So I didn't want to waste two years in doing post-graduation when I feel my aptitude is for ACIO.

President : How do you know that?

Vikas : Sir, I have always dreamt of this job in my life; and moreover, my father has inspired me since my childhood to be an intelligence officer.

(**Comment :** It is obvious that after initial nervousness and hesitation the candidate has gathered courage enough to answer the questions boldly. It seems his nervousness was the result of his external features some beyond his control like dark brown complexion, rough hair, short neck etc. but others quite within his control like dress, shoes which could have been high-heeled to raise his stature and so on. Even in the case of his hair and moustaches, he could have taken certain positive steps if he had given thought to the matter. In any case, now his inner self has come out and he is likely to display his real knowledge and talent. This is what the board wanted. That is why for the present the board has started with very simple questions.)

President : How is it Mr. Vikas that even when you haven't done post-graduation you are qualified for appearing in this examination as far as your age is concerned ?

Vikas : Sir, from your question I understand that your honour wants to ask why I have done my graduation rather late. Of course there is no gap in my studies after doing matriculation but my studies were disturbed in my primary classes due to transfer of my father from one place to the other. Some people suggested that while filling up the school board form for the matriculation examination my date of birth could be changed to show me younger than what really I was. But my father, being an honest man to the core, refused to twist the facts.

President : What do you now feel about it?

Vikas : Sir, I highly appreciate my father's honesty and integrity not only in this but in all matters and have always tried to emulate him in my life.

President : (Changing the course of questions to a different track) How is that there have been a number of disastrous railway accidents during the past few years?

Vikas : Sir, of course in spite of all the scientific precision aimed at, human errors cannot be totally avoided. However according to world standard Indian Railways are some of the safest means of communication. Unfortunately for quite sometime the railway department is facing an acute financial crunch.

President : What has been the adverse effect of this financial crunch?

Vikas : Sir, the railway tracks in many parts of the country are out-dated and so is the case with other equipment like signalling system etc. The replacement of the old equipments by the new ones or even repairing these requires a lot of funds.

President : Mr. Vikas what are the two main kinds of democracy?

Vikas : Sir, they are direct democracy and indirect democracy.

President : What will you like to say about them?

Vikas : Sir, direct democracy was there in the ancient Greek city states when the number of voters was not large. In one form, such democracy existed in ancient India in the matter of selection of Sabhas and Samities.

Even at present voting is done in our parliament partly through raising of hands. In the present times, democracies are too large states where direct raising of hands is not possible.

President : What are most important kinds of democracies which exist in the modern world?

Vikas : Sir, they are the Parliamentary form of democracy and the Presidential form of democracy.

President : In which countries are these democracies most efficiently working?

Vikas : Sir, the parliamentary form of government is most efficiently working in the United Kingdom and the Presidential form in the United States of America.

President : What kind of government do we have in India?

Vikas : Sir, in India we have the Parliamentary form of government.

President : Is it not working efficiently?

Vikas : Sir, no doubt this form of government has got firm roots in our soil and the people are very enthusiastic about it. But there are certain apprehensive, if not negative factors, which cause some suspicion or doubt about the future in the minds of certain people.

President : What are those factors?

Vikas : Sir, I can just mention a few of them :
1. Corruption on a large scale
2. High rate of illiteracy
3. Vast disparity in incomes
4. Machinations and selfishness of politicians
5. Utter neglect of the poor and weaker sections of society
6. Multiplicity of political parties
7. Rise of regional parties on an unprecedented scale
8. Abysmally low level of morality especially among the political and affluent sections of society
9. Squandering away of precious money on petrol, luxuries etc
10. Huge foreign debt
10. Failure of law and order
11. Successive disenchantment of the people with the voting and electoral system
12. Common people's successive erosion of faith in judiciary and the judicial process
13. Disenchantment of the people with the conduct of our legislators in the parliament and assemblies and their promises and activities outside

President : Then do you think that India should switch over to the Presidential form of government?

Vikas : Sir, of course in the Presidential form the head of the government has a fixed tenure of four or five years or so. During this period, he can do a lot of good to the country with a one track concentrated mind. For example the President of America is supreme in doing his duties during his tenure. There is no question of toppling his government or hung parliament, or coalition governments. In India a lot of time, energy and money are wasted on such things as are no better than horse trading.

President : Then what is your objection to it?

Vikas : Sir, there can be a number of objections but I list only a few of them :

1. The President does not have a proper consultative machinery and thus he can commit some blunders.

2. As the government has a fixed tenure without any fear of getting toppled, it can go against the

wishes of the people and become tyrannical.

3. As the president has great powers of patronage, he can use them as a matter of favouritism and nepotism.

4. The Presidential form of government can degenerate into dictatorship as happened in Philippines in the case of President Marcos.

5. As the president has absolute powers of war and peace, he can, if he lacks insight or foresight, plunge the country or the whole world into the chaos—or a war without much reason. And we know, modern warfare is diabolical.

6. As in this form of government the state powers are highly compartmentalized into an inviolable division between the executive, the judiciary and the legislature, there can be a severe tussle among the three vital organs of the government.

7. This system of cheeks and balances can cause a great embarrassment to the President when he does not have a majority in the Parliament. This is what happened in America a number of times and even with President Bill Clinton when he found it difficult to get the budget passed and even to pay salaries to the government employees.

President : What are the most glaring negative sides of Indian budgets?

Vikas : Sir, one can list a number of such glaring deficiencies in the Indian budgets, but I'll just name a few:

1. Too little expenditure on education, that is, about three per cent of G.D.P. instead of the ideal six percent. Elementary education is the field which has particularly been neglected, though now efforts are being made to make up for this deficiency.

2. Too little allocation to defence, that is, just about 2.5 per cent when Pakistan spends about 17 percent of the budget on it. Now amends have been made to some extent in view of the Kargil conflict. So far, India had been one of the countries who spend the lowest amount on defence.

3. Deficit financing. Sir, there are several other lacunae in our budgets about which one can talk at great length.

President : So, you have made some good use of the economics subject at the graduation level.

Vikas : Thank you, Sir, for the appreciation.

President : All right, now please tell us how fiscal deficit can be reduced in your opinion.

Vikas : Sir, the government must prune its day-to-day expenditure on the one hand and raise its revenue on the other, not by hiking the tax rates but by lowering them. And secondly, the government must undertake a massive disinvestment programme in the public sector units, closure of the loss making ones and privatisation of those that are profitable.

President : How should the proceeds from disinvestment be used?

Vikas : In my opinion, the proceeds from disinvestment should be used to develop infrastructure and to retire public debts to reduce interest payment liability. The government's capacity to spend on the social sectors will also improve. No country, aspiring to become a high growth economy, can afford to ignore building human capital which will determine the competitiveness of an economy in the global economic order or the globalised world.

President : What, in your opinion, is the dilemma about the public sector in India.

Vikas : Sir, the dilemma is that in the "heyday of socialism" the public sector was supposed to provide the maximum number of jobs, and become a model employer for the private sector to emulate.

Making profit was never a major criterion for successful operation. In this era of liberalisation and reforms, the public sector is now being called upon to be competitive, but without shedding its social burden.

President : You may go now, Mr. Vikas.

Vikas : Thank you, Sir.

(He rises slowly and goes out with much more confidence than he had while coming)

(**Comment :** There is no doubt the candidate has given good account of himself but certain negative factors like awkwardness, lack of self-confidence and initial nervousness etc. still keep his fate hanging in the balance, although he has some positive qualities like honesty, a sharp intellect, interest in studies etc.)

MODEL INTERVIEW NO. 5

Mr. Brahmananda Mahapatra as a candidate is appearing for the interview before the board.

Mr. Mahapatra is a well-built young man of about 23 years. He is M.A. in Political Science from Delhi University. He has a fair complexion which enhances the charm of his black hair and also, it adds grace to his thin black moustaches. His features—chin, lips, nose, ears, eyes and cheeks—look well-sculptured by nature to give his oval face an edge in a crowd and attract on-lookers.

As his name is called by the peon, Mr. Mahapatra who was exchanging brief pleasantries mixed with witty remarks with other candidates, takes leave of them. He enters the interview room, after seeking permission, in a confident manner and greets the President.

Mahapatra : Good morning, sir.

President : Good Morning, Mr. Mahapatra. Please be seated.

Mahapatra : Thank you, sir.

(Mr. Mahapatra occupies the chair in front of the President. He makes least disturbance and sits erect in relaxed posture with a smile on his cheeks and a glint of expectation in his eyes).

President : Mr. Mahapatra, your parents have given you quite an amusing name. Haven't they?

(The candidate feels slightly puzzled as he had never expected such a question. He had heard and read that normally the interviewers ask home-spun stereotyped biographical questions for the first few minutes but hardly any personal question)

(**Comment:** Probably the President noted that the candidate was quite relaxed even in the very beginning. Hence, such a rare question was asked at the very outset. In any case, the candidate shows no signs of confusion as the President stares at him).

Mahapatra : Sir, I belong to a highly religious family. Moreover, the word Brahmananda is in tune with our old culture which is steeped in faith and spirituality that was so consummately brought out by our matchless scriptures. However, it does not mean any stress on superstition or fanaticism or even any particular religion. Indian scriptures are conspicuously secular in essence. They do not profess the superiority of a religion over any other.

President : The Mahapatras mostly live in Orissa and Brahmananda is especially a name smacking more of a resident of Uttar Pradesh or Bihar. Do you agree that there is a difference?

Mahapatra : Sir, it is true that my father is an Oriya and my mother hails from Uttar Pradesh. Further, she is the most religious person in our family, although, as I said earlier, our entire family is religiously-minded. It got this name because it was my mother's desire and my caste is after my father's. I think it is a good thing since it evinces a disregard for regionalism and casteism which are great obstacles on the path to our goal of national integration.

President : Give your suggestions how national integration can be effected?

Mahapatra : Sir many people, particularly foreign rulers, have tried to convey the impression that India has never been a nation in the past. It is true that India has been only a loosely knit political entity in the past. But, we know nationality comprises the spirit of oneness and cultural, religious or racial unity. In India since earliest times, our great ancestors, who had good foresight, devised several means of creating and maintaining this unity.

President : Mention any of such means?

Mahapatra : Sir, since ancient times, there has been a belief among the Indian people to go on pilgrimage to different religious places which are situated in different parts of the country. They visit Amaranth, Badrinath and Kedarnath in the north, Haridwar, Mathura and Kurukshetra in the central plains, Puri in the east, Dwarka in the west and Rameshwaram, Tirupati and several others in the south. The Adi Shankracharaya established his ashrams in all four corners of the country. He certainly had a clear perception of Singular India. Lord Shiva's temples are situated in all parts of the country. Our national festivals are celebrated, with minor variations, in all parts of the country.

President : Name some great Indian leaders in the modern times who have contributed to the idea and reality of national integration?

Mahapratra : Sir, all of our great modern leaders have strived to keep alive the spirit and reality of national integration and projected plausible means to give shape to their dreams. Lokmanya Tilak started the famous Ganesh Festival in Mumbai. Mahatma Gandhi spread his idea of an independent India in all parts of the country. Jawaharlal Nehru spread the message of India's unity in diversity through his writings and speeches. Rabindranath Tagore and Sri Aurobindo also contributed to the idea of India's independence and integration. Tagore's famous lyric in the Gitanjali : "Where the mind is without fear......" is too well-known to be recited in full.

President : What, in your opinion, has been the impact on people of various wars after independence?

Mahapatra : India has had to fight five wars with Pakistan and one with China after Independence.

President : How do you say India had to fight five wars with Pakistan?

Mahapatra : Sir, In 1947 Pakistan attacked Kashmir which signed the Instrument of Accession with India and became a part of our country and thus India had to defend this state. In 1948, Pakistan again attacked Kashmir. In 1965 and 1971 Pakistan again attacked India and she had to fight. In 1999, Pakistan, taking advantage of sub-zero temperature, occupied the high mountain peaks of Kargil, Batalik and Dras in Kashmir, under the cover of Mujahiddin and Afghan mercenaries. Some people may call it "Kargil Conflict," but I consider it a full-fledged war, since it involved skills and expertise of a major war. The impact of these wars on the minds of the Indian people can be felt even today. We have emerged as a stronger nation after the five wars.

President : Then do you think the war to be a good thing for our country?

Mahapatra : I don't think so, Sir. We Indians are peace-loving people. We believe in *"Sarve Bhavantu Sukhina"*, that is, welfare of all. But, if war is forced on us, we know how to answer it, as we had answered Pakistan each time in five wars and inflicting a crushing defeat on the enemy.

President : Can you name the four recipients of the Param Vir Chakra in the Kargil war?

Mahapatra : The four recipients of Param Vir Chakra in the Kargil war were Captain Vikram Batra, 13 Jammu Kashmir Rifles; Captain Manoj Kumar Pandey, 1/11 Gorkha Rifles; Rifleman Sanjay Kumar, 13 Jammu and Kashmir Rifles; and Grenadier Yogender Singh Yadav.

President : Which of these four recipients got the award posthumously?

Mahapatra : Sir, Captain Vikram Batra and Lieutenant Manoj Kumar Pandey got the award posthumously.

President : What have you to say about Yogender Singh Yadav?

Mahapatra : Sir, the army made a major goof-up in announcing a posthumous Param Vir Chakra for Grenadier Yogender Singh Yadav, but Mr. Yadav was still alive and under treatment for injuries in the Army's Base Hospital in Delhi Cantonment. Later, the then chief of the Army Staff, General Ved Prakash Malik visited the hospital to enquire about Mr. Yadav's health.

President : Can you enlighten us about the Param Vir Chakra?

Mahapatra : Sir, the Param Vir Chakra, also called the PVC, is the highest award for gallantry in India. It was designed by a lady of foreign origin who had married an Indian Army officer and had an undying fascination for India.

The distinguished lady who designed the medal was Eva Maday who was renamed Savitri Khanolkar after marriage.

Ms. Savitri Khanolkar's father was Hungarian and mother, a Russian. From her early childhood, she was fascinated by India and in due course she married Capt. Vikram Khanolkar, an Indian Army officer who graduated from Sandhurst and joined the Sikh regiment. She was then just 15 while her husband was 27.

Ms. Khanolkar, who died in 1990, went on to study Hindi and Sanskrit at Patna University. Later, she studied the Vedanta and became a follower of Ramakrishna.

It was perhaps due to her intense study of India that soon after independence, she was asked by the Army's the then adjutant general Major General Hira Lal Atal to design a medal for the highest award for valour.

She took her inspiration from the mythical Rishi Dadhichi who donated his thigh bone to the gods to make Vajra (thunder bolt). On either side of the Vajra, she put Shivaji's sword Bhawani and thus, the PVC came into being.

Ironically, the first PVC was awarded to her only daughter's brother-in-law Major Somnath Sharma, a 4 Kumaon officer, who was posthumously awarded for the brave act that he had done on November 3, 1947 during the 1947-48 Indo Pak war in Kashmir.

President : How did you gather all this information about the award?

Mahapatra : Sir, I had read this in a newspaper.

President : Good, It seems you read the newspaper regularly.

Mahapatra : Yes, sir. I subscribe to a number of newspapers and journals to keep myself abreast of all kinds of the latest knowledge.

President : We are pleased to hear it. Then, you must be able to enlighten us about India's nuclear doctrine.

Mahapatra : Sir, in the third week of August 1999, India made public her draft nuclear doctrine, spelling out the minimum nuclear deterrent, command and control system and the broad thrust on nuclear forces, even while reiterating her strict adherence to the objective of "no-first use" and "non-use against non-nuclear weapon states."

President : Can you spell out briefly what India means by "minimum nuclear deterrent."

Mahapatra : Sir according to the doctrine document, we shall have sufficient, survivable and operationally prepared nuclear forces; a robust command and control system; effective intelligence and early warning capabilities; comprehensive planning and training for operations in line with the strategy and the will to employ nuclear forces and weapons.

President : Should we change the doctrine as China has also become a friend?

Mahapatra : Sir, If we have good relations with China, it does not mean that we should relegate our nuclear programme to a back-seat. Rather, it would be suicidal to do so. Our nuclear programmes can help us at any point of time in the future. If China is a friend today, she can be an enemy (once again) tomorrow. Further, even if the Chinese remain friendly towards us, other countries can become hostile towards us. Myanmar is an example in this context. We have to be prepared for all dangers at all times. But we shall use nuclear power for only peaceful purposes.

President : Thank you, Mr. Mahapatra. You may go now.

Mahapatra : Thank you, sir. A good day to you all sirs.

(He bows slightly as he rises up from the chair and comes out of the room confidently and in a calm manner, making least noise).

(**Comment :** The candidate has played his cards nicely and created a very positive impression on the members of the board. The members of the board are quite convinced of his knowledge and positive attitude towards life. Besides, he is well groomed and is convincingly a responsible lad. Certainly, he can be selected.)

TIPS FOR PERSONALITY DEVELOPMENT

One must develop his personality in every possible manner. Everyone can improve his personality with the help of the following useful tips:

- Honestly analyze the traits of your personality and character.

- Enlist your bad habits and try to get rid of them.

- Listen to everyone politely, even if their ideas are not of your interest.

- During conversation, do not keep talking about yourself too much.

- Keep your morale high in case of defeat and be more polite on being victorious.

- Solve your problems in a creative way.

- Positive attitude is of great importance in our personality.

- The real beauty of man lies not in his physical appearance but in his work and good qualities.

- Keep improving your physical appearance also as it is the first thing anyone notices about you, even before you speak and work.

- You should respect and appreciate others but do not try to copycat them.

- Have a close analysis of your own behaviour. If you are young, your friends should like you and more should befriend you.

- Your attitude should be broad, confident, respectful and ready-to-take-criticism.

- Smiles help us communicate better, keep smiling.

- Observe and improve your sitting and walking postures.

- Inculcate healthy eating, living and sleeping habits.

- Develop good reading habits, viewing news channels and debates and analyse them yourself.

- Develop habits of discussing on various topics and practise giving lectures before friends and family members.

- Improve your knowledge of English and practise good conversation with your friends.

- Listen with utmost care to your critics and improve yourself.

- Develop good listening and comprehending skills.

- Improve your memory and concentration of mind.

- Start doing everything in a planned manner.

- Form a group of friends and organise help, relief and charity works.

- Interact with different types of people and know their views.

- Organise some small and big activities.

- Try to solve small and big problems at home and around.

- Start participating in different social activities.

- Start doing some voluntary social work.

- Start playing some indoor and outdoor games.

- Start doing physical exercise and yoga daily.

- Observe the personality, mannerism and good habits of the people you like or admire and keep improving yourself.

Remember, we are individuals and each individual has his/her own unique personality. One can lack in some but can be good at some. Try to better the good ones and inculcate the one which you don't have. Bring out a lovely personality and make your presence felt everywhere.

If you take care of these small but very useful tips, you will be able to develop an impressive and influential personality abundant in Officers Like Qualities (OLQs).